RETHINKING THEOLOGY AND SCIENCE

Rethinking Theology and Science

Six Models for the Current Dialogue

Edited by

Niels Henrik Gregersen
and
J. Wentzel van Huyssteen

William B. Eerdmans Publishing Company
Grand Rapids, Michigan / Cambridge, U.K.

© 1998 Wm. B. Eerdmans Publishing Co.
255 Jefferson Ave. S.E., Grand Rapids, Michigan 49503 /
P.O. Box 163, Cambridge CB3 9PU U.K.

Printed in the United States of America

03 02 01 00 99 98   7 6 5 4 3 2 1

Library of Congress Cataloging-in-Publication Data

Rethinking theology and science : six models for the current dialogue /
    edited by Niels Henrik Gregersen and J. Wentzel van Huyssteen.
         p.   cm.
    This book grew out of a series of discussions at various
conferences of the European Society for the Study of Science
and Theology (ESSSAT), and the Forum for Theology and
Science, Univ. of Aarhus, Denmark, and four of these
contributions were presented as lectures at the Aarhus Forum.
    Includes bibliographical references.
    ISBN 0-8028-4464-2 (pbk : alk. paper)
    1. Religion and science. 2. Knowledge, Theory of. I. Gregersen,
Niels Henrik, 1956- . II. Van Huyssteen, J. Wentzel.
BL240.2.R48   1998
291.1'75 — dc21   98-15995
                                                                CIP

Contents

Contents

Acknowledgments

THIS BOOK GREW out of a series of ongoing discussions and happy interactions between the different authors in various challenging and stimulating European settings, particularly the conferences of the European Society for the Study of Science and Theology (ESSSAT), and the Forum for Theology and Science at the University of Aarhus in Denmark. Four of the six present contributions have been presented as lectures at the Aarhus Forum.

We as the editors are deeply grateful to Princeton Theological Seminary and the Faculty of Theology at the University of Aarhus for creating such superb working environments for studies in the field of science and theology. Niels Henrik Gregersen also expresses his thanks to the Center of Theological Inquiry, Princeton, for welcoming him as a member at the Center for the academic year 1996-97, which also greatly helped to facilitate the editorial process.

The William B. Eerdmans Publishing Company has shown a sustained interest in issues in theology and science, and has been extremely supportive in making this project a reality. We are indeed grateful for this kind of professional encouragement, and in particular would like to thank Mr. William B. Eerdmans, Jr., for his ongoing sensitivity for contemporary issues in interdisciplinary theology. We are especially indebted to him for including in his imaginative vision those of us who believe that a book like this could be an important vehicle for bringing together North American and European thought on a subject that touches the heart of Christian theology today.

Finally, we want to thank Dr. LeRon Shults, at Princeton Theological Seminary, for his careful and meticulous editorial assistance.

Niels Henrik Gregersen
J. Wentzel van Huyssteen

Theology and Science in a Pluralist World: An Introduction

Niels Henrik Gregersen
and J. Wentzel van Huyssteen

THOSE OF US WHO commit much of our energy and of our lives to "theology and science" are unquestionably living in exciting times. Gone are the days in which any attempt to relate theology and science to one another could still possibly — and mistakenly — be seen as a rather esoteric, intellectualist exercise limited to a privileged few. "Theology and science," as a very focused interdisciplinary venture, is indeed alive and well today on both sides of the Atlantic, as theologians, scientists, and philosophers are joining this complex cross-disciplinary conversation with its ever-new challenges and configurations. It seems that this ancient and enduring dialogue has managed to successfully transform itself, in our present Western culture, into a sustained and dynamic contemporary discourse with its own prevailing identity for our times.

Contrary to popular misconceptions, the dialogue between theology and the sciences is rarely about conflict and dissensus: those who actively participate in this dialogue are in fact mostly deeply committed to both religion and science as two of the most dominant and shaping forces in our culture. But an important part of our popular culture can certainly also be found in the enduring legacy of the success and prestige of the natural sciences, which still serves to substantiate the aura of science, and the myth of the universal superiority of natural scientific rationality. The dialogue between theology and science has therefore suffered from the so-called modernist dilemma, where "objective," uni-

1

versal scientific claims are typically and severely contrasted with subjective, "irrational" theological beliefs, often resulting in a relentless pressure to contrast religion and theology with manicured forms of "pure" science. It is therefore especially significant that it is a small group of scientists, who also happen to be theologians, who have taken the lead in breaking through the audacious claims of contemporary scientism to become the dominant pioneers in the theology and science dialogue of our day. Scientist-theologians like Arthur Peacocke, Ian Barbour, and John Polkinghorne have indeed been towering figures in the second half of this century and are still shaping much of the current dialogue in our field. All three of these prominent figures have rightly insisted on protecting the intellectual integrity of reasoning strategies as diverse as theology and science, while at the same time they have also pursued a quest to harmonize these two discourses into a viable unifying account of human knowledge.

This common ground and shared concern was clearly and admirably explicated in John Polkinghorne's recent *Scientists as Theologians* (1996), where Polkinghorne compares his own contributions to the theology and science dialogue with those of his peers Ian Barbour and Arthur Peacocke. In spite of important differences, these three scientist-theologians have indeed set the stage for the ongoing dialogue between theology and science. John Polkinghorne has rightly called all three of them revisionists: all three attempt to break through the modernist polarization of religion and science by defending the thesis that religion (and therefore also theology, as a reflection on religious experience) makes important and novel cognitive claims. All three also acknowledge that modern discoveries about the nature and history of the physical world have had important modifying effects on the tone of contemporary theological discourse (cf. Polkinghorne 1996, 81f.). All three agree on how important it is to realize that scientific concepts should be allowed to mold and influence theological thought, but significantly differ on where they would want to place themselves on a spectrum reaching from varying forms of epistemological consonance, on the one end, to methodological and conceptual integration on the other. Although Peacocke, Barbour, and Polkinghorne all see themselves as critical realists, their well-known differences on theological issues like God, christology, and divine action, can be related to their different understandings of how theology relates to philosophy and to contemporary culture in general.

This "first generation" of important and influential scientist-

theologians have in fact always been admirably aware of how the articulation of both theological and scientific thought has consistently been
influenced by the prevailing culture. From this has grown a strong and
increasing awareness of how deeply theology and science, as two very
different reasoning strategies, are embedded in contemporary culture.
Polkinghorne also briefly refers to the prevailing influence of postmodern thought, and how it is threatening to move us away from
"knowing the way things are" to the complete relativism of functionalist,
constructivist thought (1996, 2). In spite of this kind of relativism — or
maybe even because of this relativism — our scientist-theologians still
see theology as the great integrative discipline, revealing a strong commitment to interdisciplinary reflection as it seeks to explore the many-
layered reality of our experience. Polkinghorne finally calls theology
"metaphysics practised in the presence of God" (1996, 1). And in their
strategy of aligning theology and science in a common struggle against
"a twentieth-century despair of any knowledge of reality" (Polkinghorne
1996, 4), Barbour, Polkinghorne, and Peacocke have developed their
variously nuanced versions of critical realism as the most plausible
methodological approach to the challenges of the current theology and
science dialogue. A host of younger theologians, philosophers, and
scientist-theologians has since taken this on as a tremendously important challenge, and in this sense have revealed Ian Barbour's fourfold
taxonomy for relating theology and science through either *conflict,
dialogue, independence, or integration* (cf. Barbour 1990, 3-30), as possibly
one of the most enduring legacies of our "first generation" of scientist-
theologians.

It is precisely at this point that the authors of this book take their
cue for "rethinking theology and science." In following the lead of our
first generation of scientist-theologians, we are taking on anew the task
of rethinking, and remodelling, the dialogue between science and theology under the challenge of a growing cognitive pluralism. We are,
therefore, also very well aware of the fact that the broader cultural
context in which the dialogue between theology and science is pursued,
has become increasingly local, diverse, and complex.

This pluralism is not just apparent in everyday life. Also within
the natural sciences we observe a tendency towards a diversification of
conceptualities, methods, approaches, paradigms, and cognitive values.
A discipline like biology, for instance, is organized in historical as well
as in experimental departments, and among its methods we find historical inference, morphological description, chemical analysis, refine-

ment of the theory-structure of Darwinism, and so on. Hence, even
within the natural sciences disunity has indeed become a matter of fact.
Whereas the catch-word between the 1930s and the 1960s was the
"unification of science," an increasing number of today's philosophers
of science are focusing upon the pluralism of conceptual disunities and
the manifold of competitive theories (cf. Galison and Stump 1996). It
is not surprising, therefore, to witness an even stronger plurality of
paradigms within social sciences such as economy or sociology, and in
the humanities and theology as well.

Cognitive pluralism has thus become one of the primary challenges to both science and theology. This demonstrates clearly that the
construal of polarizing and contrastive thought models, which dissoci-
ates the "objective" sciences, on the one hand, from the subjective and
"prejudiced" studies of the humanities and theology, on the other hand,
is all too simplistic. A diversification of cognitive models, and a variety
of styles of reasoning, therefore, emerge in all fields of academic life.
Acknowledging these forms of disciplinary pluralism, however, does not
necessarily imply the uncritical acceptance of a syncretistic attitude
where just "anything goes." As Ian Hacking recently pointed out (cf.
Galison and Stump 1996, 73), not only has each style of reasoning inside
the sciences created its own "self-stabilizing techniques," but some are
also more effective for specific purposes than others. Moreover, Hacking
emphasizes that even if the idea of a unified conceptualization of all
fundamental aspects of reality is often out of place, the demand for
establishing interconnections and facilitating a communication between
different cognitive systems remains as necessary as ever.

Seen within this perspective, some of the trends in contemporary
theology might not be all that different after all. On the one hand, the
inescapability of theological pluralism has rendered it almost impossible
to talk about the "theology" side of "theology and science," as if the
existence of one true theology could still be posited in such a generic,
uncomplicated way. The postmodern jettisoning of the grand metanarratives of modernity has in fact been a severe blow for the reigning
theological paradigms of our day, a blow from which they have hardly
recovered. In addition to this, the recognition of the importance of
discrete experiences and specific traditions has also resulted in the
inevitable emergence of so-called local theologies (cf. Byrne 1994, 6).
Not only have liberation theologies, womanist, feminist, and eco-
theologies claimed the intrinsic theological importance of particular
experiences, but also post-liberal, as well as various forms of evangelical

theology, today raise the same claim with respect to their own background communities. Here the specific contents of theology is to be found *within* the contexts themselves, and not only as derived from tradition. Nevertheless, it seems that a majority of these emphatically contextual forms of theological reflection have in fact, and even to an increasing extent, involved a serious and conscious choice for very specific aspects of Christian tradition, or of neglected aspects of Christian life and reflection. A strengthening of cross-connections, and a growth in cross-disciplinary awareness between the concerns of "local" theologies and the concerns of more classical types of theology, also seem to be very typical of contemporary theological reflection. In a variety of ways, the urge towards pluralization has also led contextual theologies into taking responsibility for specific human concerns, and for theological agendas that transcend the boundaries of specific groups.

At least two forms of pluralism, therefore, seem to be at stake in recent debates called forth by the postmodern challenge to theology. There is, on the one hand, a *syncretistic pluralism* that indifferently endorses any cognitive scheme (often while denying the reality claims inherent in cognitive models such as those of science). On the other hand we find new proponents for a *perspectival pluralism* which is still committed to some kinds of realism, even if only in modest and truncated forms. The dilemma for the theologian interested in interdisciplinary conversation with the natural sciences is, of course, the collapse of the unifying discourse systems of Western metaphysics. Postmodernity has rightly unmasked the illusions created by epistemological foundationalism. We now know that any issue is always seen from a particular interpreted point of view, and that our epistemic practices therefore constitute contexts in which our very participation is a precondition for our observations. Under these conditions the suggestion that theology could still be "the great integrative discipline" (cf. Polkinghorne 1996, 1), has become increasingly implausible, if not untenable. But if the idea of one homogeneous metanarrative description for science and theology fails, what then are the alternatives?

One option, quite popular among some contemporary theologians is to take refuge in the insular comfort of internally closed language-systems. We are convinced, however, that everyone committed to public interdisciplinary dialogue — between church and society, and between the academy and the churches — cannot consistently sustain a purely intra-communal view of the role of Christian churches and

Christian theology. Strong theological commitments in fact also speak against such a "re-tribalization" of theology. First, the realm of nature and society constitutes a shared space for common concerns between Christians and non-Christians. According to traditional Christian understanding, nature and society are part of God's creation, and thus objects of both preservation and transformation. Hence, all ethical questions as well as questions pertaining to the interpretation of science in relation to other important affairs in the world (including religion), are always shared questions of humanity, even if we as Christians and non-Christians may disagree as far as our various approaches are concerned. Furthermore, the presupposition that the cognitive systems of some preferred theologies are able to answer just any question and uncover all aspects of reality certainly amounts to an epistemic arrogance which cannot be justified on general or theological grounds. The assumption that a specific Christian language tradition, lived out "craftfully" by certain communities, can claim this language as God-given and "sealed" by God, leads to a fatal conflation of the Word of God and the words of tradition. Trying to overcome the modernist individualism of perennial decision-making by this kind of "postmodern" communitarianism can easily end up meaning that "we (as a group) decide who God is." Such a move certainly does not overcome the deeper theological problem of idolatry (cf. Dalferth 1996, 416-430). To make a strong plea for a Christian counterculture, therefore, does not at all imply that one is speaking from an allegedly God's-eye perspective.

The authors of this book agree that there are good reasons for furthering the interdisciplinary dialogue between theology and the natural sciences. But they do not share a common view on science, or on theology, or on the best viable way to pursue this dialogue. This book is explicitly not intended to offer one monolithic answer to the question which haunts so many of us: how is it possible for theology to credibly join other modes of knowledge in some form of interdisciplinary, public discourse? And how can the resources of theology enrich this discussion, and also benefit from the astonishing effectiveness of the scientific understanding of nature? Precisely the interdisciplinary and crosscultural nature of the dialogue between theology and science forms a very specific challenge to rethink the cultural ramifications of this dialogue, as we reevaluate the epistemology which undergirds our conversations in this intellectual context. If both theology and science are so concretely embedded in culture, then it would be only normal and natural that different epistemic and non-epistemic values would shape our different perspectives in this interdisciplinary dialogue. In this sense, of course, "theology and science" is really just a subset of a much broader issue, that is, the problem of theology's interdisciplinary status in the current academic situation.

This book now suggests six different and rather diverse models for the ongoing dialogue between science and theology. The authors were first asked to present "position papers" of the approaches they were representing. Following this, the papers were circulated among the authors in order to facilitate an internal criticism, which afterwards was incorporated into the individual chapters. The reader should therefore be aware of interaction between the authors, sometimes approvingly, sometimes critical, sometimes tacitly, and sometimes in more explicit conversation. The purpose of the book from the beginning has been, therefore, to offer a clear outline of various different models, some of which are already at play in the contemporary dialogue. We therefore hope that the present book will facilitate a helpful orientation for newcomers to the field, and that it may prove helpful in channeling some of the important discussions on methodology and epistemology.

The six models that are presented here are the following: (1) postfoundationalist epistemology, (2) critical realism, (3) scientific naturalism, (4) non-integrative pragmaticism, (5) complementarity, and (6) contextual coherence theory.

J. Wentzel van Huyssteen argues for postfoundationalism as a third option beyond the extremes of a modernist, foundationalist epistemology on the one hand and skeptical, nonfoundationalist forms of postmodernism on the other. According to van Huyssteen, postmodernism does not leave us without rational criteria in either the sciences or in theology. Human rationality in fact has many faces, many dimensions, and complex resources: some are cognitive, others are evaluative, while still others are pragmatic. While the natural sciences may be paradigmatic for the cognitive aspects of human reasoning, other dimensions also define the core of rationality. Taking a cue from Harold Brown's theory of rationality, van Huyssteen argues that it is the concept of the rational person (rather than rational ideas) which is pivotal for creating a safe, interdisciplinary space for the shaping of the dialogue between theology and the sciences. As rational agents we are never separated from our social and historical contexts, and in a very specific sense, therefore, tradition seems to be both the source and destiny of human rationality. Rational persons should also be willing, however, to reach beyond the limits of their own epistemic traditions.

By recasting the theology and science discussion in postfoundationalist terms, an interdisciplinary space is cleared, which now enables a radical revisioning and rediscovery of the shared resources of theological and scientific rationality.

Kees van Kooten Niekerk presents a case for preserving what is often regarded as the standard model for the dialogue between theology and science, critical realism, while also refining it at the same time. First he points to the different levels on which the realist claims of the sciences are raised (observation statements, statements of mathematical or primary relations, and theories). Van Kooten Niekerk pursues his analysis by opting for a qualified form of critical realism. "Science" in general cannot legitimately raise realist claims. The case for approaching reality has to be established for each statement and theory in particular. Admittedly many theories remain doubtful, since we often may have good reasons to assume *that* the referents of theories exist while we do not know *what* they are. It is a distinctive mark of science, however, that while theories and paradigms may come and go, primary statements persist. Van Kooten Niekerk also points to the difficulty in transferring the model of critical realism from the sciences to theology. Whereas scientific statements purport to be statements of facts, theological statements normally contain both statements and evaluations. Consequently, theology is primarily an existential and only secondarily a theoretical enterprise.

Willem B. Drees offers a defense of scientific naturalism as the basis for the dialogue between theology and science. What Drees calls the "wildness of experience" is often taken to imply epistemic pluralism. According to Drees, however, this should not be taken to mean that the explanatory potential of science is deficient in principle. Historically, the "scientific images" of the world have again and again superseded the "manifest images" of everyday life. A scientific naturalism thus claims that no supernatural or spiritual realm distinct from the natural world shows up within our natural world. Our scientific explanations, however, do not by themselves explain the framework that is given by the natural world as a whole. Hence, on the boundaries of science, limit-questions arise that are open for religious interpretation. Furthermore, in the human appreciation of the local qualities that appear within evolutionary history there is also potential room for a religious wondering, as long as religion does not presume to explain the characteristics of the world by reference to a god-of-the-gaps. Religious life, however, is more a way of life than a theory about the world. And since humans are situated in different worlds, they are likely to develop a religious variety which may be both acceptable and valuable in a naturalist perspective.

Eberhard Herrmann presents a case for a nonintegrative pragmaticism for science and theology. On this view, religion is to be understood as one of many "views of life," rooted in the continuous need of human beings to cope with the contingencies of their lives in a very practical sense. In two important ways Herrmann presents an alternative to critical realism as normally defined. First, he does not think that science and religion really do have a common referent, for instance, nature or God. The statements of science and religion do not lie on the same logical level. Statements are always context-bound, and since religious and scientific statements are derived from very different epistemic contexts, they have radically different meanings which are not comparable and therefore remain incompatible. Second, religion is more about a human approach to reality than about reality in itself. Herrmann's approach is therefore nonintegrative when it comes to comparing statements of science and religion. But Herrmann sees in this no reason for alarm. For even if religious language is not regarded as making inferences about God as an external and faraway reality, God may still be (in Hilary Putnam's sense) the "internal object," that is, the reality which is intented by religious stories. If religious narratives are felt as existentially adequate expressions of experiences, then religions do function as real-life options, and do so legitimately. On this basis, Herrmann recommends a "division of work" for science and theology. Science and theology both wrestle with questions all important for human survival. We need both the knowledge of the nature of the world that science provides us and a guidance for the values by which we shape our lives provided by views of life.

Fraser Watts presents a model of complementarity for science and theology. Following the general thrust of critical realism, Watts takes both science and theology to be referential discourses. He departs, however, from the assumption that the worlds to which science and theology refer are identical. Theology is to be regarded instead as a higher-level discourse, while the sciences are concerned in more detail with particular aspects of the wider reality which falls under the purview of theology. According to the proposal put forth by Watts, the relation between science and theology can be modeled in analogy to the well-known need for dual description of mental/brain events. This analogy is more illuminating for the complementarity model than the usual wave/particle analogy of quantum processes. For while the latter belongs to the same overall discourse system, the mind/body problem demands two different (though not unrelated) set of descriptions: the first-person perspective and the third-person perspective. According to this model, theology should not be perverted into a discipline improperly close to the empirical sciences, although theology has to take the empirical sciences into account. The model of complementarity liberates theology from seeing itself as an alternative to scientific explanations, as has recently been attempted in theological appropriations of the anthropic principle of the "fine-tuned universe." Theology is not competing with the sciences on the same level. As a higher-level discipline, however, theology may be able to explain why the naturalistic explanations work as well as they seem to do.

Finally, **Niels Henrik Gregersen** outlines a contextual coherence theory for the dialogue between theology and science. Building upon Nicholas Rescher's pragmaticist coherence theory, he points to the criterion of coherence as a critical norm inside all forms of knowledge, including forms of knowledge that are not strictly speaking empirical. All epistemic systems are in need of a theoretical self-substantiation but must also demonstrate their pragmatic applicability to particular domains of reality. Using the challenge of Darwinism as a test case for a theology of creation, Gregersen shows that the continuous attempt to establish a cognitive equilibrium between science and the particular concerns of Christian theology has in fact shaped the self-understanding of theology on a variety of levels. Not only have scientific data such as the age of the earth been fully appropriated, but also different levels of theory-building, thought models, metaphors, and worldviews have been involved in the dialogue. A contextual coherence theory that takes seriously the different kinds of data for science and Christian theology is workable since it has been operative, and still is. The contextual coherence theory may be seen as a via media between a critical realism (which uses its energy in the external relation to "reality") and nonintegrative models (which do not allow for cross-fertilizations between science and theology). While coherence theories share with Quine and others a holistic theory of knowledge, Gregersen argues, in a critical discussion with Nancey Murphy's empiricist program for theology, that the rationality of theology is given with its ability to connect with other modes of knowledge rather than in its direct empirical nature.

References

Byrne, James M. 1994. "Theology and Christian Faith." In "Why Theology?" ed. Claude Geffré and Werner Jeanrond. *Concilium* 6.

Dalferth, Ingolf. 1996. "Was Gott ist, bestimme ich! Theologie im Zeitalter der 'Cafeteria-Religion.'" *Theologische Literaturzeitung* 121:5.

Galison, Peter, and David J. Stump. 1996. *The Disunity of Science: Boundaries, Contexts, and Power.* Stanford: Stanford University Press.

Polkinghorne, John. 1996. *Scientists as Theologians: A Comparison of the Writings of Ian Barbour, Arthur Peacocke, and John Polkinghorne.* London: SPCK.

Postfoundationalism in Theology and Science: Beyond Conflict and Consonance

J. Wentzel van Huyssteen

THE REMARKABLE DIVERSITY and dynamic nature of the current dialogue between theology and the sciences, especially in the United Kingdom, Europe, and North America, can undoubtedly be seen as one of the most exciting and controversial intellectual projects of our time. The extreme complexity of the historical relationship between these two dominant forces in our culture should caution us, however, against too simplistic generalizations about this enduring dialogue. Precisely the subtlety of the cross-disciplinary interaction between these two very different modes of reflection will have profound implications for any attempt to identify the specific rationality and interdisciplinary character of *theological* reflection today. Theology, I think, has suffered much from the fallout of the modernist dilemma in which "objective," universal scientific claims were highlighted in glaring contrast to allegedly less superior and subjective, "irrational" theological beliefs, and which always resulted in the relentless pressure to completely polarize science and all forms of religion (cf. Bell 1996, 197). For those of us who are theologians, and who care passionately about theology's public, interdisciplinary face, trying to find a safe epistemological space for the dialogue between theology and the sciences therefore forms a very specific challenge. But before we take the easy way out and succumb to the temptation to treat "theology" and "science" as two very separate, discrete entities, a careful and responsible approach to this problematical relationship should first of all reveal an epistemological sensitivity to the continually shifting boundaries between these two disciplines,

13

and to the way both disciplines are shaped by their social and historical embeddedness in specific cultures.

This kind of epistemological sensitivity should, first of all, include a heightened awareness, true to our postmodern sensibilities, that "theology" and "science" actually never exist in a generalized, abstract sense, but always in quite specific social, historical, and intellectual contexts. This will irrevocably locate the rationality of both theological and scientific reflection within the context of living, developing, and changing traditions. To abstract either "theology" or "science" from a specific time or from specific contexts, and then to try to establish their mutual relationship, therefore, would indeed be a highly artificial and fruitless endeavor. Furthermore, contemporary philosophy of science with its sharp focus on ever-evolving models of rationality has clearly shown that the boundaries between theological and scientific modes of reflection have not only shifted with time, but that the very nature of these boundaries is today challenged, questioned, and deconstructed in ways that were not possible before. This is another important reason why it has become more difficult than ever to speak of *the* relationship between theology and science (cf. Brooke 1991, 321). Of course, the realization that theological rationality is always located within the living context of developing and changing traditions makes possible a diversity of theological responses to scientific rationality. It also challenges us to try to discover in imaginative ways what this fact may mean for the problem of the shaping of rationality in theological reflection.

Furthermore, anyone who takes time today to reflect on the interdisciplinary status of theology, and thus on the current context of the enduring but troubled science and theology dialogue, will inevitably find the intellectual and spiritual mood of our contemporary Western culture at the heart of this complex debate. This mood is radically pluralist and postmodern, and as such resists any attempt to catch it in one name, or one overarching description. Yet, I do believe that we still have good reasons for calling our culture at least a decidedly empirical culture: a culture determined by a tradition where the sciences — especially the natural sciences — not only dominate the way we live our lives, but ultimately still function as the paradigm and apex of human rationality. That religion and religious faith — let alone theology — are often and in many ways intellectually marginalized in this situation is by now a fact of life and as such taken more or less for granted. Many theologians, and also scientists who are believers, have, of course, taken the ongoing conflict between science and religion as a special challenge to identify possible models for creative dialogue, and even consonance or harmony between theology and science (cf. Barbour 1990, 1-30). In many ways this reflects an enduring attempt to identify religious faith as an autonomous moment in human experience, which can never be completely reduced to science, or even to metaphysics or morality. From this perspective, religion has its own integrity, with religious belief, reflection, and practice seen as valid expressions of the religious dimension of life (cf. Proudfoot 1985, xiiif.).

Strong pleas for the autonomy and unique nature of religious faith and religious experience will, of course, always fuel the ongoing theology and science dialogue, but they also reinforce some important — and confusing — stereotypes that have kept alive some of the typical "problems" of this debate. The most important of these problems reveals strong contradictions and even conflict (cf. Theissen 1984, 4ff.) between scientific thought and religious faith, and can be stated as follows (cf. van Huyssteen 1997, 239f.):

- scientific statements are hypothetical, fallible, and tentative, while statements of religious faith are dogmatic, ideological, and fideistic;
- scientific thought is always open to critical evaluation, justification, or falsification, while religious faith goes against the facts and often defies empirical evidence;
- scientific thought delights in critical dissent and constructive criticism, while faith more often than not depends on massive consensus and uncritical commitment;
- scientists therefore seem to base their beliefs on evidence and rational argument, while religious beliefs appear to be founded on "faith" only;
- scientific rationality is thus revealed as not only a very manicured and disciplined form of human reflection, but as also incommensurable with, and vastly superior to, religious faith and theological reflection.

It comes as no surprise that, on this view, science emerges as the great alternative not only to religious faith (cf. Midgley 1992, 139), but especially to theology as a reflection on this faith. Many of us, in fact, did grow up learning an account of our intellectual history as the story of the steady triumph of science over superstition and ignorance (cf.

Placher 1989, 14). Almost all of these stereotyped contrasts between science and religion, however, assume far too simple a picture of what both science and theology are about. When we dig deeper into this complex issue, therefore, much more is revealed about the philosophical and epistemological complexities of trying to contrast theology and science in this way. What emerges — often surprisingly — is a common or shared epistemological pattern: a reductionist notion of superior empiricist science is, after all, philosophically not all that different from an equally foundationalist conception of biblical literalism or religious fideism. Though scientism and scientific materialism seem often to be at the opposite end of the spectrum from biblical literalism or theologies that claim self-authenticating notions of divine revelation, their foundationalist approaches may share several characteristics (cf. van Huyssteen 1997, 240):

- both believe that there are serious conflicts between contemporary science and religious beliefs;
- both very specifically seek knowledge with secure and incontrovertible foundations, and find this in either logic, sense data, and experiment (science), or in an infallible scripture or self-authenticating revelation (theology);
- both end up claiming that science and theology make rival claims about the same domain and that one ultimately has to choose between them.

Ian Barbour has convincingly shown that both these typical conflictual approaches to the differences between theology and the natural sciences not only prolong a stereotyped conflict model between theology and science, but that they actually represent a misunderstanding of what science and theology are about (cf. Barbour 1990, 1ff.). The fact that theology and science may in actuality share foundationalist views while at the same time claiming to be in conflict also reveals why genuine conflicts between religion and science are exceedingly difficult to detect and specify accurately: in retrospect many of the serious clashes between religion and science turn out to be not so much clashes between religion and science as clashes between incompatible, even incommensurable, worldviews or philosophies (cf. Lash 1985, 277). I hope to show in this paper that the current dialogue between religion and science at the very least implies a fall from epistemological innocence as far as this complex and fascinating issue goes.

The Postmodern Challenge

The complexity of this kind of epistemological challenge becomes even more fascinating when we take note of remarkable shifts in the minds of scientists who seem to come up against the limits of scientific rationality in their own work. In his important *God and the New Physics* (1983), we find Paul Davies still working from a fairly simplistic but strong contrast between science and religion. The implied conflict between these two explains his reductionist use of scientific explanations to assess religious claims, his startling assertion that science offers a surer path to God than religion (cf. Davies 1983, ix), and his opting for a "natural God" who would be wholly within the universe, constrained by physical laws and accessible — at least in principle — to scientific investigation (cf. 209). Because of the theory of relativity and quantum theory, the "new physics" not only demands a radical reformulation of the most important aspects of reality but is uniquely placed to provide answers even to ultimate questions formerly reserved for religion. Now in a more recent work, *The Mind of God* (1992), Davies seems to make some important shifts: where previously he came up against a "natural God" by pushing the logic of scientific rationality as far back as it would go in search of ultimate answers, Davies now acknowledges the "mystery" at the end of the universe (cf. Davies 1992, 223ff.). He now seems to be arguing for the possibility of alternative modes of knowledge — even mystical knowledge — as valid ways of understanding the universe, its existence, and properties in categories that may lie outside the categories of regular scientific thought.

In a similar vein, Bernard D'Espagnat has stated that scientific rationality has its own very specific and inherent limitations, and then argues for a "window" within scientific rationality that seems to point to a "more" beyond the limitations of this kind of rationality: if someone would want to move beyond the limitations of empirical observation and experimentation, that is, the domain of the natural sciences, in a focused concern for the whole of reality, such a project could therefore not in advance be judged to be incoherent, illegitimate, or irrational (cf. D'Espagnat 1989, 205). This window, even if epistemically very small, is an opening made by rational means on the basis of the experienced limitations of scientific rationality, and suggests a richer notion of rationality that transcends the purely cognitive dimension of our human knowing. Along the same lines, much of modern physics is understood to have done away with the essentially classical ideal of an objective world existing securely out there, waiting to be measured and analyzed by us. Instead, quantum mechanics and relativity challenge the possibilities and limits of empirical knowledge and expose us as inalienable — but also limiting — participants in the world we are trying to understand (cf. Lindley 1993, 54).

It is, however, quite fascinating to see that, in spite of such a nuanced awareness of the limitations of natural scientific rationality, scientists like Paul Davies are also — and at the same time — seriously criticized by feminist thinkers for creating and prolonging a new form of "postmodern" patriarchy that grows out of revolutions in cosmology, mathematics, and quantum physics. James F. Moore (1995) has recently argued that precisely the highly visible and ubiquitous presence of quasi-theological ideas in the work of contemporary cosmologists like Paul Davies (1992), Frank Tipler (1994), Stephen Hawking (1988), and Steven Weinberg (1992), while an enticing new opportunity for dialogue between theologians and cosmologists, may also be a revisioning of traditional forms of patriarchy. Feminists have indeed long contended that science is especially resistant to the sort of feminist critique that might lead to the critical rethinking of science as a discipline (cf. Moore 1995, 614). Natural science's amazing isolation from feminist critique makes it especially difficult to assess whether a pattern such as patriarchy is indeed produced in the quasi-theologies emerging from much of contemporary cosmology. However, it also makes it especially difficult to evaluate what a truly *postmodern* form of science would look like, and how that would link up to, and possibly merge with, the postmodern challenge to contemporary philosophy of science.

For James Moore, the components of this patriarchy are so well established that we not only can accurately identify a white, middle-class, male worldview in science, but can also predict with uncanny precision what might be present in the thinking of anyone who accepts this worldview (cf. Moore 1995, 615). To this I would add that patriarchy thus surfaces in science as a typically modernist, foundationalist metanarrative and reveals itself primarily in science's innate conviction that natural scientific rationality is not only superior, but in its controlling, patriarchal grasp can actually claim to know and understand everything, and as such be totally rational, logical, and objective. Margaret Wertheim (1995) has recently argued that physics is the great bastion of patriarchy, and if this is even remotely true, then the ideas emerging from contemporary cosmology could indeed reflect the general contours of a patriarchal view of God. In this typically modernist, patriarchal view of God, God — in modernist science, as in modernist theology — emerges as the primary holder of power, fundamentally transcendent and separate from our world. God is the one in control of this universe, and this power and control is pointedly reflected in the laws and order of nature as parameters of this divine power (cf. Moore 1995, 617). What we find, then, are either chauvinist attempts at "theories of everything" as the projection of science's capacity to explain all aspects of the relation between the four primary forces of the universe, or more nuanced attempts like Paul Davies's to appeal to God as the mystery at the end of the universe. Even in this image, however, feminist critique would like to reveal the not-so-subtle image of the stereotypical male as the master in control of a well-designed universe.

It is at this point — the very serious challenge of the notion that there is one and only one true view of reality — that feminist critique fuses with other forms of postmodern criticism in philosophy of science and theology, and explodes the fantasy of a superior scientific rationality (cf. Moore 1995, 632). Nuanced views of the limits of scientific rationality such as these become a special challenge to theologians and also scientists who want to move away from the false certainties provided by overblown foundationalist epistemologies. However, moving away from the narrow focus on a strictly scientific rationality to broader and alternative ways of understanding may turn out not to be enough, and serious issues remain that need to be addressed. Special attention needs to be given, for instance, not only to differences and apparent contrasts between science and religion, but also to the important distinction between religion and theology. For instance, it will not suffice to allow only for crucial differences between, say, mysticism and scientific rationality, when theological reflection also presents itself as a form of knowledge, and then as a form of rational reflection, that not only may differ from mysticism in important ways, but which may in fact even overlap significantly with scientific rationality. Theology, in this reflective mode, may turn out to share more with scientific reflection than with mystical experience. Paul Davies may want to take human reasoning as far as it will go and not opt for mysticism and revelation, even if these — in transcending human reason — may indeed turn out to be valid alternative routes to a more comprehensive form of human knowledge (cf. 1992, 24ff.). However, in a nuanced notion of theological rationality we may for good reasons choose to see theology (as a reflection on religion and religious experience) not as bypassing human reason at all, and therefore not as an *alternative* to scientific rationality. It may still transcend and be different from a strictly scientific rationality, but it may at the same time in very important ways turn out to overlap with scientific rationality, and as such share in the human quest for intelligibility and ultimate meaning: a quest that has always been crucial for defining scientific rationality.

At the heart of the contemporary "religion and science" problem, then, lies the deeper problem of how the epistemic and other values that shape the rationality of religion and of theological reflection will be different from, or similar to, those that shape the rationality of science. The challenge of postmodernist pluralism, of course, makes it virtually impossible even to speak so generally about "rationality," "science," "religion," or "God." And even if we should want to embrace and appropriate positive, constructive forms of postmodern thinking, the crucial question still remains whether the rationality of science is in any significant way superior to other forms of rationality. Mainly as a result of the pervasive influence of the classical or positivist model of rationality in our culture, the natural sciences — especially the physical sciences — are indeed still regarded by many today as the paradigm for rationality. Postmodern philosophy of science has indeed, along with feminist critique, severely challenged this special status of the natural sciences (cf. Rouse 1991). Postmodern philosophy of science understandably rejects epistemological foundationalism as well as all metanarratives that would claim to legitimate scientific knowledge, practices, and results. In its extremist form this leads to the dismissal of philosophy of science itself as our traditional means of gaining an understanding of science (cf. Lötter 1994, 153ff.). This perspective replaces traditional philosophy of science with a postmodern reconstruction of the local activity of scientists, where scientific claims, explanations, procedures, and experiments are seen as part of a series of activities situated within the narrative field of science. On this view, then, all global legitimation of the epistemic status and ontological standing of science through philosophical argument is seen as typically modern, and challenged as such.

Postmodernism, however, has proved to be as protean and multiinterpretable as it is challenging. Not only in philosophy of science, but also in the theology and science dialogue, alternative interpretations of postmodern themes, as well as constructive appropriations of some of these, have become viable options. In his seminal work on the nature of human rationality, Harold Brown also rejects all forms of epistemological foundationalism and argues persuasively that an adequate model of rationality should indeed be exemplified by those disciplines that we, with good reasons, take to be paradigm cases of rational endeavor (cf. 1990, 79ff). This ultimately brings us face to face with the important question: is there a special sense in which the natural sciences — in spite of the pervasive influence positivism and the resulting challenge of postmodernism in contemporary philosophy of science — still provide us with a crucial test case in our quest for the nature of rationality, since scientific reflection currently still seems to stand as our clearest example of a rational enterprise?

Today, in a post-positivist and post-Kuhnian age, we know about the interpreted character of all knowledge, about the rediscovery of the hermeneutical dimension of scientific knowledge, and that the rules according to which scientific decisions are made change as science itself develops (cf. Bernstein 1983, 30ff.; Dean 1988, 88). And the fact that the rules change shows that they do not meet the conditions of universality and necessity imposed by the classical, modernist model of rationality. The historicist turn in philosophy of science initiated by Thomas S. Kuhn has thoroughly replaced the foundationalism of the classical model and has opened the way to various attempts at non- or anti-foundationalist models of rationality in philosophy of science. In his most recent work *Rationality and Science* (1993), Roger Trigg, on the other hand, wants to alert us to the dangers of complete relativism that may follow the necessary move away from objectivist notions of truth and verification. In a strong reaction against a modernist notion of rationality that stresses universality and necessity, nonfoundationalism could indeed easily align itself with a relativist mode of postmodern thinking and as such highlight the fact that every group and every context has its own rationality.

If this nonfoundationalist view were true, then any social or human activity could in principle function as a test case for rationality. This notion would leave us with an extreme relativism of rationalities: a relativism that not only forms the opposite of the classical model's objectivism, but a relativism that would also be devastating for any intersubjective truth-claims in both scientific and theological reflection. Proponents of the relativism of this "many rationalities" view hold that the rules which govern science are internal to science in the same way that other human activities (religion, business, magic, etc.) are also governed by rules internal to them. In the relativism that flows from this nonfoundationalism, it is therefore maintained that each area of human activity has criteria internal to a specific culture or social group. Since each area can therefore claim its own criteria of rationality, there can be no independent framework for deciding whether one framework is more rational than another (cf. Brown 1990, 113). For this way of thinking, the sciences, along with religion, are seen as just one more feature of postmodern Western society, where all cultures or societies create cognitive structures that explain the world around them. It is also obviously denied that the body of beliefs developed by science could be in any way cognitively superior to other beliefs.

Over against the objectivism of foundationalism and the extreme relativism of most forms of nonfoundationalism, I would like to propose *a postfoundationalist model of rationality* which would be thoroughly contextual, but which at the same time would reach beyond the limits of one's own group or culture in interdisciplinary conversation (cf. van Huyssteen 1997, 1ff., 238ff.). This view of rationality will aim to capture those features of science which indeed make it a paradigmatically rational enterprise without falling back into the kind of epistemological foundationalism so typical of the classical view of rationality. It is only within a postfoundationalist view of rationality very similar to this that Harold Brown can persuasively argue that, while science did indeed develop in the Western world, there are still powerful grounds for maintaining that science has a significance that transcends the particular culture in which it first appeared (cf. Brown 1990, 114). Whatever else a postfoundationalist model of rationality might mean, it certainly means at least the following: while we always operate in terms of concepts and criteria that appear within a particular culture, we are nonetheless able to transcend our specific contexts and reach out to more intersubjective levels of discussion. Over against the relativism of a nonfoundationalist "many rationalities" view, a postfoundationalist model of rationality aims to show that scientific reflection, as a highly contextualized reasoning strategy, can indeed be a potential and reliable source of knowledge that not only transcends the cultures in which the various sciences first appeared, but can also epistemically relate to broader and different notions of rationality.

This relates closely to the fact that the post-Kuhnian philosophy of science has shown us that there can be no sharp line of demarcation between scientific rationality and other forms of rationality (cf. van Huyssteen 1989, 63ff.). In fact, scientific rationality relates to a pre-analytic reasonableness of a more basic kind of human rationality that informs all goal-directed action. Within this broader context Christian theology too should seek a knowledge as secure as it can possibly achieve, a form of knowledge that will allow an optimal understanding of that to which Christian believers are committing themselves in faith. In the end this epistemic goal of theological reflection, more than anything — and in spite of important differences between a theological and a strictly scientific rationality — will determine the shaping of the rationality of theological reflection. And if in both theology and science we strive to explain better in order to understand better, then surely the epistemological problem of the nature of rationality should be one of the most important foci of our attempts to relate religion and science to one another meaningfully today. The complexity of the nature of human rationality, and the way this plays out differently in theology and the sciences, reveals that there are no easy ways to bridge the gap between these two in terms of models of "conflict," "dialogue," or even "consonance." In his own careful consideration of the complex history of Western thought, John Brooke very convincingly alerts us to the epistemological fallacy of directly inferring from contemporary science to theological doctrine (cf. Brooke 1991). Both theology and science are cultural phenomena: as modes of theoretical reflection they may not only mean different things in different times, but — since both are located in living, developing, evolving traditions — the boundaries between them are constantly shifting.

As theologians we should therefore take very seriously the theories of contemporary physics, biology, and the other sciences: not to exploit or to try to change them, but to find interpretations that could reveal important epistemological overlaps between theological and scientific modes of reflection. Only then would it make sense to explore some forms of hypothetical consonance with the Christian viewpoint. The theologian can never separate his or her science from his or her theology, but she or he should learn to distrust epistemological shortcuts from one discipline to the other. One way to do this would be to find a conceptual framework that would yield a broader, more flexible notion of human rationality.

The Move to Postfoundationalism

As a first step towards a broader and richer idea of rationality, we can follow the lead of Nicholas Rescher (1988, 1992) and identify at least three resources of rationality that are highly relevant not only for the natural, the social, and the human sciences, but also for theology as a reflection on religious experience: the *cognitive context,* the *evaluative context,* and the *pragmatic context* (cf. also van Huyssteen 1997, 249f.). None of these resources of rationality has priority over any of the others, even if cognitive rationality, or the cognitive dimension of rationality, is often dominant in intellectual issues. In both science and theology we are therefore challenged to make sound, rational judgment in our quest for intelligibility: finding good reasons for hanging on to certain beliefs, good reasons for making certain moral choices, and good reasons for acting in certain ways. Within a postfoundationalist epistemology these three go together as a seamless whole and merge in the common task of uniting the best reasons for belief, evaluation, and action.

In his move to an alternative, postclassical model of rationality, Harold Brown stresses the evaluative resources of rationality by highlighting the role of *critical judgment* in human cognition (cf. van Huyssteen 1997, 247ff.). Judgment in this broader epistemic sense is the ability to evaluate a situation, assess evidence, and then come to a reasonable decision without following rules (Brown 1990, 137; cf. van Niekerk 1990, 180). In Brown's concept of rationality, judgment plays a crucial epistemic role, and its focus on the particular and the contingent — instead of the general and the necessary — is a very definite step beyond the classical model's foundationalism. Brown argues persuasively that we cannot understand human knowledge fully without recognizing the role that judgment plays at key epistemic junctures. Judgments must be made by individuals who are in command of an appropriate body of information that is relevant to the judgment in question. Brown therefore develops the idea of rational judgment and intersubjective criticism as epistemic skills that should be performed by experts (cf. Brown 1990, 137).

Within the rule-governed context of the classical/positivist model of rationality, scientific statements would clearly be seen as rational because they are normally judged to be objective, impartial, and based on empirical evidence alone. Values, and value judgements, on the other hand, are normally seen as nonscientific and therefore as subjective, partial, the expressions of individual feeling, religious belief, or social convention, and as such, necessarily nonrational, because there is no objective way in which they could ever be justified. I believe this view implies not only a gross misrepresentation of what values are, but also of what science is (cf. Wavel 1980, 43ff.). Not only can scientific knowledge and a strictly scientific rationality be unopposed to values and value judgments in this way, but science — and therefore all scientific knowledge — is in fact always based on value judgments. In science, the acceptance and rejection of hypotheses, and also theory choice, are indeed based on evaluation and deliberation and place certain kinds of value judgments at the heart of the scientific method itself. This obviously means that the context of personal decisions forms a crucial part of the strategies of present-day science (cf. Hoering 1980, 127). And because science is so rational, its unavoidable dependence on values and value judgments implies that these too must be an integral part of the process of rational reflection. In fact, it could be argued that decisions by individual scientists to work on one problem rather than another already imply value judgments about the superiority of knowledge to ignorance, intelligibility to unintelligibility, and truth to error.

I think it is quite clear now that science not only employs value judgments at crucial epistemic junctures, but also that their role in science is so basic that the commonsense procedures of evaluation and deliberation, which are based on value judgments, are in fact essential to scientific rationality. The crucial role of value judgments in all rational reflection also reveals that, in both scientific and theological reflection, theory appraisal and theory choice will always imply complex and sophisticated forms of value judgment. Theory choice, on this view, can no longer be seen as the result of rule-following, as in the classical model of rationality, but instead reveals the influence of both empirical and extra-empirical factors. Included in these extra-empirical influences that shape the rationality of science are epistemic values such as predictive accuracy, coherence, simplicity, and so on, but also a host of non-epistemic values that scientists could hold on to, for example, naturalism, various forms of empiricism, pragmatism, and feminism (cf. also Jones 1994). And as in theological reflection, these epistemic and nonepistemic values that shape the rationality of scientific reflection are never just a chaotic collage of random beliefs or values, but are normally fairly coherent and reflect our fundamental commitment to specific worldviews and research traditions. These research traditions and broader worldviews are mostly tacitly assumed, are rarely produced through rational reflection alone, and reveal that scientific reflection — like theological reflection — is a very specific cultural and human phenomenon.

Because of the complete breakdown of any stark opposition between scientific and other forms of rationality in a postfoundationalist epistemology, it can thus be argued that there is no necessary difference between the epistemic uses of values and value judgments in science, and between their uses in other modes of rational inquiry like the humanities, ethics, and theology. What is more, the fact that in ethics or theology, for example, value judgments sometimes are more subjective than in science actually says nothing about how more or less rational a judgment in each of these fields of inquiry would be: it merely reveals a different epistemological focus and a broader experiential scope. This again reveals the cognitive, evaluative, and pragmatic resources of rationality, as well as the fact that theology and science, along with other modes of intellectual inquiry, share these common rational resources and are both capable of rational value judgments.

Harold Brown's specific perspective on the role of judgment in rational decision-making is exciting because it also frees us from the idea that only infallibility or perfectability counts in epistemic matters. When at any point in time we make a decision for something in the light of the best reasons available to us, there need be no incompatibility between accepting a set of fallible claims for a substantial period of time and being prepared to reconsider them when we have good reasons for doing so. On this view the development of cognitive skills is closely analogous to the development of physical skills, and the conscious, explicit rule-following that has long been taken as the paradigm of intelligent mental life captures only a small portion of our cognitive resources (cf. Brown 1990, 177). Earlier we saw that perhaps the most central idea in our commonsense notion of rationality is that we normally have good reasons for our rational beliefs and actions. Precisely because our rational beliefs are based on good reasons, we regard them as more rational than nonrational or irrational beliefs. Next to *rational beliefs*, however, we also need to identify who *rational persons* are, that is, persons who can exercise good sense and good judgment in difficult and complex circumstances. We expect a rational person to be open to new ideas, and — as Harold Brown puts it — to function well in the context of discovery (1990, 183). Brown therefore wants to retrieve neglected features of the classical concept as a possible basis for an alternative model of rationality. He does this in three steps:

1. In the first place the notion of the *rational agent* is taken as fundamental, and notions like "rational belief" are seen as derivative, in the sense that a rational belief will be one that is arrived at by a rational agent. Moreover, the classical notion of rationality stresses the idea that a belief's rationality is connected with the way we arrive at

that belief, that is, by way of a body of appropriate evidence, which then makes it a rational belief. This aspect of the classical model of rationality is now included by Brown in his own model, but it is developed very differently. In the classical model, the central emphasis is placed on the logical relations between the evidence and the belief, while the role of the agent is minimized. In the new, alternative model, the agent is taken to be basic, and the way that an agent deals with evidence in arriving at a belief will determine the rationality of that belief for him or her (Brown 1990, 185).

2. The ability to make judgments in those situations in which we lack sufficient rules to determine our decisions is seen as a characteristic feature of a rational agent. As in Rescher's view, the evaluative dimension and the accompanying notion of judgment become central to this model of rationality. It futhermore entails that our ability to act as rational agents is limited by our *expertise* (Brown 1990, 185). This does not mean that only experts can be rational, but it does mean that in cases where we may lack expertise, there may be only one rational decision open to us: to seek expert advice.

3. The third step required for Brown's alternative model is the introduction of a *social or contextual element* (Brown 1990, 187): rational decision-making is a socially mediated rather than a rule-governed process (cf. van Niekerk 1990, 184). For a belief based on judgment to be a rational one, it must be submitted to the community of those who share the relevant expertise. This demand, that rational beliefs be subject to evaluation and criticism, is in conformity with our normal understanding of rationality. Brown now correctly argues that this idea can be developed without its foundationalist implications, precisely by taking rationality to be a social phenomenon. Judgment therefore becomes necessary exactly when no general rules are available, and rationality thus always requires other people. And not just any other people, but people with the skills needed to exercise judgment on a particular issue within a specific context.

Brown here differs significantly from Thomas Kuhn and his consensus model of rationality. For Kuhn, the social aspect replaces positivist rules as the basis for scientific research and decision-making, rational decisions are those made by the scientific community, and in normal science these become embodied in communally approved and transmitted practices (Brown 1990, 191). Kuhn thus holds to the position that when the majority of a relevant scientific community reaches agreement, we have a rational decision. Brown, however, differs from

Kuhn precisely at this point: agreement with the majority does not automatically make a belief rational. Brown's model requires only that individuals submit their judgments for evaluation by their peers, and that they take this evaluation seriously. This is also much closer to real-life situations where, as academics and even as Christian theologians, we often hardly agree at all. Brown's model thus does not require that each member of the community agree with the majority, since agreement with the majority view is neither necessary nor sufficient for rationality (cf. 1990, 192). Scientific practice clearly demonstrates that rational disagreement is a pervasive feature of science. Brown's model therefore allows for and accepts the fact that human judgment is always fallible, and that our best chance of eliminating error is by exposing our judgments and decisions to the critical scrutiny of other people. In a postfoundationalist notion of rationality, therefore, the predicate "rational" characterizes an individual's decisions. It does not — in the first place at least — characterize beliefs, propositions, or communities. Even if a community of experts is necessary for an individual to arrive at a rational belief, it still is the individual's choice that is rational, and not the community (cf. Brown 1990, 193). Brown's alternative model of rationality makes the human agent who exercises judgment central to rational procedures, and it is the fallibility of this judgment that leads to the requirement of critical evaluation. And because of the way judgment is exercised here, our interpreted and traditioned experience enters the process that leads to rational judgment, even if we cannot always capture the experience in propositions.

At this point, however, we are faced with an important question: how does a postfoundationalist model of rationality get us beyond the social relativism of nonfoundationalism? If rationality involves nothing more than judgment and critical evaluation by the members of an appropriate community, then we may find rational belief and decision-making in communities that normally may even be characterized as irrational. For Brown, theologians are a case in point: "Various groups of theologians who belong to different religions may all be engaged in a fully rational endeavor, and the same may hold for, say, Azande witch doctors" (1990, 194). Brown is fully aware of the fact that this possibility follows from his model of rationality, and therefore argues along the following lines: (1) to claim that a belief is rational is not the same as to claim that a belief is true; (2) while rational acceptance of a claim indeed depends on the assessing of evidence, some forms of evidence provide a stronger warrant for belief than other forms of evidence. In his own words: "Thus while questions of denominational theology may be capable of a rational solution, it does not follow that we have no basis at all for choosing between, say, a scientific and a theological world-view at those points at which the two views conflict" (195). Although on this view theological rationality still seems to come a distant second to scientific rationality, Brown's argument for a richer notion of rationality does show that rationality in the classical sense is not enough when it comes to the cognitive assessment of knowledge-claims.

An even more careful analysis of this postfoundationalist move becomes possible when we realize that rationality not only involves evaluation against the standards of a community of inquiry, but also assures that the personal voice of the individual rational agent is not silenced in this ongoing process of collective assessment. In an important paper, Philip Clayton and Steven Knapp (1993) have outlined exactly what the epistemological ramifications for relating strong individual, personal convictions to the broader standards of a community of inquiry would be. Clayton and Knapp also confirm that rationality in general, and properly understood, always involves evaluation against the standards of a community of inquiry (cf. 1993, 151). Of course, the standards for what we see as good or bad reasons are never independent of our specific social and cultural contexts. This contextualist view of rational agency is enhanced by the fact that in a postfoundationalist epistemology the modernist distinction between "objective," empirical (read: scientific) reasons and more "subjective," ethical, religious, or aesthetic reasons is revealed as nonsensical. In all our reasoning strategies — and therefore in theology and the sciences too — this interactionist epistemology implies that we need to move beyond the forced separation of "purely objective" factual issues and "purely subjective" religious or theological issues. The responsible judgments that we hope to make, and the strong personal convictions that will flow from this, should substantiate the claim that some of our convictions are binding to us as rational agents *precisely* as a consequence of our commitment to rationality. This again confirms that rationality and context are more than just compatible: they are in fact inseparable (cf. also Clayton and Knapp 1993, 151f.). In trying to make a responsible judgment, the rationality of a given claim lies in its relation to an ongoing process of collective assessment. On this view a necessary condition for my claim that a judgment or belief is rational is that it has been subjected to — or is genuinely open to — criticism by the "experts," that is, those whom I take to be the relevant community of inquiry.

But what of the individual who sees beyond the available community, the gifted visionary or prophet who may be severely misunderstood by the community's ongoing collective assessment of his or her judgments, beliefs, and strong convictions? In an innovative twist Clayton and Knapp here open the door to another possibility: the rationality of a given claim is indeed to be found in an ongoing process of collective assessment, but at the same time there is no reason to hold that *any* presently existing community fully represents a rational agent's sense of what a community is or should be (cf. Clayton and Knapp 1993, 152). When a visionary, a genius, or a prophet relies almost exclusively on the standards of an as-yet-nonexistent communal rationality, the very specific limits of communal rationality are revealed. This also reveals the richness of the resources of human rationality, as the cognitive, pragmatic, and evaluative dimensions of rationality merge in the rational agent's own reasons for believing, acting, and judging. This means that our good reasons for making certain judgments, which will lead to certain strong convictions that will and should be critically evaluated in our epistemic community's ongoing process of collective assessment, are first of all evaluated against the standards implicit in each rational agent's *self-conception* (cf. Clayton and Knapp 1993, 152). By recognizing how a rational agent's personal judgments, beliefs, and actions are shaped by his or her self-conception, we have truly moved beyond any modernist attempts to argue for a universal, context-free, general account of human rationality. As human beings we are characterized by self-awareness, and our individual, personal motivations or reasons for believing, acting, and choosing are not only closely tied to some sense of who this "I" is but are indeed epistemically shaping the value judgments we make in terms of this self-conception. For Clayton and Knapp the notion of an individual's self-conception provides the indispensable starting point for an account of ethics (cf. 1993, 152).

I want to claim the same for our reflection on human rationality: the rational agent's self-conception and self-awareness are not only intrinsically connected to rationality; they are an indispensable starting point for any account of the values that shape human rationality. In the absence of the availability of modernist rules, metanarratives, or transcendental standards for rationality, each of us is left with only one viable option: in assessing what rationality is, I must assess it as I see it, from where I stand. As a human being with a distinct self-awareness, and a very specific quest for intelligibility, I can step into the reality of communicative praxis only from where I stand, and begin any intersubjective conversation only by appealing to *my* rationality (cf. Rescher 1993, 110). Thus, not only rationality and context, but also rationality and strong personal commitments inextricably go together. And as long as I participate in a rationally conscientious way in the back and forth of the feedback process that make up our communal discourse, I am rationally justified in holding on to my commitments and strong convictions.

As a rational agent I can enter any conversation only from my own perspective on what the rational explanation of experience is. It does *not* follow from this, as we will see, that for my standards to be rational, they should ultimately also be in agreement with those of others who are differently situated (cf. Rescher 1993, 110). Rationality, therefore, does not presuppose consensus. The epistemic tolerance that emerges from this pluralism flows from the experiential and contextual nature of rationality, but it should never lead to relativistic indifference. Precisely on this point Nicholas Rescher has argued persuasively that when it comes to making good rational choices for the right reasons, all perspectives that are taken to be normative are *not* going to be equally acceptable. If the experiential bases and the values that shape our judgments are at issue, then the pattern of our own ongoing, contextualized experience are going to be altogether decisive — for us at any rate — in communal discourse. And because rationality requires that we attune our beliefs and judgments to our own self-conception and self-awareness, rationality also requires that we attune our beliefs, convictions, and evaluations to the overall pattern of our experience. From this perspective, it should be clear that a postfoundationalist notion of rationality could never be some kind of superimposed metanarrative but rather develops as an emerging pattern that unifies our interpreted experience without totalizing it (cf. Schrag 1992, 154ff.). In this sense, the claim that rationality is always embedded in the rational agent's self-awareness also implies that one's own experience is always going to be rationally compelling (Rescher 1993, 119).

Rationality cannot be adequately understood if we do not completely accept the ramifications of the fact that every person has some form of self-awareness, some image of the kind of self he or she has been or wants to become. This self-conception always shapes what we regard as the most plausible reasons for the choices we make, the beliefs we commit ourselves to, and the actions we take. But this trust in our personal convictions must always be open to intersubjective assessment as we walk the fine line between our personal standards and the standards of what we regard as the ideal epistemic community. What is suggested here is a necessary "feedback relationship" between the self-aware individual and his or her social context (cf. Clayton and Knapp 1993, 153): an epistemic relationship in which we learn with discernment to acquire rational beliefs, not just about our worlds, but also about ourselves. Both individual and communal rationality therefore have necessary limitations, but for a full picture of the richness of human rationality it is necessary to see how they enhance one another. Communal consensus by itself cannot completely define rationality, but it also would not be rational for an individual to insist (without good reasons) on holding beliefs that conflict completely with the epistemic community's ongoing process of collective assessment. Rationality thus clearly entails an unavoidable investment in the interest of others. Because our epistemic communities never exist in complete isolation from one another, it will be important to realize that an adequately contextualized notion of rationality is necessary to facilitate intersubjective, cross-disciplinary conversation.

A postfoundationalist notion of rationality therefore does not return us to the relativist position, according to which every group or language game is automatically rational in terms of its own internal rules. This model involves tighter constraints and consequently moves beyond agreed-upon rules to submitting results for critical evaluation by experts in the field. On this view it is not rationality but rational beliefs that are always situated contextually. The thesis that what is rational to believe or do is relative to a particular situation should therefore not be confused with the thesis that rationality itself is relative. In a pluralist and cross-disciplinary dialogue, then, we begin our conversations by bringing our views, convictions, and judgments to those that make up our epistemic communities. The epistemic movement in a postfoundationalist evaluation of opinions and viewpoints therefore goes from individual judgment to expert evaluation to intersubjective conversation. Because each judgment always takes place in some community, and each community has a particular history, the broader research tradition(s) in which communities are embedded will now epistemically shape, but not completely determine, the questions one asks, the assumptions one makes, and the arguments one finds persuasive.

The very obvious relationship between rationality and context now invariably raises the question of the relation between rationality and truth. It does seem that the notion of truth is so deeply embedded in our thinking about cognitive matters that we can barely get along without it (Brown 1990, 198). In the classical notion of rationality there is a close tie between rationality and truth, and for this reason false propositions could never be rationally accepted. Contemporary anti-foundationalist and postmodern thought, on the other hand, emphasizes that people from different societies can accept radically different sets of claims as true, and that it is impossible to determine which of these claims are really true. Both Kuhn (1970) and Laudan (1977) have also shown that human beings have managed to function very successfully on the basis of beliefs that they later reject as false. It is extremely difficult, however, to dispense with the notion of truth completely (cf. Brown 1990, 197). Whatever we say or claim about truth or true premises does us little good unless we have reasons for believing that they are indeed true. This, according to Brown, is where rationality enters the picture, since rationality is concerned with assessing reasons and making value judgments for believing one claim or another (cf. 1990, 201). This, of course, is the great attraction of the classical model and makes the search for foundations so understandable. The epistemic failure of foundationalism, however, has left us without any strong truth-claims: the only reasons we now have for hanging on to our cognitive claims are that we judge them the best ones available to us.

The point here is that notions of truth and rationality are indeed distinct in the sense that achieving one of them in no way entails that the other has also been achieved — something that both theologians and scientists have notoriously found difficult to accept. There is, however, the possibility of a weaker but vital tie between rationality and truth: we proceed rationally in attempting to "discover" truth, and we take those conclusions that are rationally acceptable in terms of our own judgments as our best current estimates of the truth. Harold Brown argues that the search for truth is a long-term process and that we need coherent procedures to carry out this pursuit for optimal intelligibility, which for Brown is the ultimate function of rationality (cf. Brown 1990, 202). Brown's argument for a weak tie between truth and rationality turns out to be very persuasive for any attempt to arrive at a plausible postfoundationalist notion of progress in science. Even if we are committed to the view that later theories are better theories, it does not have to imply a closer-to-the-truth position. In his argument against such a theory of verisimilitude, Nicholas Rescher also warns against the temptation to think of *improvement in warrant* (having better reasons) in terms of *improvement in approximation* (moving closer to the truth; cf. Rescher 1992, 48). In fact, since we now accept that science often progresses through revolutions and radical shifts, there is no way that we can still think of scientific truth as developing by way of convergence or accumulation.

What is achieved in scientific inquiry is therefore not an *approximation of truth* but an *estimation of truth:* scientists form, as best as they can, a reasoned judgment of where the truth of the matter lies. In this way we may not manage to get nearer to "the truth," but we do present our best estimates of what we believe the truth might be within a specific context (cf. van Huyssteen 1997, 255). On the level of scientific theorizing, our present world picture thus represents a better estimate than our past attempts only in the sense that it has accommodated, comparatively speaking, a wider range of data. This fallibilism is also strengthened by Rescher's consistent and helpful distinction between a *better estimate* (one that has fewer deficits and may be based on fuller information) and a *closer estimate* (one that claims to be closer to the "real truth"): in scientific theorizing we must settle for a qualitative "better" because there is obviously no way of monitoring the issue of a measure "closer" (cf. Rescher 1992, 53). The fact that scientific knowledge also moves through radical changes and discontinuities invalidates any talk of successive approximation. Our accepted truths — in both science and theology — should therefore be viewed as nothing more than the best estimates that we are able to make in the present moment. For pragmatic reasons, however, it might still make sense to talk about "pursuing truth" (cf. Rescher 1992, 56).

A postfoundationalist model of rationality thus preserves the idea of progress and the idea that rational beliefs are based on good evidence, although there are now different sources of evidence for different claims. This becomes even clearer when we take a closer look at the concept of objectivity. Obviously we first need to disassociate ourselves from the view that objectivity requires that we approach our subject without any preconceptions. What Brown argues for is that objectivity means at least this: that the evidence or good arguments supporting an objective belief must derive from a source that is independent of that belief (Brown 1990, 203). The example that Brown uses to illustrate this is taken from physics: a physicist, working within a certain historical and social context, might claim that all matter is constructed of electrons, neutrons, and protons. What is normally claimed here is that these are actually features of the physical world. Of course these claims, like all intellectual or specifically scientific claims, are made from a certain historical and social context. Brown correctly argues, however, that such claims are nevertheless not solely claims about that context, culture, or language. One of the things that language permits us to do is precisely to make claims about items that exist apart from us and our language (cf. Brown 1990, 203).

So, once we have acknowledged the cultural, linguistic, or social context of a claim, the point remains that many claims make assertions about some state of affairs that is independent of those claims. For Brown these are paradigm examples of the pursuit of objectivity (cf. 1990, 204), and as such come very close to what Nicholas Rescher has called the pursuit of truth. It is, of course, important to remember that not all matters can be studied objectively: some subjects may not have what Brown has called a "required ontological status" (1990, 205). We have, for example, no objective basis for evaluating ethical claims. This, however, does not by itself block the exercise of rationality in these fields, for there may be other considerations that can provide the basis for rational evaluation. One may, for example, have good reasons for believing that an ethical system ought to have a certain degree of coherence (cf. also theology), and that this should provide grounds for rational analysis.

This argument for a weak notion of objectivity is certainly not meant to function as a basis or "foundation" for a strong metaphysical realism. The point is that we normally study items or issues that are relatively independent of the claims we make about them. It is even more crucial, however, always to distinguish carefully between rationality and objectivity: rationality (cf. in theology) is indeed possible even in the absence of regular scientific objectivity. Still, objectivity remains epistemically important because it provides us with an especially powerful body of evidence to be used in the rational assessment of our claims.

Theology and Science as a Case Study for Interdisciplinary Reflection

This discussion of the role and characteristics of truth, progress, and objectivity in science brings us to the problem of the status of science, and of how much we can hope to achieve through scientific knowledge vis-à-vis theological knowledge. The key question here is: how far can the scientific enterprise advance toward achieving complete intelligibility or a definite understanding of nature? The fallibilism implied in a postfoundationalist notion of scientific rationality necessarily leads to what has been called the imperfectability of science (cf. Rescher 1992, 77f.). A fallibilist epistemology necessarily implies that our knowledge — even our scientific knowledge — can never be complete or perfect. For Nicholas Rescher this *fait accompli* invites a description of the cognitive situation of the natural sciences in theological terms: expelled from the Garden of Eden, we are deprived of access to the God'-eye point of view. We yearn for absolutes but have to settle for plausibilities; we desire what is definitely correct but have to settle for conjectures and estimates (cf. 1992, 85). The ideal of a perfected science, though unattainable, is nevertheless epistemically highly useful. Rescher calls this idea of a perfected science a *focus imaginarius* whose pursuit channels and thereby structures our scientific inquiry: "As such it represents the ultimate telos of inquiry, the idealized destination of an incompletable journey, a grail of sorts that we can pursue but not possess" (Rescher 1992, 94).

We have again returned to one of our most important initial questions: if scientific knowledge itself is so imperfect and essentially fallibilist, why does it provide such an important test case for our reflection on rationality, and for our attempts to discern a meaningful epistemological consonance between science and theology? Having moved beyond the foundationalism of the classical model of rationality and its restrictive notions of verification and empirical evidence, it now becomes possible to claim the following: rationality, specifically a post-foundationalist notion of rationality, still requires serious assessment of evidence, and we should therefore find our clearest examples of cognitive rationality in an area or field where the most reliable evidence is systematically gathered and deployed. Objective procedures still provide the richest and most reliable evidence, and one of the most important features of science is precisely its systematic pursuit of objective evidence (cf. Brown 1990, 207).

With this, I think, the selection of scientific reflection as possibly our best available and clearest example of the cognitive dimension of rationality at work is indeed still justified. This special position of the sciences, which now, in a much more qualified and weak sense, is still the paradigm of rationality at work, is ultimately also the reason why contemporary philosophy of science still forms the most important epistemological link in the current religion and science debate. What is not justified, however, is any claim that uncritically extends the nature of such a strictly scientific rationality to the rationality of religious or theological reflection. Because of the nature and the comprehensive resources of human rationality, the rationality of science and the rationality of religious reflection do seem to overlap at some very crucial junctures. The theologian shares with the scientist the crucial role of being a rational agent, of making the best possible rational judgments within a specific context and for a specific community. The theologian also shares with the scientist the fallibilism implied by the contextuality of rational decision making and thus the experiential and interpretative dimension of all our knowledge. The experiential and interpretative roots of religious knowing, however, are much more complex than the mostly empirical roots of scientific knowledge. Rationality in religion and in theological reflection is, therefore, a broader and more complex affair than a strictly scientific rationality (cf. Moore 1994). The lingering imperialism of scientific rationality should not close our eyes, however, to the remarkable epistemic consonance between scientific and theological ways of thinking. At the same time some scientists and philosophers of science, as we saw before, are acknowledging the limitations of scientific rationality (cf. D'Espagnat 1989; Davies 1992), and are thereby also opening the way to the acknowledgment of broader notions of rationality.

The close ties between science and rationality, of course, present the religion and science debate with yet another challenging question: *why is natural science possible at all?* What happens so that the lawful order of nature becomes intelligible to us in the conceptual terms that we have devised? Philosophers such as Nicholas Rescher and scientists such as Paul Davies have persuasively argued that the problem of the intelligibility of nature is eminently expressed in the question of the cognitive accessibility of nature to mathematizing intelligence (cf. Rescher 1992, 99). In fact, the belief that the underlying order of the world can be expressed in mathematical form lies at the very heart of science, and as such is rarely questioned (cf. Davies 1992, 140). Rescher's answer to this crucial question not only reveals a postfoundationalist move to an interactionist or relational model of rationality that enables him to transcend the rigid realism/antirealism debate but also gets him to a position that is very close to what Jerome Stone (1992) has called *transactional realism:* the answer to the question of the cognitive accessibility of nature to mathematizing intelligence can only be found in a somewhat complex, two-sided story in which both sides, intelligence and nature, must be expected to have a part (Rescher 1992, 99). This, of course, is consonant with the most basic thrust of a modest or weak form of critical realism: it is precisely the interaction between our thoughts and the world which conditions our sense of order, beauty, regularity, symmetry, and elegance. Evolutionary pressure thus coordinates the mind with its environment. For Nicholas Rescher, this leads to a crucial epistemological insight: the mathematical mechanisms we employ for understanding our world reflect the structure of our (interpreted) experience. In this sense it is no more a miracle that the human mind can understand the world through its intellectual resources than that the human eye can see it through its physiological resources (Recher 1992, 100).

A model of rationality that in this interactionist way allows us to acknowledge that we devise our mathematics and science to fit nature through the mediation of experience reveals an unexpected epistemological consonance between theology and science. I have argued before that all religious (and certainly all theological) language reflects the structure of our interpreted experience (cf. van Huyssteen 1993, 253-265). In science our concepts and theories can therefore be seen as products of an interaction in which both nature and ourselves play a formative role. Talking abstractly about the intelligibility of nature, about the regularities of nature and the laws that express them, indeed remains incomplete until we answer the more basic question: *intelligible for whom?* This frees us to realize that science, like all intellectual endeavors is, in Rescher's words, *our* science. This implies that reality can never be described or presupposed in any absolute way, but is known through investigator-relative results that will differ with different modes of interactions between our world and us (cf. Rescher 1992, 111).

What is at stake in this postfoundationalist model of rationality is not so much the ontological question as to the existence or not of the "real world" (mind-independent or not, as in the realism/antirealism debate), but rather the status of our knowledge of reality as presupposed in the epistemic process. Rescher also convincingly argues, in his own way, that regardless of the extent to which reality may be "mind-independent," our knowledge of this reality represents information yielded only by the ongoing interpretation of our experience (1992, 119). What is relevant and important for us, therefore, depends on how we go about experiencing our world, and how we interact with what we see as reality. For the theology and science discussion a plausible epistemological consonance emerges only on this level: as we have seen, the resources of rationality are indeed broader than just cognitivity. But epistemological fallibilism and rational accountability become viable options only when we realize that our exclusive cognitive access to reality is through the construction of a "world picture" or models in which our own intellectual resources play a crucially conditioning and shaping role.

Obviously the issue of objectivity (in the sense of mind-independence) is pivotal for any form of realism. Rescher argues that realism in this broad sense has two inseparable and indispensable constituents — the one existential and ontological, the other cognitive and epistemic (cf. 1992, 256). The former maintains that there is indeed a real world, a realm of mind-independent, physical reality. The latter maintains that we can to some extent secure information about this mind-independent realm. What is crucial about Rescher's position on realism — vis-à-vis strong forms of scientific realism (that argue for realism on the basis of the success of science) and also some forms of critical realism that attempt to ground reference to reality in a correspondence view of truth — is that the ontological component of this philosophical realism is not a matter of discovery or the result of argument, but rather a functional or pragmatic presupposition for our inquiries (257). Without this presupposed conception of reality it would be hard to maintain a fallibilist epistemology. The justification of this fundamental presupposition of objectivity is not evidential, and therefore not foundationalist: it is, rather, a functional one.

This account of the pragmatic basis of a weak form of critical realism results in a truly postfoundationalist move: *on this view realism is a position to which we are constrained not by the push of evidence, but by the pull of purpose* (cf. Rescher 1992, 270). Realism in this mode does not represent a discovered fact or a justified position, but rather the methodological presupposition of our praxis of inquiry. Traditional realists see the basis for realism in the success and progress of science (cf. Leplin 1984, 1-8). Because of its necessary fallibilism, however, a pragmatic form of critical realism implies an epistemic humility that pivots on the inevitable provisional character of all our knowledge and on the idea that — whether in theology or science — there is more to reality than we can actually know. A postfoundationalist notion of rationality, shared as a rich and mutual source by both science and theology, thus reveals an epistemic consonance and epistemological overlap that transcends the important differences between scientific and theological reflection. In so doing, it honors the provisional, contextual, and fallibilist nature of all human knowledge while at the same time enabling us to retain our ideals of truth, objectivity, rationality, and progress.

Thus, once again, a broader and richer notion of human rationality is revealed with its distinct cognitive, evaluative, and pragmatic dimensions. Whether in religion or science, in each of these fields we have good reasons for hanging on to certain beliefs, good reasons for making certain judgments and moral choices, and good reasons for acting in certain ways. In theology, as a critical reflection on religion and religious experience, rationality implies the ability to give an account, to provide a rationale for the way one thinks, chooses, acts, and believes. Here too theory-acceptance has a distinct cognitive dimension. When we ask, however, what besides belief is involved in theory-acceptance, the pragmatic and evaluative dimensions of theory-acceptance are revealed (cf. van Fraassen 1980, 3ff.). Here the rationality of science and of theology very much overlap in that both exhibit what intellectual practice would be like for those who adopt a specific model of thought. From this it does not follow that the natural sciences are "just like" theology. Furthermore, what sets science apart is certainly not that decisions between scientific theories are made by some objective procedure, a procedure forever unavailable to theological decision-making (cf. Placher 1989, 50).

In both theology and science, then, rationality pivots in the deployment of good reasons: an act of judgment in which we, through believing, doing, and choosing the right thing for the right reasons, become rational persons. Being rational is therefore not just a matter of having some reasons for what one believes in and argues for, but having the strongest and best available reasons to support the rationality of one's beliefs within a concrete context. The hazy intersection between the diverse fields of theology and the other sciences is therefore not in the first place to be determined by exploring possible methodological parallels or degrees of consonance between theology and science. What should be explored first is a common and shared resource found in a richer notion of human rationality, even if these important epistemological overlaps sometimes are overwhelmed by equally important differences beween religion and science. Thus are revealed the unacceptable epistemological shortcuts that come into play when the rationality of science is contrasted with the so-called irrationality or nonrationality of religion, or even when the rationality of religion, and of theological reflection, is proclaimed to be radically different in every possible respect from scientific rationality. We now know that rationality cannot be narrowed down to a strictly scientific rationality, and scientific rationality cannot be reduced to natural scientific rationality.

I would therefore like to claim that the quest for intelligibility and ultimate meaning in theology is also dependent on broader resources than just the purely cognitive, that is, on the evolving nature of the epistemic and non-epistemic values that have shaped theological rationality throughout history. But what does this imply concretely for theology? At the very least it implies that the realist assumptions and faith commitments of experienced Christian faith are relevant epistemological issues to be dealt with seriously in the theology and science discussion. By doing this, theology could move away from the absolutism of foundationalism as well as from the relativism of nonfoundationalism. This can further be achieved by showing that because theology is an activity of a community of enquirers, there can be no way to prescribe a rationality for that activity without considering its actual practice, along with the way this reflective practice grows out of the way Christian believers live a daily life of faith.

The theology and science dialogue in a very specific way reveals how the explanatory role of interpreted experience in theology can only be adequately appreciated in terms of an experiential epistemology. This not only means that religious experience is better explained theologically, but that in explaining the role of experience, the philosophical theologian will have to move from the question of rationality to intelligibility, from intelligibility to the question of personal understanding, and from personal understanding to personal experience. This is something the scientist need never do when doing science. Dealing with personal commitment in this way may show that the rationality of religion, and therefore of theology, is often shaped by epistemic values different from those of science. The dependence of theology on this kind of experiential adequacy for determining and maintaining its explanatory adequacy, however, need never again mean that theology is less rational, or less contextual for that matter, than science.

The nature of the ongoing discussion between theology and science should help us to realize that, in spite of a promising and emerging new field of study, the complex relationship between scientific and religious epistemology is more challenging than ever. This becomes all the more clear when we keep in mind not only the deconstruction and discovery of the limitations of the natural sciences in the post-Kuhnian era, but also when we focus carefully on the nature of the natural sciences. The sciences are eminently competent when it comes to theory construction and to experimental and pragmatic enterprises, but they are unqualified when it comes to finding answers to our deepest religious questions. In religion, and in theological reflection, we go beyond strictly scientific reflection when we focus on the role of story and ritual, and on the often noncognitive functions of religious models in evoking attitudes and encouraging personal transformation (cf. Barbour 1990, 66ff.).

The fundamental differences between theology and science should therefore be respected, as well as the differences between different forms of explanation, not only between the different sciences, but also between theology and the other sciences. However, in spite of important differences and sometimes radically different levels of explanation, theology and science do share common resources of rationality. A theology and a science that come to discover this mutual quest for intelligibility in spite of some very important differences will also be freed to discover that nothing that is part of, or the result of, natural scientific explanation need ever be logically incompatible with theological reflection. Science can tell us little or nothing about our experience of subjectivity, about the astonishing emergence of human consciousness and personhood, and about why we have an intelligible universe. God is the name that Christian believers give to the best available explanation of all that is (cf. Peacocke 1990, 134).

In focusing on the importance of the natural sciences, we should then have an openness for that which reaches beyond the world of the natural sciences, that is, to the world on which the social sciences, history, philosophy, and theology focus. In this wider context we could discover that theology and science both share not only a mutually enriching quest for intelligibility, but also the importance of tradition and of the explanatory role of interpreted experience. An honest analysis of the differences between the sciences and between theological and scientific explanations might then yield more intelligibility in the apologetic attempt to understand our postmodern world as truly God's own world.

Conclusion

In this paper I have tried to deal with two powerful challenges that underlie the current theology and science dialogue: first, the rationality of theological reflection is primarily and definitively shaped by its location in the living context of the contemporary interdisciplinary discussion; second, this interdisciplinary context is — epistemologically at least — significantly shaped by the dominant presence and enduring influence of scientific rationality on our culture. Theologians, often focusing on what is perceived to be the unique hermeneutics of theological reflection, have notoriously neglected this profound epistemological challenge by ignoring or not seeing the pervasive influence of the sciences on the epistemic and other values that shape theological reflection.

Rediscovering the fact that the theology and science dialogue is only part of a larger and more comprehensive conversation about the interdisciplinary status of theological reflection has therefore enabled us to address three important questions:

1. Are there good reasons for still seeing the natural sciences as our clearest available example of human rationality at work?
2. If so, does the rationality of theology and of theological reflection have anything in common with scientific rationality, and what would the significance of these epistemological overlaps be?
3. Even if there are large and impressive overlaps between these two modes of rationality, how would the rationality of science and the rationality of theological reflection be different?

My conclusion has been that science can still, but only in a very qualified sense, be seen as the clearest available example we have of the cognitive dimension of human rationality at work (cf. van Huyssteen 1997, 263f.). This does not mean that science or scientific rationality is in any way superior to other modes of rationality. On the contrary, a postfoundationalist notion of rationality reveals rich and complex resources for human rationality that are shared by scientific and theological reflection. With this it also has been possible to reject a nonfoundationalist "many rationalities" view in which science and religion represent radically different and often incommensurable forms of life. Today, in our postmodern culture, not only religion but also science turn out to be surprisingly pluralist subjects (cf. Placher 1989, 14f.). With the demise of positivism and the classical model of rationality, the claim that the problems of pluralism and relativism in science can be solved by appealing to universality and objectivity on the basis of scientific method is long gone. Different modes of rationality should therefore today be judged not in terms of a superior scientific rationality, but by the way in which they share in the common cognitive, evaluative, and pragmatic resources of human rationality.

It would therefore not be justified to extend the nature of a strictly scientific rationality to the rationality of religion or theological reflection. The theologian, in her or his reflection on the meaning of religious experience does, however, share with the scientist the following:

1. the crucial role of being a rational agent, and of having to make the best possible judgments within a specific context, and within and for a specific community;
2. the epistemological fallibilism implied by contextual decision-making;
3. the experiential and interpretative dimension of all our knowledge;
4. the fact, therefore, that neither science nor theology can ever have demonstrably certain foundations.

The methods of science, as our best example of cognitive rationality at work, are therefore unique: but not unique in the sense of providing a uniquely rational or uniquely objective way of discovering truth. Science is unique because of its history of success in coping with the problems of empirical reality. Beyond the fact that theology and science share the rich resources of human rationality, it always remains important to take note of the equally important differences between scientific and theological rationality. William Stoeger has recently and very successfully argued that we should move away from simplistic contrasts between theology and science which often try to pinpoint the difference between the two in terms of their very different objects (cf. Stoeger 1988, 232f.). The difference between these two claimants to human rationality is not, for instance, based only on the difference between "empirical problems" and "God's revelation." The difference between the two is a much more refined one, and is found rather in significant differences in *epistemological focus, experiential scope,* and *heuristic structures.* What is important here is more than just differences in object, language, and method. The theology and science dialogue indeed turns out to be at the heart of the debate on the interdisciplinary nature and location of theological reflection, and clearly presents itself as a plausible context for a contemporary apologetics for the Christian faith.

A postfoundationalist notion of rationality should, therefore, be able to open our epistemological eyes to broader and more complex notions of rationality, where scientific rationality — even if still our clearest example of the cognitive dimension of rationality at work — cannot and should not be taken as normative for religious faith. And although theology, as reflection on this religious faith, shares with science the contextual, experiential, and interpretative dimension of all human knowledge, the experiential and interpretative roots of religious knowing are always much more complex than the experiential and interpretative roots of empirical, scientific knowledge. Religious beliefs cannot, therefore, be easily likened to empirical hypotheses, because they grow out of much more complex situations. Religion and religious faith (and theological reflection, in spite of important epistemological overlaps with scientific reflection) are in many ways not like science at all: for the adherents of many religious traditions, faith involves not just a way of looking at the world, but also a personal trust in God. An ultimate faith commitment to God is, in this respect, more like trust in a friend or a spouse than like belief in a scientific theory (cf. Placher 1989, 141). On this very personal level, theology and science indeed seem to be very different kinds of activities, each with their own rules in their own domains, but neither one necessarily less rational than the other.

A postfoundational model of rationality thus focuses not only on the experience of knowing, and therefore on the experiential and hermeneutical dimensions of rationality, but also implies for both theology and the sciences an accountability to human experience. Despite important differences in epistemological focus and experiential scope, theology and all other modes of inquiry do seem to be shaped by the epistemic value of experiential accountability. I see this experiential accountability playing out as only a gradual difference between empirical adequacy in science and experiential adequacy in theological reflection. This shared experiential accountability reveals that in both theology and the sciences we relate to our world epistemically through the mediation of interpreted experience. In theology this will be the final and decisive move beyond fideist strategies: strategies which still claim theology's own "internal logic" or self-authenticating notions of divine revelation as a basis for disciplinary integrity and then proceed to set up a dualism between naturalism and supernaturalism with a demand for a reductionist choice between these two. In both theology and science, experiential adequacy pivots, rather, on the deployment of good reasons: an act of responsible judgment in which we, through believing, doing, and choosing the right thing for the right reasons, become rational persons.

Finally, in this paper I have also briefly touched on the fact that postmodernism, as a contemporary cultural phenomenon, has clearly been unable to come to terms with the issue of rationality in any positive way. As a result of the postmodernist challenge, however, many of the stereotyped ways of relating theology and science through models of conflict, independence, consonance, harmony, or dialogue are revealed as simplistic generalizations about the relationship between these two dominant forces in our culture. The challenge so typical of postmodernist pluralism not only implies a heightened awareness, and a historical sensitivity, to the shifting boundaries between theology and science, but in fact makes it impossible even to speak so generally about "rationality," "religion," "theology," "God," or "Divine action." It has therefore become clear that "theology" and "science" do not exist in such a generalized, abstract sense, but always only in quite specific social, historical, and intellectual contexts. We have also seen that the rationality of both theological and scientific reflection is thus situated within the context of living, developing, and changing traditions, and that it is necessary to distinguish between constructive and deconstructive modes of postmodern reflection.

To find a safe epistemological space for theology and science beyond the postmodern challenge, I have proposed the rediscovery and revisioning of the shared resources of theological and scientific rationality by recasting the theology and science discussion in postfoundationalist terms. In a postfoundationalist Christian theology the focus will always, and first of all, be on a relentless criticism of uncritically held crypto-foundationalist assumptions. This should allow us to explore freely and critically the experiential and interpretative roots of all our beliefs, and to be open to the fact that, even in matters of faith, religious commitment, and theological reflection, we relate to our world only through interpreted experience. The theologian is thus freed to speak and reflect from within a personal faith commitment, and in cross-disciplinary conversation with the scientist, to discover patterns that might be consonant with the Christian worldview.

References

Barbour, Ian. 1990. *Religion in an Age of Science*. San Francisco: Harper and Row.

Bell, Catherine. 1996. "Modernism and Postmodernism in the Study of Religion." *Religious Studies Review* 22:3.

Bernstein, Richard J. 1983. *Beyond Objectivism and Relativism*. Oxford: Basil Blackwell.

Brooke, John H. 1991. *Science and Religion: Some Historical Perspectives.* Cambridge: Cambridge University Press.

Brown, Harold. 1990. *Rationality.* London: Routledge.

Clayton, Philip, and Steven Knapp. 1993. "Ethics and Rationality." *American Philosophical Quarterly* 30:2.

Davies, Paul. 1983. *God and the New Physics.* New York: Simon and Schuster.

_____. 1992. *The Mind of God: The Scientific Basis for a Rational World.* New York: Simon and Schuster.

Dean, William. 1988. *History Making History: The New Historicism in American Religious Thought.* New York: State University of New York Press.

D'Espagnat, B. 1989. *Reality and the Physicist.* Cambridge: Cambridge University Press.

Drees, Willem B. 1990. *Beyond the Big Bang: Quantum Cosmologies and God.* La Salle: Open Court.

Hawking, Stephen. 1988. *A Brief History of Time.* New York: Bantam Books.

Hoering, Walter. 1980. "On Judging Rationality." *Studies in the History and Philosophy of Science* 11:2.

Jones, Stanton. 1994. "A Constructive Relationship for Religion with the Science and Profession of Psychology: Perhaps the Boldest Model Yet." *American Psychologist* 49:3.

Kuhn, Thomas S. 1970. *The Structure of Scientific Revolutions.* Chicago: The University of Chicago Press.

Lash, Nicholas. 1985. "Production and Prospect: Reflections on Christian Hope and Original Sin." In *Evolution and Creation,* ed. E. McMullin. Notre Dame: The University of Notre Dame Press.

Laudan, Larry. 1977. *Progress and Its Problems: Towards a Theory of Scientific Growth.* London: Routledge and Kegan Paul.

Leplin, Jarrett. 1984. *Scientific Realism.* Berkeley: University of California Press.

Lindley, David. 1993. *The End of Physics: The Myth of a Unified Theory.* New York: Basic Books.

Lötter, H. P. P. 1994. "A Postmodern Philosophy of Science?" *South African Journal of Philosophy* 13:3.

McMullin, Ernan. 1981. "How Should Cosmology Relate to Theology?" In *The Sciences and Theology in the Twentieth Century,* ed. A. R. Peacocke. Notre Dame: University of Notre Dame Press.

Midgley, Mary. 1992. *Science as Salvation: A Modern Myth and Its Meaning.* London: Routledge.

Moore, Gareth. 1994. "A Scene with Cranes: Engagement and Truth in Religion." *Philosophical Investigations* 17:1-13.

Moore, James F. 1995. "Cosmology and Theology: The Reemergence of Patriarchy." *Zygon* 30:4.

Peacocke, Arthur. 1990. *Theology for a Scientific Age*. Oxford: Basil Blackwell.

Placher, William C. 1989. *Unapologetic Theology: A Christian Voice in a Pluralist Conversation*. Louisville: Westminster/John Knox.

Proudfoot, Wayne. 1985. *Religious Experience*. Berkeley: University of California Press.

Rescher, Nicholas. 1988. *Rationality*. Oxford: Clarendon.

_____. 1992. *A System of Pragmatic Idealism*. Vol. 1. Princeton: Princeton University Press.

_____. 1993. *Pluralism: Against the Demand for Consensus*. Oxford: Clarendon.

Rouse, Joseph. 1991. "The Politics of Postmodern Philosophy of Science." *Philosophy of Science* 58:607-627.

Schrag, Calvin. 1992. *The Resources of Rationality: A Response to the Postmodern Challenge*. Bloomington: Indiana University Press.

Stoeger, W. R. 1988. "Contemporary Cosmology and Its Implications for the Science-Religion Dialogue." In *Physics, Philosophy and Theology: A Common Quest for Understanding*, ed. Robert J. Russell, William R. Stoeger, and George Koyne. Rome: Vatican Observatory.

Stone, Jerome. 1992. *The Minimalist Vision of Transcendence: A Naturalist Philosophy of Religion*. New York: State University of New York Press.

Theissen, Gerd. 1984. *Biblical Faith: An Evolutionary Approach*. London: SCM.

Tipler, Frank J. 1994. *The Physics of Immortality*. New York: Anchor Books/Doubleday.

Trigg, Roger. 1993. *Rationality and Science: Can Science Explain Everything?* Oxford: Blackwell.

van Fraassen, Bas. 1980. *The Scientific Image*. Oxford: Clarendon Press.

van Huyssteen, J. Wentzel. 1989. *Theology and the Justification of Faith: The Construction of Theories in Systematic Theology*. Grand Rapids: Wm. B. Eerdmans.

_____. 1993. "Critical Realism and God: Can There Be Faith after Foundationalism?" In *Intellektueel in Konteks*, ed. A. van Niekerk, W. Esterhuyse, and J. Hattingh. Pretoria: HSRC Publishers.

_____. 1997. *Essays in Postfoundationalist Theology.* Grand Rapids: Wm. B. Eerdmans.

van Niekerk, A. A. 1990. "To Follow a Rule or to Rule What Should Follow? Rationality and Judgment in the Human Sciences." In *Knowledge and Method in the Human Sciences,* ed. Johan Mouton and Dian Joubert. Pretoria: HSRC Publishers.

Wavel, Bruce B. 1980. "The Rationality of Values." *Zygon* 15:1.

Weinberg, Steven. 1992. *Dreams of Final Theory.* London: Hutchinson Radius.

Wertheim, Margaret. 1995. *Pythagoras' Trousers: God, Physics and the Gender Wars.* New York: Times Books.

A Critical Realist Perspective on the Dialogue between Theology and Science

Kees van Kooten Niekerk

1. Critical Realism

Critical realism is a philosophical view of the nature of knowledge. On the one hand, it holds that it is possible to acquire knowledge about the external or physical world as it really is, independent of the human mind or subjectivity. That is why it is called *realism*. On the other hand, it rejects the claim of so-called naive realism that the external world is as we experience it. Valid knowledge of the real world can only be acquired through critical reflection upon experience. That is why it is called *critical*.

Historically, the term has been used in connection with different philosophical positions. In German philosophy, it designates those positions which take account of Kant's critical epistemology but deny that the subjectivity of our experience makes it impossible to acquire valid knowledge of the external world as it is in itself. In Anglo-American philosophy, Critical Realism from 1920 onwards became the name of a movement that purported to integrate insights of both idealism and the so-called New Realism, which was a naive realist reaction to idealism. In contrast to New Realism, it acknowledged the mediation of the mind

I want to express my thanks to Niels Henrik Gregersen, Eberhard Herrmann, Wentzel van Huyssteen, Henrik Jørgensen, Poul Martinsen, and Jitse van der Meer, for taking the trouble to read a draft of this article and giving me many valuable comments.

in our access to the external world, but regarded it as possible to accommodate for the distortions due to that mediation.[1]

As far as I know the concept of critical realism was introduced into the dialogue between theology and science by Ian G. Barbour. In 1966 he opted for a critical realist epistemology in connection with both science and religion, which "must acknowledge both the creativity of man's mind, and the existence of patterns in events that are not created by man's mind" (172; cf. 248). Later, he was followed in this respect by Arthur Peacocke and John Polkinghorne, among others.[2] Actually, critical realism has been the dominant epistemology in the science-theology debate for several decades. In the following, I want to endorse this tradition. That is, I want to defend critical realism as the most appropriate point of departure for the dialogue between science and theology. However, I do not want to do so without modification, because I think it is necessary to point to some limits in the application of critical realism to science, and particularly to theology. Finally, I want to consider the consequences of a limited critical realism for the dialogue between theology and science.

a. Metaphysical Realism

Critical realism presupposes metaphysical realism. That is, it assumes that the world we meet in normal sense experience (as distinguished from dreams, hallucinations, etc.) exists as a real physical world independently of our experience.[3] Metaphysical realism expresses our natural belief about the world. Prior to reflection we all believe in a real

---

1. See Ritter and Gründer 1971 s.v. "Realismus," vol. 8, pp. 157f. and 163f.; and Audi 1995 s.v. "critical realism," 169f.
2. See Peacocke 1979, 17-22 (with a reference to Barbour on 22 n. 38) and especially Peacocke 1984. Cf. Peacocke 1993, 11-23. Furthermore: Polkinghorne 1987, chs. 2 and 3.
3. "Metaphysical realism" is understood here in the sense in which it is defined in Audi 1995, viz., as "the view that (a) there are real objects (usually the view is concerned with spatiotemporal objects), (b) they exist independently of our experience or knowledge of them, and (c) they have properties and enter into relations independently of the concepts with which we understand them or of the language with which we describe them" (488). It may be appropriate to note that this definition claims much less than Hilary Putnam's, according to which metaphysical realism holds: (1) The world consists of some fixed totality of mind-independent objects; (2) there is exactly one true and complete description of "the way the world is"; (3) truth involves some sort of correspondence relation between words or thought-signs and external things and sets of things (Putnam 1981, 49; cf. Putnam 1992, 30).

world "out there." This is, however, no sufficient reason to regard this belief as true. Natural beliefs may turn out to be mistaken (e.g., the belief that the sun moves around the earth). Actually, some philosophers (first and foremost Bishop Berkeley) have denied the existence of a physical world. Therefore, we should not accept metaphysical realism without some form of argumentation.

The principal reason why those philosophers reject the existence of a physical world is that we are only acquainted with the world through our experience of it. In a fundamental sense, we can only be sure of the world as an experienced world, that is, as an appearance in our minds. Therefore, they argue, it is not warranted to assume the existence of a physical world which is independent of our mind. The only world is a mental or ideal world.

Berkeley is are right that I only have acquaintance of the world through experience as a function of my mind. But that does not necessarily mean that the world I am acquainted with does not exist independently of my experience. My mind might be an instrument which brings me in contact with a physical world outside myself. Whether this is the case cannot be proved, since I have no access to a possible physical world except through experience. But I can reflect upon the world as it is experienced in order to see whether it contains features that point beyond my mind.

The question is: how can we best explain the existence and character of the experienced world? It seems that there are only two reasonable possibilities. Either this world is a mere product or creation of my mind (pretty much like dreams, for example), or it is the mental appearance of a physical world outside my mind. Sure, there is a third possibility. According to Berkeley the appearing world must be understood as a partial participation in an ideal world in God's mind. But this possibility is hardly acceptable, since it makes use of postulations (participation, God's mind), the character and existence of which are at least as much in need of explanation as the world they intend to explain.

Now, I think the experienced world has many features which are hard to explain as mental creations but make good sense as appearances of a mind-independent physical world. This article is not the place for a comprehensive exposition of them. I restrict myself to the features I regard as most convincing.[4]

4. A classic defense of metaphysical realism is offered by Russell [1912] 1920, ch. 2, which is a part of the inspiration behind the following exposition.

The first feature is that the world again and again behaves contrary to my expectations and wishes. It exhibits a curious stubbornness. For example, I am on my way to my work. When I arrive at the railway station I see my train just leaving. I have to wait a quarter of an hour for the next train. I enter my working place in a mood of irritation. Therefore I don't notice the glass door, which normally stands open. I hit my head and I am plagued by a bad headache the rest of the day. In my opinion it is very hard to explain these experiences as creations of my mind. Why should I create such events that counteract my intentions and leave me in a state of irritation and pain? By far the most plausible explanation is that I move in a world with physical trains and glass doors which exist and behave independently of my experience of them.

The second feature is that my mind confronts me with my body. On the one hand, my body appears as a part of the world: it is there as an object in (mental) space and time among other objects. On the other hand, my mind turns out to be intimately tied to my body. This appears from the fact that I do not only experience my body as a part of the world but also from within (e.g., in feelings of warmth and pain). Moreover, my empirical knowledge of the world is dependent upon bodily movements in and through it, which are directed by my mind. The natural explanation of these experiences is that my mind through my body is situated in a physical world that exists independently of it. The alternative explanation that these experiences are created by my mind is very problematic. For why should such a sovereign mind create an illusory body as a necessary condition for the acquisition of knowledge of a world that is its own creation?

We can take one more step. My world is not only populated with foreign physical objects. It is also populated with bodies similar to mine. I can talk with those bodies about a common world and usually we understand each other. Moreover, they teach me many new things that I did not know before. Therefore, I can hardly evade the conclusion that they are human beings like me. In that case, my mind is only one among other minds, not the sole comprehensive creator of the world. Of course, it is logically possible to understand the other human beings as mere creations of my own mind. But this understanding raises overwhelming problems. How could my mind be able to create human beings that turn out to contain a wealth of knowledge and insight which is initially hidden to itself. Why should it do so? And above all: why should it create a world that is such as to give rise to the illusion that it is not the sole, all-creating mind?

The conclusion must be that the experienced world is very hard to explain as an ideal creation of my mind, whereas it is easy to explain as the mental appearance of a physical world that exists independently of my mind. Therefore, in my view, there are good reasons to accept metaphysical realism, though it cannot be proved to be true. Hence I assume, with critical realism, that in normal sense experience I meet a real physical world. Moreover, I think my argument has demonstrated that I myself, through my body, am a part of that world and that some of its inhabitants are human beings in possession of minds like mine. Thus, the argument so far has ascertained the existence of an external physical world and of fellow humans as parts of that world.

b. Epistemological Realism

Critical realism is right *that* we meet a real physical world in sense-experience. But this does not necessarily mean that it is possible to know *what* that world is like.[5] The world I experience is after all the world as it appears in my mind. And it is easy to see that this appearance is no simple reflection of the real world.

This can be expounded by an analysis of the phenomenon of perception. Normally, we perceive something *as* something. I see the thing in the middle of my room *as* a table, I hear the sound outside *as* a siren. I do so because I am acquainted with tables and ambulances in advance. It can, however, be imagined that I have no knowledge of ambulances and sirens whatsoever. Then I merely hear a sound without understanding what it is. In that case it is more appropriate to speak of a sensation. Thus, we can make a distinction between a sensation and a perception, the former being the sensual phenomenon as such, and the latter being an understood or interpreted sensation.[6]

Now, sensations (at least of the exemplified type) confront me with a world which I have good reasons to believe is a real, external world, and which exists independently of me. At the same time, however, they cannot be precise reflections of that world. This appears from the fact that I can have different sensations of the same thing in different

5. Cf. Drees's contention that the debates on scientific realism are not debates about the existence of an outer reality but about the quality of our knowledge (1996, 7f.).

6. A similar distinction is the distinction between "object perception" and a "fact perception" (see Audi s.v. "perception," 569). For the sake of clarity I prefer the terms in the text.

situations. My table looks different from different angles. Its color changes with the light. The siren sounds different when I grow older, because I catch fewer overtones. An apple is difficult to taste when you have caught a cold. Et cetera. These differences mean that at least the majority of sensations cannot be precise reflections of external objects. And even if some should happen to be, we could not know which ones, because we do not have a mind-independent access to the external world enabling us to compare our sensations with it.

But even if sensation would give a precise reflection of the external world, perception would not. For in perception we understand our sensations by means of concepts that structure them in certain ways. If I do not know very much about trees I may perceive a particular tree merely as a conifer. But if I am interested in trees I may perceive it as a spruce rather than a pine, or even as a Norway spruce. And at Christmas time I may perceive the same tree as a potential Christmas tree without noticing what kind of tree it is in a botanical sense. Thus, in perception we *do* something with our sensations. By means of our concepts we focus on some aspects of our sensations rather than others and associate them with aspects of the knowledge we have in advance. Thereby, we transcend the world as it makes itself felt in sensation. Also for this reason perception cannot be held to give a precise reflection of the external world.

The concepts by which we structure our sensations are not our private inventions. They are part of the conceptual system that we inherit through the language of our society. It is well known that different languages conceptualize the world differently in some respects. For example, whereas English has eleven primary color terms, Hanunóo (a Philippine language) has only four, each covering several English designations. On the other hand, whereas French makes a distinction between a river flowing into the sea ("fleuve") and a tributary river ("rivière"), English has only one concept ("river"; cf. Leech [1974] 1977, 28-31). Which conceptual possibilities we have at our disposal for structuring the world is relative to the society we live in. That is especially apparent with a concept like "Christmas tree." This concept presupposes, and is linked with, a complex social practice, and without a rudimentary knowledge of this practice it is impossible to understand it. People unacquainted with Western culture cannot perceive a spruce as a Christmas tree. This social dependence of our conceptualization confirms that perception does not give a precise reflection of the world.

However, the fact that conceptualization is individually and socially conditioned does not mean that perception and perception-related knowledge are completely arbitrary. First, conceptualization is constrained by the character of our sensations. Our sensations permit different conceptualizations of trees and rivers, but unification of trees and rivers under one common concept would ignore many obvious differences and therefore hamper communication and understanding. Second, given a certain conceptual system, only relatively few statements are permitted as faithful expressions of what is experienced. I am free to call the observed tree a conifer, a Norway spruce, or even a Christmas tree, but I am not allowed to call it a river. If I do so, my statement is false. Thus, in combination with my conceptual system, sense-experience sets narrow limits to what can be accepted as faithful (or true) statements about the (mental or internal) world.

On this subject, I agree with the main line in Nancey Murphy's thought when she writes that "while concepts are human contrivances and not pictures or representations, they are shaped by a real world. And *given* a stable set of concepts, we can go on to formulate sentences, most of whose criteria for acceptance (or acceptance as true) can best be described as a combination of coherence and empirical adequacy. . . . *given* a stable conceptual system, truth is in part a function of the way the world is" (1993, 354). However, I think it is confusing to speak of "a real world" and "the way the world is." For this way of speaking gives the impression that we have a direct access to the external world — though that is hardly what Murphy means.

This problem is avoided by Hilary Putnam's "internal realism," since it determines the objects of the world from "*within* a theory or description" (1981, 50). I do not, however, agree with Putnam's rejection of any correspondence theory of truth. Of course, he is right that "you cannot single out a correspondence between our concepts and the supposed noumenal objects without access to the noumenal objects" (73). But that does not exclude the possibility of singling out a correspondence between statements and perceptions of *internal* (in contradistinction to external or noumenal) objects, as I did above. That "*too many* correspondences exist" (73) — because of different possibilities of conceptualization — is no good argument. For this does not alter the importance of being able, on the basis of the different conceptual possibilities, to separate statements which correspond with (conceptualized) experience from statements which notoriously do not (and therefore must be considered as false).

Critical realism, then, is an attempt to do justice to both the mental nature of the appearing world and the experiential constraints upon it. The recognition of the role of sensation and conceptualization leads critical realism to the rejection of the naive realist claim that experience conveys a precise reflection of a real, external world. On the other hand, it interprets the experiential constraints upon the mental world as the impact of an external world. Therefore, it regards it as possible to acquire valid knowledge of that world. It is, in other words, a form of epistemological realism. But according to critical realism, valid knowledge of the external world can only be acquired in and through a critical attitude, which attempts to distill the real from the mental. How far that is possible cannot be decided in advance. It depends upon the convincing power of concrete critical procedures and their results. Hence, it is not surprising that critical realism is particularly interested in science. For it is first and foremost there that we meet a successful critical treatment of the world of our experience.

2. Critical Realism with Regard to Science

a. Science as a Critical Enterprise

Before we look at critical realism in connection with science, it is good to keep in mind that "science" is a very abstract concept. In reality, there is not such a thing as science. The concept of science covers a manifold of different activities, which in different ways attain different kinds of results about different aspects of the natural world. I shall not attempt to give a characterization of science in all its diversity. I only want to draw attention to a few more or less general features of science that are of importance for the purpose of this article.

The principal interest that underlies science is a basic human interest in cognition, in knowing what the world is like and understanding why it is as it is.[7] Of course, science can be practiced for different reasons. One important reason is undoubtedly a striving for technological control. But this can hardly be the principal reason, since many branches of science cannot be explained by it (e.g., theoretical physics, astronomy, and evolutionary biology). Such kinds of science can only be understood as expressions of a cognitive interest. And I suppose that this interest often also plays a part for people who practice science for other reasons (cf. Barbour [1966] 1971, 149f.).

7. Cf. Spiro's contention with reference to the universal applicability of the Rorschach test: "I believe that it can be shown that everywhere man has a desire to know, to understand, to find meaning" (1966, 109).

The human interest in cognition has brought about an impressive body of scientific knowledge. With regard to the question of critical realism it is useful to distinguish different categories of statements within this body. I adopt the distinction of Olaf Pedersen between observation statements, statements of primary relations, and scientific theories. Observation statements report single events observed at a certain place and time and may include measuring results (e.g., temperature). Statements of primary relations affirm simple natural laws like "The boiling point of alcohol is 78° Celsius at a pressure of one atmosphere." Scientific theories are networks of statements which may contain concepts like force and energy that have no direct counterparts in the world of phenomena (Pedersen 1988, 127).

The body of scientific knowledge has come about as the result of a critical procedure. Let me mention a few characterististics of it. Science is a corporate enterprise. It develops in interaction between many individual scientists. In this interaction ideas and results are subjected to intersubjective assessment. Only ideas and results that stand firm in intersubjective criticism are accepted as valid. And only provisionally, since in principle they always can be subjected to new criticism (Barbour [1966] 1971, 151-156; Chalmers [1978] 1983, 119f.; cf. Drees 1996, 237-244).

The central (though not the only) criterion in the intersubjective assessment of scientific ideas and results is conformity with experience. The application of this criterion is relatively straightforward in connection with observation statements and statements of primary relations, provided that they refer to phenomena which are publicly available (e.g., the appearance of a new comet) or which can be reproduced experimentally (e.g., the boiling of alcohol). Empirical assessment is more complicated in connection with theories. The reason is that scientific theories normally have a general and abstract character and therefore are far removed from the concrete world of experience. An important demand here is that proposed theories be tested on their ability to account for data that do not belong to the basis of their formulation. If possible, such testing takes the form of an experimental manipulation of nature in such a way that it produces data which can be compared with logical consequences of the theory at stake. A good example is G. F. Fitzgerald's discovery that Clerk Maxwell's electromagnetic theory predicted the existence of radio waves, a consequence Maxwell himself had not realized. After this discovery Fitzgerald succeeded in generating radio waves, thereby providing an experimental confirmation of Maxwell's theory.[8]

The application of the conformity criterion ensures that only those scientific results and ideas are accepted as valid that are essentially in accordance with the intersubjective world of experience. Of course, conformity with experience is in itself no sufficient reason to believe that accepted scientific knowledge tells us something about the real world. As we have seen above, the world of experience, though connected to the real world, is not the real world itself. Moreover, intersubjective agreement about accordance with experience is dependent upon prevailing paradigms, which change with the course of history.[9] Nevertheless, the critical procedure of science promotes empirical adequacy and restricts arbitrariness. The question is, how far can the application of this procedure support reality claims for accepted scientific knowledge?

This question cannot be answered in general. Scientific reality claims must be judged from case to case. That cannot be done here, of course. But I think it is possible to make some general remarks about the realist bearing of the different categories of scientific statements. However, before I do so I want to say something about the linguistic aspect of the reality problem.

b. Language and Reality

The reality question is always asked with regard to the content of a statement or a combination of statements. The realistic plausibility of what you are saying is the realistic plausibility of *what* you are saying. Now, language contains a great semantic flexibility. This flexibility enables us, among other things, to formulate statements with different degrees of precision. And the precision of formulation affects a statement's realistic plausibility. For example, when I come home from my work I can tell my wife that I hit my head against a glass door. But I can also content myself with saying that I bumped into a solid thing. The expression "a glass door" can hardly be taken as a precise description of the external object that (literally!) made itself felt. For the

8. See for the assessment of scientific theories and the problems connected with it Barbour [1966] 1971, 144-148 and McMullin 1984, 30f. The Fitzgerald example is mentioned in Chalmers [1978] 1983, 117.

9. See for the paradigm concept Kuhn [1962] 1970, especially ch. 2 (pp. 10-22) and the postscript (pp. 174-210).

concepts of "glass" and "door" are deeply embedded in my human and cultural way of experiencing the world (they depend, for example, on seeing, touching, and entering rooms). The expression "a solid thing" is also experience-related. But it is sufficiently vague to serve as a plausible description of an aspect of the real world. That the real world contains a thing that is solid enough to block my way and leave me with a bad headache does not tell us very much about it, of course. The realistic plausibility of what I say is paid for with lack of precision. Nevertheless, something is said, which is more than nothing. And at any rate the example shows that it is possible to make statements about the real world which have a certain plausibility of being true.

Another aspect of the semantic flexibility of language is the possibility of the use of metaphors. Generally speaking, in metaphorical language a word or a phrase is used to denote a thing other than that which it denotes literally. In science, well-known concepts can be used as metaphors for hidden entities, as vehicles of a partial understanding. For example, a physicist can use the familiar concepts of particle and wave to denote quantum entities, although he is aware that those concepts (as mutually exclusive) can only apply partially. An important extension of metaphorical language in science is the use of models. Models are more complex than metaphors. In models, well-known structures, relations, and processes function as analogies for hidden ones. They are applied in the expectation that they can convey a better understanding of the represented things. A classic example of a model in science is Niels Bohr's planetary model of the atom, which aided him to formulate the equations for the energy levels of the electrons and to relate the "spring" of an electron from one "orbit" to another to the frequency of emitted or absorbed light (cf. Barbour 1990, 41f.).

Metaphors and models are not considered as precise descriptions of the entities, structures, relations, and processes they intend to illuminate. They figure only as approximations. This approximative, unfixed character makes them suited to function as parts of statements about the real world — just as the vague expression "a solid thing" is better suited for that purpose than the precise expression "a glass door." If metaphors and models are used that way, they do not claim to give a precise description of a part of reality. What they tell is necessarily unfixed or vague. But a vague content is not the same as no content. For example, Bohr's atomic model does not claim to give a precise description of atoms. But it claims in any case that atoms consist of a nucleus (whatever it is) and one or more electrons (whatever they are) in fixed states, between which they can change position, thereby emitting or absorbing a quantum of light. That may not be much, but it is more than nothing. And it is precisely because of this moderate claim (in connection with its explanatory force) that Bohr's model can be regarded as a plausible representative of the real atom. As Barbour puts it: "Models . . . are neither literal pictures nor useful fictions but limited and inadequate ways of imagining what is not observable. They make tentative ontological claims that there are entities in the world something like those postulated in the models" (1990, 43).[10]

c. Observation Statements

The first part of this article has argued that conceptualization plays an essential part in perception. This applies to science as well. Scientific observations are dependent upon the scientist's conceptuality and thereby linked to his theoretical ideas. Consequently, there are no neutral observation statements in science. Observation statements always make use of concepts that are part of the observer's theoretical frame of reference (see Chalmers [1978] 1983, 22-37).

What this means for the realist bearing of observation statements can be explained by means of the example of the discovery of oxygen. Thomas S. Kuhn relates that the British scientist and theologian Joseph Priestley in the 1770s collected a gas released by heated red oxide of mercury. In 1774 he identified this gas as nitrous oxide, but in 1775, after further tests, he revised the identification to common air with less than its usual quantity of phlogiston. The latter description presupposed the theory of combustion current at that time which regarded burning as the result of the emission of a special "flame-stuff" called phlogiston. Subsequently, the French scientist Lavoisier by the same experiment isolated the same gas. But, being skeptical of the phlogiston theory, he described it in 1775 as "air itself entire without alteration." Later, in 1777, he concluded that the gas was a distinct species, one of the two main constituents of the atmosphere — the gas we now call oxygen. But unlike us, he regarded the gas as the product of an atomic "principle of acidity" and "caloric," the matter of heat (Kuhn [1962] 1970, 53-56).

This example neatly shows the dependence of observation state-

10. See for the use of metaphors and models in science McMullin 1984, 30-35; Peacocke 1984, 29-34 (cf. 40-44); and Barbour 1990, 41-45.

ments on the observers' theoretical presuppositions. And the historical change of such presuppositions (including our own!) must make us wary not to mistake a theory-dependent description for a precise reflection of reality. On the other hand, there can be no doubt that Priestley's and Lavoisier's different descriptions referred to the same (internal) stuff, since it was released by the same kind of experiment. Therefore, it is essential to distinguish — both in observation statements and in descriptions — between reference as such and the way of referring. Whereas the latter is always dependent upon theory (except for the use of pure signs like "this" or "that"), the former may be unambiguous and continuous in spite of changing theoretical interpretations.[11]

This distinction makes it possible to consider the question of the reality of the referent of an observation statement independently of the statement's way of referring to it. To stick to my example, in Kuhn's account there are at least two elements that make it plausible that the gas we call "oxygen" really exists. First, Priestley's change in understanding from "nitrous oxide" to "dephlogisticated air" can hardly be explained otherwise than as the impact of external constraints upon his thought, which pulled him away, so to speak, from the familiar to the unknown. Second, the fact that the gas also appeared to Lavoisier, though his theoretical intuitions were quite different from Priestley's, shows that its appearance cannot have been a pure projection of Priestley's theoretical ideas. Therefore, there are good reasons to believe *that* oxygen really exists, although we cannot say exactly *what* it is. And I suppose that similar remarks can be made with regard to most other scientific observation statements. If so, they tell us something about the real world. But how far their descriptive content corresponds to the real world depends upon the realist bearing of the whole theoretical framework they presuppose.

d. Statements of Primary Relations

Statements of primary relations are particularly interesting in connection with the reality question. Let me also explain this by means of an example. Pedersen tells us that he once as a schoolteacher made eleven-year-old pupils weigh and measure pieces of lead. He noted the num-

---

11. Cf. Soskice 1988, 177-179, who mentions the interesting point made by Saul Kripke that reference can even be successful when the descriptive content of the referring statement is false!

bers they found in two parallel columns on the blackboard. Afterwards he asked them to make calculations with the parallel numbers. Addition, subtraction, and multiplication gave no significant results. Then when the pupils ventured to perform the most difficult calculation they had mastered, division, approximately the same result (11.4) appeared for each pair of numbers. The pupils were very surprised. They had found a constant relation in nature, the existence of which they had no idea of before the experiment.

Pedersen characterizes the pupils' experience as a "fundamental scientific experience." And he continues by quoting statements of eminent scientists like Heisenberg and Hubble, which express the same kind of experience. He concludes: "Both Heisenberg and Hubble shared the same conviction that the fundamental scientific experience is so strong because something from a world beyond the human mind is fed into it in some way which it is difficult to explain and communicate. The mind is certainly full of operations and bustling with activity; but what it really has to work upon is something not provided by itself" (Pedersen 1988, 131-133).

What is fascinating in Pedersen's example is that the pupils _discovered_ a relation in nature they had not dreamt of before. Of course, their discovery was conditioned by sense experience, the use of man-made measuring apparatus and the performance of mathematical operations devised by the human mind. But it cannot be explained as a pure product of these conditions. Application of the same procedure to other substances would have given other results. It is, moreover, hard to imagine that the number 11.4 could be due to a hidden a priori of the human mind. How could such an a priori be able to control the pupils' weighings and measurings of lead so as to produce that number for each pair of results? The only plausible explanation is that the procedure enabled the pupils to discover something that lay beyond their minds — namely the _real_ specific gravity of lead in proportion to water!

If this conclusion is right, it must in principle be valid for all similar primary relations that can be established intersubjectively. In that case, statements of such primary relations express real relations in nature. Their realist bearing is supported by the fact that they, as Pedersen puts it, "show a remarkable resilience to the passage of time. Once critically established they are preserved as a treasure from which very little is again discarded" (Pedersen 1988, 129). In other words, they represent a lasting strand of scientific knowledge across historical changes in scientific theories. This is another indication that they express real relations which exist independently of the human mind.

e. Scientific Theories

As far as science is concerned, realism has been discussed mainly with regard to scientific *theories*. That is natural, since theories are the most interesting part of science. Unlike observation statements and statements of primary relations, scientific theories give, or purport to give, an explanation of many natural phenomena which otherwise would be unintelligible. They do so by means of postulated hypothetical entities, structures, and processes (McMullin 1994, 81f.). For this reason they are essentially creations of the human mind, which are often far removed from the world of experience. As a consequence, realism is more problematic with regard to scientific theories than with regard to the other kinds of scientific statements.

It cannot be denied that the theories of science are very successful. That is, they enable us to predict, to understand, and to manipulate many phenomena and processes of the natural world. The question is whether this success is a sufficient indication that scientific theories tell us something about the real world. According to *scientific realism* it is. Scientific realism claims, in the words of Ernan McMullin, one of its principal advocates, "that the long-term success of a scientific theory gives reason to believe that something like the entities and structure postulated by the theory actually exists" (McMullin 1984, 26). *Antirealism* denies this. Antirealism can go together with an instrumentalist view of science, which regards scientific theories as pure instruments of intellectual and practical control of the world, without ontological import.[12]

Antirealist criticism of scientific realism can take a logical or a historical form. The logical point is that scientific theories are underdetermined by the data they explain. That is, a given set of data permits different theories that can explain them. And since such theories can be ontologically incompatible it is not justified to conclude from their explanatory success that they are true. Hilary Putnam gives the example that all physical events can be explained by action at a distance across empty space (as Newton did) and by interactions mediated by electromagnetic fields. These theories are ontologically incompatible, since

---

12. See Ritter and Gründer 1971 s.v. "Instrumentalismus," vol. 4, pp. 424-428; and Audi 1995 s.v. "instrumentalism," 379.

action at a distance excludes mediated action. Therefore, at least one of them must be false. Consequently, the fact that a theory explains all data is an insufficient reason to assume that it is true (Putnam 1981, 72-74).

The antirealist argument from history is to the effect that many successful scientific theories in the course of time have been replaced by other successful theories. Therefore, success is no reason to believe that something like the entities and structures postulated by the theory really exists. Insofar as "success" means "explanatory success" this argument can be regarded as a historical documentation of the logical point that conformity with the data does not warrant truth. Larry Laudan has listed a great number of once successful theories which are now rejected. One example is a whole family of theories, the etherial theories of eighteenth- and nineteenth-century physics and chemistry. Those theories were once highly successful. Nevertheless, the existence of the ether, their central entity, is generally rejected in our time. Laudan concludes: "I daresay that for every highly successful theory in the history of science that we now believe to be a genuinely referring theory, one could find half a dozen once successful theories that we now regard as substantially nonreferring" (Laudan 1984, esp. 225f., 232).

To this criticism McMullin replies that scientific realism is no global thesis. The realist bearing must be assessed for each theory in particular. Conformity with the data is in itself no sufficient criterion. It must be supplemented with other criteria such as coherence, consonance with other parts of science, and fertility over a longer period of time (McMullin 1994, 98-104). An example of a fruitful theory is the development from the continental drift hypothesis to the plate tectonic model in geology. This model has become able to explain so many phenomena so well that it must be held to approximate real structures of the world (McMullin 1984, 30-35). McMullin believes that his version of scientific realism rules out most of Laudan's historical examples as instances against it. As for Laudan's ether-examples, he replies that the postulation of ether often was a mere addition of a "carrier" that was not required by the equations themselves. However, he grants Laudan's criticism the value "that it warns the realist that the ontological claim he makes is at best tentative, for surprising reversals *have* happened in the history of science" (McMullin 1984, 17f.).

The argument for the realist bearing of scientific theories has the logical form of an *abductive* (or, as McMullin calls it: retroductive) *inference*. The term was introduced by C. S. Peirce, who characterizes an abductive inference as follows:

> "The surprising fact, C, is observed;
> But if A were true, C would be a matter of course,
> Hence, there is reason to suspect that A is true." (Peirce 1960, 117)

Applied to science this kind of inference means, that if a scientific theory explains the phenomena, there is reason to believe that it is true (McMullin 1984, 8; McMullin 1994, 81f.).

Now, Laudan contends that basing scientific realism on the success of science is committing a *petitio principii*. The question is whether the application of abduction to scientific theories warrants their truth. According to Laudan, scientific realism attempts to substantiate that claim by means of a new, second-order abduction. This abduction treats realism itself as an explanatory hypothesis, the ability of which to explain the success of science is regarded as a good reason to assume that it is true. According to Laudan, this argument is a *petitio principii*, since the validity of the abductive inference for scientific theories cannot be substantiated by an argument that presupposes that validity (Laudan 1984, 242f.).

Put in this way, Laudan's criticism is right, of course. But, as far as I can see, it does not affect McMullin's version of scientific realism. For McMullin does not attempt to substantiate the realist bearing of scientific theories with reference to the truth (or plausibility) of realism as an explanation of the success of science in general. As we have seen, he stresses that the realist claim has to be justified for each scientific theory in particular and that explanatory success (in the sense of conformity with the data) alone is not sufficient. It must be supplemented by the application of other criteria like fruitfulness, coherence, and so on. Since those other criteria do not include an abductive inference, McMullin's scientific realism cannot be blamed for committing a *petitio principii*.[13]

I agree with McMullin that realism cannot be a general claim of scientific theories but has to be established for each theory in particular. However, I think we should take one more step on the path of differentiation. It can also be necessary to distinguish *within* a particular theory. For example, quantum mechanics postulates different kinds of theoretical entities (electrons, quarks, gluons, etc.). But among these, electrons have a special status, since they are used routinely in experimental practice as tools to produce effects that can extend our understanding of elementary physical processes. Ian Hacking regards this use as the best proof

---

13. Cf. McMullin's own commentary to Laudan's criticism in 1994, 98-100.

that they exist. "We are completely convinced of the reality of electrons when we regularly set to build — and often enough succeed in building — new kinds of device that use various well understood causal properties of electrons to interfere in other more hypothetical parts of nature" (Hacking 1984, 161). Hacking makes the same distinction between reference and the way of referring that we made in connection with observation statements. This distinction is particularly relevant with regard to electrons, since they are the subject of mutually incompatible descriptions as "clouds" and "particles." Yet, there is no doubt that these descriptions refer to "the same kind of thing, the electron" (157f.).[14]

The return of this distinction reminds us of a limit of scientific realism, which concerns both scientific theories and theory-dependent observation statements. Often we have good reasons to assume *that* the (internal) referents of our concepts or descriptions really exist. But *what* they precisely are, remains hidden. This applies to more robust theoretical entities like tectonic plates as well as to electrons and even to directly observable entities like stars and trees. The reason is that all science in a fundamental sense remains dependent upon the human mind, which has no direct access to the external world. But within the body of scientific knowledge it seems that the nonfigurative mathematical statements of primary relations, somewhat paradoxically, bring us most closely to a precise picture of the real world!

3. Critical Realism with Regard to Theology

a. Theology as Critical Reflection on the Christian Religion

In this article, I use the concept of theology to mean critical reflection on the Christian religion. This is not the place to give an account of

---

14. Hacking adopts the distinction between reference and the way of referring from Hilary Putnam's *Mind, Language and Reality* (1975). He remarks that Putnam's account of reference there "was intended to bolster scientific realism," before his rejection of "metaphysical realism" in favour of "internal realism" (Hacking 1984, 159). Therefore, I suppose that Hacking by the electron as a referent means the real, external thing. But strictly speaking, one should distinguish between the electron as an internal referent and an external thing, the former being the one target of different descriptions, the latter being the real electron that explains the appearance of that target and its experimental effects.

the Christian religion, but in order to explain my understanding of theology it is necessary to mention some central doctrines of Christian belief. The core of Christian belief, at least in its traditional form, consists of the convictions that God has created the world, that he has revealed himself in the history of Israel and especially in Jesus Christ as a loving God, that he forgives our sins and promises eternal life, and that he commands us to live our lives in love for him and our neighbors.[15]

This summary shows that the Christian religion first and foremost focuses on the question of the meaning of life. On the one hand, it is concerned with the problems of evil, suffering, and death, which apparently deprive life of meaning. On the other hand, it offers an answer to those problems by pointing out that God's forgiving love, a life devoted to the love of God and our neighbors, and the promise of eternal life nevertheless make life worth living. And even apparently more theoretical doctrines like the doctrine of creation have an existential or practical orientation.

This can be illustrated with the first creation story (Genesis 1:1-2,4a). At first sight this story might seem to give a mere account of the origin of the world. But on closer inspection it turns out that it (as a mythical story) is oriented to the question of the meaning of life. Let me point out three features which substantiate that claim: (1) After almost every act of creation it is said that God regarded its results as good, and of the entire creation we are even told that God regarded it as very good (1:31). This means among other things that the earth, as God has created it, is a good place for humans to live. (2) After having created man and woman, God blessed them and said to them: "Be fruitful and increase, fill the earth and subdue it, have dominion over the fish in the sea, the birds of the air, and every living thing that moves on the earth" (1:28). Thereby, man and woman are assigned important tasks as a part of the meaning of their lives on earth. (3) Having finished his creation, God rested on the seventh day and sanctified it (2:2f.). Six days of work are followed by one day of rest. This establishes a divine model for the rhythm of human life. These features show that the story of the creation is not merely an account of the origin of the world. Of course, it is such an account too. But the story is told with a view to

---

15. When I here and below speak of God as "he" this should not be understood as the expression of a sexist bias but merely as the use of a traditional language for which there is in my opinion no satisfactory alternative.

human life on earth, and thereby it connects to the central question of
the Christian religion, the question of the meaning of life.

As critical reflection on the Christian religion, theology has an
exegetical, a historical, a systematic, and a practical branch. For the
dialogue with science, systematic theology is most relevant. Therefore, I
restrict myself to this branch of theology. Generally speaking, the task of
systematic theology is critical reflection on Christian belief with regard to
its coherence (both internal and in relation to nonreligious knowledge)
and its significance for people of our time. In this quality, (systematic)
theology concerns itself primarily with existential questions. As a consequence, its statements involve valuations. Theology speaks of evil,
suffering, and death as *bad* things, of God as a *good* God, of love as the
way of life that makes life *worth* living, and it states that we *ought to* love
God and our neighbors. And even when it speaks of the world, it speaks
of it, among other things, as God's *good* creation. Thus, generally speaking, theological statements have another nature than scientific statements. Whereas scientific statements are (or purport to be) statements of
fact, theological statements include valuations.[16] Therefore, it is prima
facie not obvious that critical realism as a theory of factual or theoretical
knowledge can be transferred from science to theology.

b. The Cognitive Dimension of Theology

The existential nature of Christian belief may tempt one to think that it
merely concerns a way of life. A classic example of such a view is R. B.
Braithwaite's interpretation of Christian belief. According to Braithwaite,
the meaning of Christian assertions — which can be epitomized in the
assertion that God is love *(agape)* — is that they proclaim the intention to
follow an agapeistic way of life (Braithwaite 1971, 81f.). In contradistinction to purely moral assertions, in Christian assertions the proclaimed
intention is connected with stories as its inspiration. But according to
Braithwaite the Christian need not believe that the stories are true: "A

---

16. That scientific statements are or purport to be statements of fact is a *formal*
assertion about the nature of scientific statements. Therefore, it does not contradict
the contention of Wentzel van Huyssteen in his contribution to this volume that
valuation plays an important part in the *process* of science as a human enterprise.
Besides, valuation in science concerns precisely the question of what the world is
like, not what its value is. Thus, scientific statements do not (purport to) speak of
what is good and bad in the world and how we ought to live, as many theological
statements do.

man is not, I think, a professing Christian unless he both proposes to live according to Christian moral principles and associates his intention with thinking of Christian stories; but he need not believe that the empirical propositions presented by the stories correspond to empirical fact" (86).

In my opinion, Braithwaite's and similar interpretations misunderstand Christian belief. When Christians assert that God is love, they essentially assert that there really exists a God who loves man. This can be illustrated with the well-known parable of the Good Shepherd (Luke 15:3-7). It can hardly be doubted that the meaning of this story, in the version of Luke, is to proclaim God's forgiving love for sinners. This meaning presupposes the existence of God. To a listener who does not believe that God exists the story loses its significance. If there is no God, there cannot be divine forgiveness. Perhaps such a listener can find a new significance in that story. If he is a Braithwaitian, he may draw inspiration from it to help people who have gone astray. But that would involve a significant discontinuity with both the original meaning and the common Christian understanding of the story.

This story shows that Christian belief does not merely concern a way of life. The Christian way of life presupposes matters of fact, first and foremost the existence of God as a loving God. For a Christian, the fact of God's existence and love is a necessary condition for the possibility of a meaningful life. It is for this reason that in Christian religious language the formulation of a way of life is connected with stories about God and his action. Those stories imply propositions, cognitive statements of matters of fact. Normally, the propositions are wrapped up in evaluative language, since the stories speak of God and his action from the perspective of their significance for man. Fact and value are intertwined. But it is possible to isolate the cognitive dimension of the stories and formulate it in separate propositions (cf. Drees 1996, 28f.).

When Christian belief includes propositional beliefs, one of the tasks of theology has to be critical reflection on its propositional or cognitive content. The primary source of theology is the biblical tradition. Theology recognizes that this tradition is an expression of human religious experience interpreted by changing categories of different times. Therefore, it cannot assign absolute authority to the cognitive claims of this tradition. It has to judge to what extent those claims can be regarded as valid in the light of the knowledge of our time. Moreover, it has to reformulate them in contemporary categories in order that they can be understood by people of our time. Logically, critical reformulations of cognitive claims are themselves propositions. Hence, theological statements, insofar as they are propositions, have the same status as scientific statements. The question is, whether this formal similarity alone justifies the application of critical realism to theology, or, more precisely, to its cognitive dimension.

It must be stressed that the cognitive dimension is only a *part* of (systematic) theology. In the critical realist tradition of the science-theology debate there is a tendency to conceive of theology primarily as a theoretical understanding of the world. The advantage of this conception for the dialogue between theology and science is, of course, that it places theology in the same category as science. Consequently, science and theology appear as "interacting and mutually illuminating approaches to reality" (Peacocke 1984, 51) or "investigations of what is, the search for increasing verisimilitude in our understanding of reality" (Polkinghorne 1987, 42).

This conception involves, however, the serious problem that it cannot do justice to the practical or existential character of theology. Illustrative is Peacocke 1993. On the basis of a critical realist understanding of theology Peacocke observes that a major difference between the use of models in science and theology is that in the latter, models have "a strong affective function evoking moral and spiritual response." They do so "because of their implied cognitive reference to that which makes demands on our wills and evokes our emotions" (14f.). In itself, this observation is not wrong. But I think it is an *inadequate* account of the existential aspects of theology, since it describes them as mere effects or functions of theoretical propositions. And it remains unclear why theological propositions have such effects when scientific propositions have not.

Those "effects" become comprehensible when we realize that theology is primarily concerned with existential questions. *Because* it offers an answer to the human quest for the meaning of life it evokes "moral and spiritual response." True, it can only do so by virtue of its implied cognitive reference to God and his redemption. But this cognitive reference derives its significance from the existential quest to which it is related. The theoretical or cognitive aspect of theology is subordinated to its practical or existential subject matter. God and the world are first and foremost conceived from the perspective of their significance for human life. A primarily theoretical conception of theology neglects that. The priorities must be reversed: theology concerns primarily existential and only secondarily theoretical questions.[17]

17. Within the critical realist tradition this is recognized by Barbour, who writes: "[Religion] . . . asks about the objects of a man's trust, loyalty, and worship, his 'ultimate concern.' . . . Religious beliefs are relevant primarily to existential questions about man's orientation in a framework of meaning, the fundamental character of man and the world, personal identity and destiny, time and history." He concludes that such differences in interest between science and religion "would lead us to expect that although there may be some parallels between their methods, the differences will in the last analysis be more significant" (1971, 266)!

c. Theology and Critical Realism

Just as with regard to scientific statements, the question of the realistic bearing of theological propositions or combinations of propositions in theories cannot be answered in general. It has to be assessed for each proposition or theory in particular. There is, for example, a prima facie difference in realistic plausibility between theological conceptions of humans (e.g., as sinners) and of God, between the claim that Jesus has existed (as a historical person) and that he was the Son of God, between a conception of God as Creator and as Redeemer, and so on. Of course, I cannot deal with those individual propositions here. I restrict myself to some general remarks about the applicability of critical realism to theology as compared to science.

Most theological propositions are either propositions about God or presuppose such propositions, for example, the statement that Jesus is the Son of God or the statement that humans are sinners (in theology "sin" is a *religious* concept concerning humans' relation to God). But even theological propositions which do not contain or imply a reference to God derive their *theological* significance from relations to propositions that do so within the context of theological theories. For example, propositions about the historical Jesus are theologically interesting because Jesus is regarded as the Son of God (or at least as uniquely related to God). This means that propositions about God constitute the core of theological propositions, to which all other theological propositions are more or less directly related. Therefore, the question of the applicability of critical realism to theology must be asked primarily with regard to theological propositions about God.

Now, in my view, it is not possible to transfer a critical realist understanding from scientific statements to theological propositions about God without modification. This is because there are considerable differences between science and theology. Let me mention three:

1. Whereas it is assumed by almost all people (including scientists and philosophers)[18] that the subject matter of science, the natural world, really exists, the existence of God is far from generally accepted. This is due to the fact that God does not make his reality irresistibly felt in sense experience as the natural world does. God is the object of

18. According to Hacking, the instrumentalist about science is "a realist about livers and chairs" (1984, 159), and according to *The Cambridge Dictionary of Philosophy* metaphysical realism is "shared by common sense, the sciences, and most philosophers" (Audi 1995, 488).

religious experience. And religious experience of God is personal experience of the Invisible, which is not given to everyone, and which already presupposes a religious frame of reference in order to be interpreted as experience of *God*.[19] God's existence can also figure as a metaphysical explanation of the existence and nature of the empirical world. In that case, the proposition that God exists is connected with sense experience in a similar way as scientific hypotheses.[20] However, it cannot be said to have a similar explanatory success as accepted scientific hypotheses. On the contrary, the legitimacy of nonnatural explanations is widely disputed.[21] Briefly, theology differs from science in that it is contested whether its core subject matter (God) exists at all. And that, of course, affects the plausibility of the reality claims that are contained in theological propositions.

2. Religious experience of God defies human control. It cannot be made present for scientific investigation by way of experiment as is most experience of the natural world. It is only accessible as past experience, through spoken or written testimony (Soskice 1988, 180). In such testimony, experience and interpretation are inextricably intertwined. And since experience and interpretation differ from person to person and from period to period, theology is confronted with a testimonial variety in which it is difficult to separate the corn from the chaff. Of course, theology as Christian theology has a criterion in the Bible. But the Bible is itself essentially testimony of past religious experience, first and foremost experience of God's revelation in the history of Israel and in Jesus Christ. Therefore, theology's resort to the Bible does not alter the fact that it is fundamentally dependent on a kind of experience which, unlike scientific experience, cannot be subjected to experimental control. And that makes its propositions about God more uncertain than corroborated scientific statements, even if it is assumed that God exists.

3. Christian religious language speaks essentially metaphorically

19. Of course, there are differences with regard to different types of religious experience. Barbour 1990 distinguishes six types (36-38). Of his types, for example, "mystical experience of unity" seems more personal than "experience of order and creativity in the world." But such differences do not alter the fact that religious experience as personal experience is a more uncertain base for the belief in God's existence than is intersubjective sense experience for the belief in the existence of the world.

20. Cf. Wolfhart Pannenberg's thesis that God can be the subject of a scientific theology only as a hypothesis (1977, 299-303).

21. Cf. Drees 1996, 141f., who endorses McMullin's observation that theological realism cannot be defended with reference to theology's explanatory success.

of God as Creator, Shepherd, Father, Rock, Love, and so on. Most God-metaphors are personal. This reflects the fact that God is primarily experienced as a subject in a personal relationship. At the same time, the change between many different metaphors displays an awareness that no particular metaphor is an adequate expression of God's being. Metaphors are so essential for Christian religious speaking of God that theological propositions, although they are the result of a more or less detached reflection, cannot dispense with them (cf. Peacocke 1984, 40f.). That does not make theological propositions less sophisticated than scientific statements. To the contrary, we have seen that science also makes use of metaphors and models as means to understand aspects of the natural world. Hence, in this respect there is an important similarity between theology and science. That should, however, not make us blind to the differences in the use of metaphors and models: (a) Metaphors and models are only a part of scientific language. Science includes observation statements, mathematical statements of primary relations, and mathematically framed theories (e.g., the theories of special and general relativity), which are not metaphorical. In theology, on the other hand, metaphors are indispensible for all substantial speaking about God. Theology lacks a counterpart of the precise mathematical statements of science. And, as we have seen, in science the most plausible realistic claims are connected with those statements.[22] (b) Whereas scientific metaphors and models concern entities, structures, relations, and processes within the natural world, theological metaphors concern a transcendent being, God. Therefore, there is a greater dissimilarity between theological metaphors and their (external) object than between scientific metaphors and models and their (external) objects. The Christian tradition has always been aware of the great dissimilarity between our speaking of God and God's being. On the religious level this is witnessed by the use of a multiplicity of God-

22. Therefore, I think Wentzel van Huyssteen parallels theology and science too much when he writes: "The strength of the critical-realist position certainly lies in its insistence that both the objects of science and the objects of religious belief lie beyond the range of literal description. I think this eventually represents a major advance in our understanding of what not only science but also theology can achieve" (1989, 156). Of course, it is true that, strictly speaking, both the objects of science and theology cannot be described literally, since we have access to them only through experience as a human or mental phenomenon. But that does not alter the fact that science in virtue of its mathematical language can give us much more precise information about its objects and their relations than theology.

metaphors. On the theological level, this appears, among other things, from the rise of a *theologia negativa* (speaking of God in negations) in the Primitive Church and from the designation of God as the "Wholly Other" in the dialectical theology of our century. Therefore, theological metaphors of God must be regarded as less descriptive or representative than the tectonic plate model or even the quantum-mechanical wave metaphor in science (cf. Drees 1996, 148f.).

It is far from obvious that God exists, the testimony of religious experience is manifold and defies experimental control, and substantial speaking of God depends upon metaphors which only poorly depict God's being. For these reasons, generally speaking, the realistic bearing of theological propositions is considerably more uncertain than that of scientific statements. This does not mean that a critical realism with regard to theological propositions cannot be defended.[23] But I think such a defense is hardly feasible from a point of view outside the Christian tradition. It presupposes a positive attitude to Christian belief. In a fundamental way it is a question of *fides quaerens intellectum* (faith seeking understanding), which remains within the context of faith. Hence, the justification of theological realism is normally regarded as a task of theology's reflection upon itself, or as a part of a philosophy of religion which is practiced within the context of faith, whereas the defense of scientific realism is usually carried out by philosophers who, as philosophers, argue from a point of view outside science.[24]

However, the differences should not be exaggerated. On the one hand, as a *critical* enterprise the justification of theological realism has to make use of a rational argumentation, which invokes reasons that are valid apart from Christian belief. On the other hand, scientific realism cannot be demonstrated in a purely rational way. The disagreements in the discussion on scientific realism reveal that belief also plays its part there. But that does not alter the fact that, generally speaking, critical realism does not have the same rational plausibility for theology as for science.

This is not the place to propose a rational justification of the realist bearing of theological propositions about God. But to give an impression of what such a

23. It should be noticed that the transfer of critical realism from science to theology affects its definition: critical realism now not only concerns the possibility of acquiring knowledge of the physical world but also of God.

24. Cf. Laudan, who with regard to scientific realism speaks of a "metascientific discourse" (1984, 242).

justification could amount to, I want to finish this section with a short account of Basil Mitchell's defence of the central theological proposition that God exists, as it is put forward in his book *The Justification of Religious Belief*. As appears from the title of the book, Mitchell's argumentation is a part of a justification of religious belief (and more particularly of Christian belief), which suggests that the defence is advanced within the context of faith (the concept of justification presupposes that you already believe in what you justify). This is confirmed by the fact that the author can characterize his enterprise as a "Christian apologetic" (Mitchell 1973, 43). But the Christian point of departure does in no way dissolve the rationality of the argumentation.

Mitchell begins his justification with the construction of what he calls a "cumulative case." Thereby he understands a combination of arguments which separately are not sufficient but which taken together make a plausible case. The case consists essentially of three elements: (1) the existence and nature of the universe as the basis of the traditional cosmological and teleological arguments for the existence of God; (2) different kinds of religious experiences and their transforming effects on peoples' lives; (3) historical claims of divine revelation. Mitchell's point is that each element is in need of an explanation and that theistic explanations of them in conjunction support one another.[25] He recognizes, however, that the problem of evil and the doubts of historical scholarship produce serious arguments against a theistic understanding of the world.

Now, the task is to find a theory that gives the best explanation of these data. The question is: can this task be accomplished in a rational way or is the outcome determined in advance by the different (here: theistic versus atheistic) perspectives of the participants in the discussion? Mitchell admits that especially in metaphysical discussions there is a considerable degree of circularity between the perspectives and the data that are considered to be relevant. But he nevertheless thinks that a rational choice is possible, since we can take alternative data into account and judge their agreement with our explanations on the basis of common sense criteria which are not determined by our different perspectives.[26]

25. Recently, I met the same type of argumentation in a scientific context in a Danish article on the question of whether there has been life on Mars. The article relates that in meteorite AHL84001 from Mars there were found three indications of life: (1) different types of hydrocarbon which belong to the building stones of life; (2) several substances that can be interpreted as waste products from bacterial life; (3) bacteria-like structures. Interestingly, it is stated that each indication can be explained separately as the result of inorganic processes, but that the most simple explanation of their conjunction is that they are traces of life.

26. See Mitchell 1973, part 2 (chs. 3-5). With regard to the dialogue between theology and science it is interesting that ch. 4 and 5 contain an elaborate discussion with Thomas Kuhn about the problem of rational choice between different paradigms.

I think that Mitchell's argumentation exemplifies both the possibilities and the limits of a critical realist understanding of the proposition that God exists — and thereby of all theological propositions that presuppose it. It shows that it is possible to support that understanding with rational arguments which refer to empirical data. On the other hand, the arguments are far from conclusive, since the legitimacy of a nonnatural explanation of the world is contested, there are alternative (e.g., psychological) explanations of religious experience and revelation claims, and the theistic explanation of the world is challenged by the problem of evil. For these reasons, in my opinion critical realism with regard to theological propositions, though not unreasonable, remains fundamentally tied to Christian belief.

4. The Dialogue between Theology and Science

a. An Asymmetry in the Relation between Theology and Science

As a view of the nature of knowledge critical realism pertains to the *cognitive contents* of science and theology. It contends that science and theology in principle are justified in claiming that their statements and propositions tell something about a mind-independent reality, since it is not impossible to attain knowledge of that reality. Now, theological propositions do not only deal with God; they also deal with the world as God's creation and the scene and object of his redeeming action. According to a critical realist view this means that theological propositions about the world concern *the same real world* as scientific statements. Thereby, the question becomes urgent as to how far theological propositions about the world are compatible with scientific statements. From a critical realist perspective this question is an important subject for interdisciplinary discussion between theology and science.

That critical realism makes a difference here can be seen from a comparison with other views of theology and science. On a Braithwaitian view, for example, Christian belief is only concerned with an agapeistic way of life. As a consequence, theology only deals with practical or moral questions. Combined with a critical realist view of science this means that theological and scientific statements cover different realms of being. There is no overlap in subject matter that could lead to a study of the compatibility of their contents. The only interest of theology in the contents of science would lie in the significance of scientific knowledge for the consideration of practical or ethical questions. It can also be imagined that a critical realist view of theology meets an instrumentalist view of science. Again there would be no problem about the compatibility of their contents, since reality claims have another status than statements that are considered as no more than useful illusions. The only possible point of contact would lie in an ethical-theological consideration of the ability of science to manipulate the natural world. The same applies to a confrontation of a purely practical understanding of theology with an instrumentalist view of science. Only when both theology and science are regarded as concerned with the same real world does the question of the compatibility of their cognitive contents become urgent.[27]

The possibilities and limitations of a content-oriented interdisciplinary discussion must be seen against the background of the different perspectives from which theology and science approach the world. Theology looks at the natural world with regard to God's creating and redeeming activity. Therefore, it is interested in phenomena that bear witness to that activity or seem to contradict it, for example, the astonishing manifold of living beings or the existence of suffering and death. Moreover, it is only interested in such phenomena insofar as they are important for the question of the meaning of life. On the other hand, science looks at the world as a whole of purely natural phenomena. It is interested in the understanding of those phenomena *as* natural phenomena. In order to do so it attempts to uncover the regularities and laws they obey, their mutual coherence, and their developments in the past and the future.

These different approaches to the world imply an *asymmetry* in the relation between theology and science. Science is not interested in theology with a view to a possible incorporation of theological ideas, since it excludes in advance, methodologically, nonnatural explanations. It may, however, be interested in theology in another way. In its inves-

27. There are, of course, other possible interpretations of the contents of theology and science. One interesting possibility is an *internal realist* understanding of both theological propositions and scientific statements. It may be asked whether the question of the compatibility of contents puts itself here in the same way as above. I do not feel competent to answer that question. I only want to remark that it seems to me that there is less at stake here. For on internal realist terms compatibility can only be a question of coherence in a subjective worldview, whereas compatibility in the case of critical realism is a question of the identity of an independent reality with itself!

tigation of the natural world it finds itself confronted with phenomena, which it must take for granted *as* science, but which at the same time raise questions of meaning that transcend science. I think of questions like "Why is there a universe at all?" "Why is the universe of this particular kind?" and "How is it possible that it has brought forth conscious human beings that are able to know the world and themselves?" (cf. Peacocke 1993, 87-90; Drees 1996, 266-272). Of course, such boundary questions need not be answered with reference to a divine being or God. But the idea of God offers at least a possible answer. And the consideration of this possibility may make the scientist interested in the theological doctrine of God.[28]

Unlike the interest of science in theology, (systematic) theology has an interest in science with regard to the performance of its proper task. The reason is the critical realist assignment of theology. This assignment involves the task of subjecting the realist claims of particular versions of a Christian worldview to a critical assessment, and in order to do so theology has to take into account the compatibility of those claims with science. Not in the sense that the scientific worldview should be considered as an absolute criterion. Science represents only one perspective on the world and its understanding of the natural world is in many respects provisional and liable to change. But that does not alter the fact that science contains a core of accepted knowledge which in many respects must be considered to have a realist bearing. Therefore, a critical realist theology has to take science seriously. This means on the one hand, that incompatibility with uncontroversial scientific views constitutes a serious challenge to theology. When for example geology, paleontology, and biology agree that there has been life on earth for at least 3.7 billion years, theology cannot reasonably stick to the view that life was created about 6000 years ago. On the other hand, scientific results may also support elements of a Christian worldview. For example, the fact that several physical constants (e.g., the expansion rate of the universe, the strong nuclear force, and the ratio between particles and antiparticles) have exactly the values necessary for the development of human life on earth may

---

28. On the basis of such boundary questions, a scientist may think like Paul Davies that "science offers a surer path to God than religion" (Davies 1984, ix; 229). But this thesis, if proposed seriously, both presupposes a dialogue with theology and challenges to its continuation. And actually Davies develops his thesis in a dialogue with theology, as appears from discussions with, e.g., Augustine, Thomas Aquinas, and William Paley.

be regarded as a scientific support of the Christian view that God has created the universe.[29]

Thus, a serious consideration of the scientific understanding of the natural world is a part of the critical assignment of a theology that purports to be realistic. This critical assignment is an aspect of the general task of systematic theology, which is critical reflection on Christian belief with regard to its (internal and external) coherence and its significance for people of our time. Seen in that comprehensive perspective, theology's consideration of science contributes to the formation of an adequate conception of the world as God's creation and sphere of action. Thereby, it assists the believers in their search for a realistic understanding of the meaning of life.

That the study of the compatibility of the contents of science and theology is held to be important does not imply, of course, that the interdisciplinary study of other aspects of science and theology should not be important. It may, for example, be fruitful to compare theology and science as *human activities,* paying attention to the social and individual interests that underly scientific and theological practice or to the significance of the scientific and theological communities. It is evident that it is important to explore the similarities and differences between the *methods* and *languages* of theology and science, not least with a view to a nuanced understanding of their realist claims. Finally, as concerned with practical questions theology also has a *moral* interest in science, for at least two reasons: (1) with regard to scientific information as a background for responsible ethical consideration (e.g., information about environmental topics); (2) with regard to the impacts of science and technology on society as the object of moral concern.[30] My focusing on the compatibility of the *cognitive contents* of science and theology is only motivated by the fact that it is on this point that a critical realist view of science and theology makes a clear difference compared with other views.

---

29. See Barbour 1990, 135f. Barbour suggests that "this fine tuning could be taken as an argument for the existence of a designer, perhaps a God with an interest in conscious life" (135). This suggestion is, however, rejected by Drees, who points to the possibility that the "anthropic" values "may be explained by future scientific theories" (1996, 271).

30. Peters 1996 distinguishes eight ways of relating science and technology (325-331). His "ethical overlap" (328-330) includes both aspects of what I call the moral interest of theology in science.

b. The Dialogue between Theology and Science

Science and theology meet their interests in the relations of their cognitive contents best in the form of a *dialogue*. Literally, a dialogue is a conversation between two or more persons. In connection with the dialogue between theology and science we use the concept in an extended sense. The two persons are replaced by two parties and the dialogue need not take place orally; it may also employ writing (letters, articles, and books). What matters is that the reflection is not restricted to one party but takes place in a continuous exchange of thoughts between the different parties.

There can be given two reasons for dialogue as the best way of reflection between theology and science: (1) It is a necessary condition for interdisciplinary reflection that the parties make themselves acquainted with at least the most elementary knowledge of the relevant subjects that belong to the others' provinces. This can be achieved partly by reading popular accounts. However, such accounts usually only convey superficial knowledge and easily lead to misunderstandings. Therefore, such reading needs to be supplemented by a dialogue with specialists in order to check and deepen lay understandings and to avoid or correct misrepresentations. (2) The acquisition of knowledge and insight is itself essentially an intersubjective process. We have noted this with regard to science, when we pointed to the decisive role of intersubjective criticism. The same applies, of course, to theology. Therefore, substantial insight in subjects which involve both disciplines cannot be achieved without a dialogue in which representatives of both sides exchange viewpoints and criticisms.

It can hardly be expected that a dialogue between theology and science will lead to definitive results. But a dialogue can narrow the range of plausible possibilities by eliminating wrong assumptions. For example, a theologian may look at the big bang cosmology for scientific support for the belief that God created the world in time. Here, in a dialogue a physicist may point out to him that physical cosmology regards time as originated *with* the universe, so that it does not hold its creation *in* time. On the other hand, a physical cosmologist may have problems with the idea of creation, because he associates it with the view of creation in time. Here, a theologian may draw his attention to the fact that creation in the Christian tradition does not necessarily mean creation in time, and that, for example, Augustine held that time was a part of the created order (cf. Drees 1996, 264). Even though the elimination of such wrong assumptions does not convey a positive understanding of a relation between a Creator and the natural world, it helps establish a framework for a reasonable discussion. And that must be considered as an epistemic gain.

In the dialogue, it is important that the parties be aware of their own and the others' different perspectives on and approaches to the natural world and the advantages and limits that are implied therein. For example, theologians should be aware that their propositions are rooted in faith and do not have the same intersubjective strength as scientific statements. On the other hand, scientists should realize that human life and the world have many aspects that cannot be described and explained scientifically. Theologians should not put forward theological explanations of natural phenomena that are at odds with accepted scientific ones. Scientists should not invest their speculations about boundary questions with scientific authority, and so on.

It is a serious difficulty for the dialogue that theology and science use different languages. Three types of language problems may be distinguished: (1) Theology and science have their own technical language. Theology uses technical terms like "incarnation" and "contingency"; science uses technical terms like "quark" and *"Picea abies L."* Moreover, science often expresses its results in mathematical language. The understanding of a discipline's technical language presupposes a basic familiarity with the discipline itself. Therefore, the parties in the dialogue will seldom be able to understand the other part's professional discourse in depth. Needless to say, this is a serious impediment to the dialogue. (2) Both theology and science use words from everyday language in a more or less technical sense. Theology speaks for example of "sin" and "love," science of "field" and "life" in specialized ways that differ from the normal use of those words. There is a gradual transition here to the metaphorical use of words like "father" and "wave." In this case, the problem is that the technical use of such words can easily be confused with the familiar use known from everyday speech. (3) The same words are used in a different technical sense in theology and science. Such words may or may not figure in everyday language. An example of the former is the use of the word "cause." Besides its different uses in everyday language there is a theological speaking of God as the first cause (as continuously communicating being), which differs from the scientific use (cause as an event leading to another event in an intelligible way) (cf. Peacocke 1993, 45). An example of the latter is the use of the word "altruism."

In (moral) theology altruism is a human being's (conscious) directedness to the good of others, whereas in sociobiology it is an animal's (unconsciously) behaving to the benefit of other animals. It does not require a big stretch of the imagination to realize that the use of such words in the dialogue between theology and science can produce serious misunderstandings.

For these reasons, recognition of the diverse linguistic pitfalls is a necessary condition of a satisfactory dialogue. The parties should be willing to reflect upon their own concepts, explain them to the others, and listen to the others' explanation of theirs. In my view, an important part of the dialogue, particularly in the beginning phase, should be a mutual conceptual clarification. That may be somewhat tedious. But I think it can prevent many misunderstandings and thereby benefit the dialogue in the long run.

The principal point of this last section was that a proper dialogue between theology and science about the relationship of their cognitive contents presupposes an awareness of the advantages and limits given with their different approaches to reality and the different languages they use. Reflection on what is characteristic of the theological and scientific approaches and languages may be a part of theological and scientific reflection itself. But it is also an object of philosophical reflection. *Philosophy of science* and *philosophy of religion* concern themselves explicitly with the question of the nature of science and theology in connection with a reflection on their approaches and languages. Hence, it may add to the methodological awareness of the parties — and thereby benefit the dialogue — if there is made room for philosophy (or the philosophical point of view) in the discussion.

There is another reason why philosophy should partake in the dialogue between theology and science — especially when conducted on critical realist terms. One branch of philosophy, *metaphysics*, concerns itself precisely with the fundamental nature, constitution, and structure of reality. As such, it addresses, for example, the question of why there exists a world at all. It is obvious that philosophical reflection on such questions has an import for the dialogue between theology and science. It may, for example, contribute with ideas that can mediate between theological and scientific conceptions of the world (e.g., the idea that the world is fundamentally contingent), or throw a critical light on unwarranted assumptions (e.g., the assumption that it is a matter of course that the world exists). Also for this reason it is to be recommended that philosophy be involved as the third party in the critical realist dialogue between theology and science.

References

Audi, Robert (ed.). 1995. *The Cambridge Dictionary of Philosophy.* Cambridge: Cambridge University Press.

Barbour, Ian G. [1966] 1971. *Issues in Science and Religion.* New York: Harper.

_____. 1990. *Religion in an Age of Science: The Gifford Lectures 1989-1991.* Volume 1. London: SCM.

Braithwaite, R. B. 1971. "An Empiricist's View of the Nature of Religious Belief." In *The Philosophy of Religion,* ed. Basil Mitchell. Oxford: Oxford University Press.

Chalmers, A. F. [1978] 1983. *What Is This Thing Called Science?* Milton Keynes, U.K.

Davies, Paul. 1984. *God and the New Physics.* Harmondsworth, Middlesex, U.K.

Drees, Willem B. 1996. *Religion, Science and Naturalism.* Cambridge: Cambridge University Press.

Hacking, Ian. 1984. "Experimentation and Scientific Realism.| In *Scientific Realism,* ed. Jarrett Leplin. Berkeley and Los Angelos: University of California Press.

Kuhn, Thomas S. [1962] 1970. *The Structure of Scientific Revolutions.* Chicago: University of Chicago Press.

Laudan, Larry. 1984. "A Confutation of Convergent Realism." In *Scientific Realism. See* Hacking 1984.

Leech, Geoffrey. [1974] 1977. *Semantics.* Harmondsworth, Middlesex, U.K..

McMullin, Ernan. 1984. "A Case for Scientific Realism." In *Scientific Realism. See* Hacking 1984.

_____. 1994. "Enlarging the Known World." In *Physics and Our View of the World,* ed. Jan Hilgevoord. Cambridge: Cambridge University Press.

Mitchell, Basil. 1973. *The Justification of Religious Belief.* New York: Seabury.

Murphy, Nancey. 1993. "The Limits of Pragmatism and the Limits of Realism." *Zygon* 28:351-359.

Pannenberg, Wolfhart. 1977. *Wissenschaftstheorie und Theologie.* Frankfurt am Main: Suhrkamp.

Peacocke, A. R. 1979. *Creation and the World of Science: The Bampton Lectures 1978.* Oxford: Clarendon.

_____. 1984. *Intimations of Reality.* Notre Dame: University of Notre Dame Press.

_____. 1993. *Theology for a Scientific Age*. Enlarged Edition. London.

Pedersen, Olaf. 1988. "Christian Belief and the Fascination of Science." In *Physics, Philosophy and Theology: A Common Quest for Understanding*, ed. Robert J. Russel, William R. Stoeger, and George V. Coyne. Vatican City State: Vatican Observatory.

Peirce, Charles Sanders. 1960. *Collected Papers: Volume V (Pragmatism and Pragmaticism) and VI (Scientific Metaphysics)*. Ed. Charles Hartshorne and Paul Weiss. Cambridge, Mass.: Harvard University Press.

Peters, Ted. 1996. "Theology and Science: Where Are We?" *Zygon* 31:323-343.

Polkinghorne, John. 1987. *One World: The Interaction of Science and Theology*. London: S.P.C.K.

Putnam, Hilary. 1981. *Reason, Truth and History*. Cambridge: Cambridge University Press.

_____. 1992. *Realism with a Human Face*. Cambridge, Mass.: Harvard University Press.

Ritter, Joachim, and Karlfried Gründer (eds.). 1971-. *Historisches Wörterbuch der Philosophie*. Basel: Schwabe.

Russell, Bertrand. [1912] 1920. *The Problems of Philosophy*. London: Oxford University Press.

Soskice, Janet. 1988. "Knowledge and Experience in Science and Religion: Can We Be Realists?" In *Physics, Philosophy and Theology*. *See* Pedersen 1988.

Spiro, Melford E. 1966. "Religion: Problems of Definition and Explanation." In *Anthropological Approaches to the Study of Religion*, ed. M. Banton. London: Tavistock Publications.

van Huyssteen, J. Wentzel. 1989. *Theology and the Justification of Faith: Constructing Theories in Systematic Theology*. Grand Rapids: Eerdmans.

The Significance of Scientific Images: A Naturalist Stance

Willem B. Drees

T HE IMAGES SCIENCE OFFERS are relevant when we reflect on religion. This conviction rests upon the judgment that science offers the best cognitive images of the natural world and on the conviction that humans are not exempt from the natural world.

If there is no opposition there is no need to carry through an argument. One possible objection might be that there is a particular kind of experience, perhaps "religious experience," or a particular source of knowledge ("revelation"), or a particular entity such as the "soul" or "spirit" which somehow falls outside the scope of phenomena dealt with by science; humans are not as fully part of the natural world as assumed here.

One might also object to the prominence given to science, an objection which is relevant to believers and nonbelievers alike: science may be unable to do justice to the richness of reality or of our experiences of it. As the novelist John Fowles expressed it in *The Tree:*

> Ordinary experience, from waking second to second, is . . . hopelessly beyond science's powers to analyse. It is quintessentially "wild," in the sense my father disliked so much: unphilosophical, uncontrollable, incalculable. In fact it corresponds very closely — despite our endless efforts to "garden," to invent disciplining social and intellec-

Various elements in this essay, especially in sections 1a, 1b, 2b, 2c, and 2d, have been discussed in more detail in Drees 1996.

tual systems — with wild nature. Almost all the richness of our personal existence derives from this synthetic and eternally present "confused" consciousness of both internal and external reality, and not least because we know it is beyond the analytical, or destructive, capacity of science. (Fowles 1979, 40f.)

Understanding human experiences and religions in the context of our scientific image of the world should not be achieved by pruning lightly, that is, by the exclusion of complex, "wild" experiences for the sake of simplicity. While a hermeneutical approach may be challenged by scientific insights, a naturalist approach such as the one presented here is challenged by the richness and "confused" character of our experiences.

A naturalist approach is not thereby a "natural theology" leading to a "God of the philosophers," as if it would imply that one passes by all religious traditions. Upon a naturalist approach traditions can be seen as rich resources of well-winnowed wisdom (even though what has been wisdom in the past needs to be evaluated again and again in new circumstances). Traditions certainly are phenomena which deserve to be taken seriously. And so are human experiences, our "inner lives." However, there too one needs to be careful; we have learned all too well that we may be deluded and may delude ourselves, offer rationalizations for behavior we exhibit, and so on. In his theological letters from prison in May, June, and July 1944, the theologian Dietrich Bonhoeffer not only wrote against using God as a stop-gap in relation to scientific knowledge; he also warned against relating God to our "inner lives" as if that were somehow religiously more significant than the world we know about and live in.

In this essay I will first defend the significance of scientific images of the world. In that context I will also address the challenge that science might be inadequate given the richness of ordinary experience. In the second half of the essay I will move on to reflections on religion in the context of a naturalist scientific image. One element in my view is that human religions are not only views of the world to be coordinated with science, but that they are phenomena in the world, and thus objects of study as well. As human phenomena they are primarily understood as functional traditions. This generates challenges to their cognitive pretensions as claims about the nature of ultimate reality. A few interesting but problematic attempts to combine an evolutionary understanding of religion with an ontological one will be discussed. In the final section

I will explicate how and why my approach differs from "critical realistic" and "hermeneutic" approaches, even though it has some affinity to both.

Part One. The Significance of Scientific Images

a. Characteristics of Science

Science is taken in a *realist* way in the sense that it is supposed to study a reality which is, to a large extent, independent of humans and of human attempts to find out about reality. Even the study of human consciousness by physiologists and psychologists is in many cases the study of other persons, and if it is of self-reflection, there still is the assumption that the reflection concerns one's own inner feelings and thoughts — a reality on which one reflects. However, such a realism does not carry us very far in debates on *scientific realism*, which are, in my view, not debates about the existence of "reality out there" but debates about the quality of our knowledge. Do our terms refer to entities out there? Can we say that these entities exist? Do our theories express relations between entities out there? Or, less generally, which theories, or which elements in our theories, can we take seriously as "depicting" the way reality is, and to what extent? What criteria should we apply when we attempt to answer such questions? Unqualified realism seems too strong, and thus too vulnerable to criticisms. Scientific explanations and concepts are provisional human constructs organizing the natural world; they are not independent of human intellectual capacities, social interactions, and contingencies of history, even though one can still speak meaningfully of *The Advancement of Science* (Kitcher 1993).

One major characteristic of the sciences is their wide *scope;* their domain seems to be without obvious boundaries. Terrestrial physics turned out to be applicable to heavenly phenomena as well, and chemistry can be applied to all processes in living beings. The domain of the sciences extends from the smallest objects to the universe at large, from extremely brief phenomena to the stability of rocks, and from heavy objects to massless light. Correlated with the extension of science is the inner *coherence* of our scientific knowledge. The coherence between different sciences has proved to be a heuristically fruitful guide in the development of the sciences, and, if temporarily strongly violated, has at least reestablished itself as a result of later scientific developments. Coherence has become a criterium which makes us reject, or at least consider with the utmost suspicion, purported knowledge which stands in splendid isolation, even if it does not conflict with the rest of our knowledge.

Science *enlarges and changes* our view of the known world. In science there is more risk involved than in formal demonstrations (as in mathematics) since the scientific theories are not in a strict sense implied by the data (e.g., McMullin 1994, 81). The development of scientific theories is also more risky than induction or extrapolation, since theories may postulate entities and concepts of a kind not found in the data; theories are more than generalizations of facts. The debate about scientific realism (see above) can also be interpreted as a debate about the way we should consider the theories of science given the "risk" involved in the process by which we come to these theories: is the process to be understood as a form of inference on which we can rely (and to what extent and for what purposes)? Whatever we think of the realist status of scientific theories, they offer us *scientific images* of the world which *differ* from our *manifest images* (Sellars 1963). This is especially relevant when we consider religion, since religion is in general intimately related to manifest images. This has to do with the importance of tradition for religion, and hence that of symbols and myths from earlier times. It has also a "public relations" side, since most religions reach out to a wide audience which understands and relates to manifest images more easily.

Contemporary natural science is *stable and provisional*. It is stable in the sense that many branches of science seem to be cumulative, building upon knowledge acquired in the last few centuries. Whereas there was a time when the existence of atoms was seriously disputed, it now seems extremely unlikely that physicists and chemists will ever abandon belief in atoms or, for instance, in the periodic table arranging the various elements. It seems equally unlikely that biologists will abandon evolution, both as a view of the natural history of organisms and as a theory explaining this natural history in terms of transmission of properties (in genes) and of differences in survival and reproduction between various variants. However, science is also provisional, and this provisionality is not merely that we may extend our knowledge into new domains (for instance, by creating and studying super-heavy elements), but also that we may reach a further understanding of domains already known, and thereby modify our views. For instance, our understanding of the particles that make up atoms (protons, neutrons) has changed; they now are taken to consist of quarks and gluons. And if one probes further "inside" the atomic realm, one comes into a domain where the physics is very speculative, and certainly not as stable as our belief in atoms.

b. Elements of the Current Naturalist "Scientific Image"

Nonmaterial aspects of reality, such as music, science, and social meanings, are not studied as such by any of the natural sciences, but they seem to be always embodied in forms which are in the domain of the natural sciences, whether as ink on paper, sound waves in the air, or neural patterns in a brain, and only as embodied do they seem to be causally efficacious. Hence, a characteristic of contemporary naturalist scientific images is their *ontological naturalism*.

> 1. The natural world is the whole of reality that we know of
> and interact with; no supernatural or spiritual realm distinct
> from the natural world shows up *within* our natural world,
> not even in the mental life of humans.

The "within" natural reality has been italicized to signal an important qualification, namely that answers to questions *about* the natural world as a whole may perhaps require reference to something beyond the natural world.

The *coherence* of our knowledge seems to correlate with the view that different entities are constituted from the same basic stuff, that is, atoms and forces. Interactions and spatial relations between constituents are, of course, included in this view of reality; contemporary physics treats forces, particles, and space-time together. Thus, a *constitutive reductionism* is part of this scientific image.

> 2. Our natural world is a unity in the sense that all entities
> are made up of the same constituents. Physics offers us the
> best available description of these constituents, and thus of
> our natural world at its finest level of analysis.

Constitutive reduction does not imply elimination, as if the entities or processes "reduced" would not be real: pain does not become less real or painful when its physiological basis is unraveled. However, in many instances (already within physics, and even more when one moves from the causal descriptions offered by physics and chemistry to the functional descriptions offered by biology and "higher" disciplines) we encounter a *conceptual and explanatory non-reductionism*.

> 3. The description and explanation of phenomena may require concepts which do not belong to the vocabulary of fundamental physics, especially if such phenomena involve complex arrangements of constituent particles or extensive interactions with a specific environment.

With respect to living organisms evolutionary biology has become a powerful pattern of explanation which is not primarily in terms of constituents and laws (physics), but in terms of interactions between organisms and their environments. Its explanatory schemes are primarily functional: within the constraints due to natural history, traits which contribute to the functioning of an organism (or, more precisely, to the propagation of that trait in a given environment) are likely to become more abundant than other traits which are functionally neutral or disadvantageous.

> 4. Evolutionary biology offers the best available explanations for the emergence of various traits in organisms and ecosystems; such explanations focus on the contribution these traits have made to the inclusive fitness of organisms in which they were present. Thus, the major pattern of evolutionary explanation is functional.

Explanations Don't Explain the Framework

Most accounts of explanation, including the traditional "covering law" model, are primarily concerned with the explanation of facts, assuming a framework (laws, mechanisms, or the like). To some extent, the framework assumed can be considered as a fact to be explained in a wider framework — as Ohm's law on electrical currents can be explained in the context of a more general theory of electromagnetism in combination with some solid state physics. There are sequences of explanations. The chemist refers to the astrophysicist for the explanation of his elements and to the quantum physicist for the explanation of bonds between atoms. Somehow, these sequences converge: various questions about the structure of reality are passed on until they end on the desk of fundamental physicists (dealing with quantum theory, superstrings, etc.) and questions about the history of reality end on the desk of the cosmologist. As an American president is said to have had written on a sign on his desk: "The buck stops here." Thus, the physicist and the cosmologist may well say "Only God knows."[1] This particular position in the quest for explanations may explain to some extent why physicists and cosmologists might get drawn into philosophical and theological disputes in a way foreign to geologists, biologists, or chemists. The point is not that it is an effective, fruitful, or feasible heuristic strategy to explain all phenomena from "first principles"; calculations and derivations may be beyond our capacities. The argument is that there are limit questions to the scientific enterprise. These limit questions show up most clearly in physics and cosmology, and — I would like to add to the example from Misner and Weinberg — in philosophy of science, since on the desk of the philosopher of science we find questions about the nature of the explanations and arguments offered, and the role of human subjects therein.

> 5. Fundamental physics and cosmology form a boundary of the natural sciences, where speculative questions with respect to a naturalist view of our world come most explicitly to the forefront. The questions which arise at the speculative boundary I will call *limit questions* (LQ).

The questions left at the metaphorical "last desk" are questions about the world as a whole, its existence and structure (and not only questions about its beginning). Such limit questions are persistent, even though the development of science may change the shape of the actual ultimate questions considered at any time. Naturalism does not imply the dismissal of such limit questions as meaningless, nor does it imply one particular answer to such limit questions. Therefore, it is not necessarily atheistic. Religious views of reality which do not assume that a transcendent realm shows up *within* the natural world but which under-

---

1. The image of handing questions from one desk to another is taken from Misner 1977; see also Weinberg 1992, 242. It may be that the distinction between structural and historical questions breaks down in quantum cosmology (see Isham 1993), but that makes no difference for the argument.

stand the *natural world as a whole* as a creation which is dependent upon a transcendent Creator — a view which might perhaps be articulated with the help of a distinction between primary and secondary causality, or between temporal processes in the world and timeless dependence of the world (including its temporal extension) on God — are consistent with such a naturalism.

To describe the field differently, we may distinguish between four views of God's relation to natural reality and its regularities, of which two can be labeled naturalist. These two are often conflated, to the disadvantage of the religious one.

(1) Some have no particular interest in the way the world operates; when God acts, God can do so against any laws of nature. You might see it as shifting from automatic pilot to manual control; whereas on the basis of natural processes one would expect A to happen, God makes event B happen. A problem with such a view of God's relation to the world is that it adversely affects our esteem for God's creation, which is apparently of such a kind that God has to interfere against God's own creation.

(2) Some authors argue that God need not act against the laws of nature; there is enough looseness (contingency) in the web God created in the first place to allow for particular divine actions. This looseness might perhaps be located in complex and chaotic systems (e.g., Polkinghorne 1991; see for my objections Drees 1995) or at the quantum level (e.g., Russell 1995). The natural order could result in a couple of different outcomes, say A, B, C, and D, and God makes C rather than A, B, or D happen. This view depends on a proper role of contingency of an ontological kind *in* nature, whether at the quantum level or elsewhere.

Naturalism need not deny the existence of such contingency *in* nature; perhaps quantum physics should be understood as making clear that natural reality is to some extent hazy and underdetermined. However, it abstains from supplementing natural reality with additional supranatural determining factors. Chance can be taken as chance, and not as hidden determination. Naturalism accepts that nature is, when we consider the level of causal interactions, complete, without relevant holes. Created reality, the natural world, has an integrity which need not be supplemented within its web of interactions. However, this integrity is not to be confused with self-sufficiency; it does not imply that natural reality owes its existence to itself, or is self-explanatory. We need to distinguish between:

(3) naturalism as emphasizing the *integrity* of the natural world, and

(4) naturalism as claiming also the *self-sufficiency* of the natural world.

The argument about self-sufficiency is quite different from any argument about explanations within the natural world, since here we have to do with the contingency *of* existence rather than contingency *in* existence. This is a difference that a polemical atheist like Peter Atkins slides over when he claims that science is about to explain everything. He can trace back everything to a beginning of utmost simplicity, but he cannot do without assuming existence and without assuming a framework where certain rules apply and where mathematics applies. A naturalist need not assume the self-sufficiency of the framework when seeing the framework itself as a whole which has integrity.

If a religious believer accepts naturalism as integrity, it is still possible to see God as the creator of this framework, the ground of its existence. This is best understood, in my opinion, as a nontemporal notion. When God is not seen as one who interferes (above, [1] or [2]), the alternative is not to see God as the creator who started it all a long time ago, but rather to think of God as the one who gives all moments and places of reality their existence and order.

c. The Significance and Limitations of Scientific Images

Strawson (1985, 38ff.) distinguishes between "soft" or "non-reductive" and "hard" or "reductive" naturalism. Upon the "soft" understanding, naturalism refers to what we ordinarily do and believe as humans, say about colors, feelings, and moral judgements. When a painting is considered "naturalist," it is so in this "soft" sense. The "hard" version attempts to view human behaviour in an "objective," "detached" light as events in nature. This distinction corresponds to some extent with the distinction made above between "manifest" and "scientific" images. Strawson argues that these two ways of viewing the world are compatible when each is considered relative to a certain standpoint; however, if he has to choose, he opts for "soft naturalism" (Strawson 1985, 95). This is similar to Fowles's remarks quoted above about the "wild" richness of ordinary experiences compared to the ordered, trimmed, and pruned reality described by the sciences. I am of the opinion that in the light of the successes of science we have to give "hard naturalism" priority

over "soft naturalism" if there appears to be a conflict; science not only
supplements but, in many instances on good grounds, *corrects* our (soft)
"natural" understanding of reality. We cannot do better than accept the
best available knowledge, and thus build upon the most stable insights
about the constitution of worldly entities and the processes by which
they came to be what they are.

An adequate scientific image should not only make intelligible the
phenomena, but also our experience of the phenomena. Thus, an
explanation of the arrangements in the solar system should not only
explain the movements of the planets (in terms of gravitational forces,
etc.), but also why we experience the Sun rising even though we know
that the Earth is turning — and, depending on latitude, at a considerable speed of well over a thousand kilometres an hour — and why we,
despite this rotation, consider ourselves to be at rest in and with our
beds when we lay ourselves down to sleep. A classic expression of the
distance between ordinary experience and the scientific image has been
given by the physicist/astronomer Arthur Eddington, when he described
the table in his study as if there were two quite different tables. The
one was solid and brown, the other mostly empty space with electrons
swirling around nuclei. An adequate scientific image of the table should
be able to explain the experience of solidity; in this case, the experience
can be understood as a consequence of repellant forces between electrons of the table and electrons of, for instance, a book placed on top
of the table.

Why Does Nature Seem "Wild"?

If "wild" nature is to be understood in the framework generated by the
sciences, we still have to understand why it appears so "wild" as to be
beyond science's power to analyze.

Sometimes, the inability is due to the models of reality we use.
For example, metaphors borrowed from technology are used to make
sense of our experiences: "letting off steam" and "being under pressure" are metaphors which depend on nineteenth-century technology;
"recharging batteries" and "tuning in" reflects the earlier electrome-
chanical technology, and the personal computer era has generated a
whole new set of metaphors. This use of metaphors derived from
current technology is fine as long as the metaphorical character is kept
in mind. However, if the analogy between humans and technical arti-
facts, from clocks to computers, is made too tight, it tends to become

ridiculous; "wild nature," including human nature, is richer than such technological metaphors can express.

As I see it, the wildness of experiences is related to various limitations which manifest themselves almost everywhere in nature. For example, with respect to human nature: we do not monitor our inner states, nor could we if we intended, and the causal webs of responding to the environment are the product of a long convoluted history — both as an evolutionary history of our species and as the development of our own being through complex interactions among and between genetic and environmental components — as to be beyond detailed analysis.

We are also limited with respect to detailed explanations of particular events. Chaos-theory has made clear what could have been obvious to students of historical evidence: we never have sufficient knowledge of all details as to provide a full account of the course of events. Besides, a full account would be so cumbersome as to be totally unmanageable and inaccessible to us. Evolutionary biology has made clear that all current forms of life are products of long sequences of earlier beings; explanations consist in one or more reconstructions of the past as it may have been, for all else we currently know — and not in having "the true account of how it happened in all detail." As long as the concept of "explanation" is not used in an overdemanding way (which would make it hard to find any cases where anything is explained), such limitations do not imply that the development of current life forms or the phenomena which actually happen in a complex and chaotic system are unexplained or inexplicable in some deep, religiously significant sense;[2] phenomena are explained when underlying causes or mechanisms are discerned (an ontic notion of explanation) and when they are located in wider theoretical framework (an epistemic notion of explanation; see for these notions Salmon 1990).

Quantum physics may be interpreted as showing that there are limitations not only to the determinateness of our knowledge but also of reality. However, even then we may consider the outcome of a quantum event to have been explained when it is understood as one of the possible outcomes given the setup of the situation. With respect to probabilistic explanations I agree with the following summary of an argument by Richard Jeffrey: "When a stochastic mechanism — e.g.,

---

2. Here I disagree strongly with John Polkinghorne who has used the unpredictability of chaotic systems as a model for divine action; for a more developed version of my objections see Drees 1995 and Drees 1996, 99-100.

the tossing of coins or genetic determination of inherited characteristics — produces a variety of outcomes, some more probable and others less probable, we understand those with small probabilities exactly as well as we do those that are highly probable. Our understanding results from an understanding of that mechanism and the fact that it is stochastic."[3]

In addition to the epistemological limitations mentioned so far there is also a limitation of a more conceptual kind: sciences describing higher, more complex levels of reality need concepts which are not adequately expressible in the concepts of physics (see in section 1b the statement about conceptual and explanatory non-reductionism); they cut the pie of reality in different ways into intelligible units and processes and the wider context may have to be taken into account in different ways (especially when it comes to issues such as the meaning of language). This shows up especially clearly in the relationship between biology on the one hand and physics and chemistry on the other. In physics and chemistry, phenomena are primarily classified in terms of what they do and of their microstructure, whereas in biology phenomena are primarily classified in terms of their purpose and function (e.g., Mackor 1994, 542; Millikan 1984, 1989). In biology there is a greater variety of types of explanations, since one may explain in functional terms what happens, in causal terms how it happens, and in evolutionary terms why the organism is structured so that this behavior can happen.

A Brief History of Science: Via the Simple to the Complex

Aristotelian physics was in many ways more immediately adequate to our experiences than modern physics. The first phase of modern physical and chemical science has been to study simple phenomena, either those with obvious regularity such as motions of the planets or those which were artificially created or approximated in experiments, such as balls rolling along inclined planes or reactions between homogeneous volumes of chemicals, passing over the complexities of friction and of surface phenomena in chemistry. An enormous amount of abstraction and simplification (compared to the real world) has taken place in order to develop science with some depth. It should be obvious that science in this phase was woefully inadequate to deal with complex phenomena

---

3. The quote is from Salmon (1990, 62), who refers to R. C. Jeffrey, "Statistical Explanation vs. Statistical Inference," in *Essays in Honor of Carl G. Hempel*, ed. N. Rescher (Dordrecht: Reidel, 1969).

from the real world. This is a criticism of those who have attached too much significance to Newtonian physics and other early variants of modern science when discussing human nature, social life, or religious convictions. However, it is at the same time a criticism of those who argue that since science failed so obviously when applied to most real world phenomena it is bound to remain so inadequate. It is easy to dismiss science as inadequate when one has erected a straw man. Scientists and authors of popular books on science have on various occasions made such a dismissal of science easy by presenting too simple cases of "greedy reductionism" — a phrase I owe to Daniel Dennett (1995, 82).

Science has not ended with the analysis of simple phenomena. Especially in this century, the scope of science has been extended enormously, studying all kinds of more complex entities and complicated processes such as those which are not in equilibrium, processes in thin layers, and so on; the study of complexity and "chaos" exemplifies (but does not exhaust) this development. Increased computing power and powerful techniques in molecular biology and physics have joined forces with interest in details of particular processes. Thus, science is more and more able to study systems which match or approximate the complexity of the real world. While scientists are in many cases able to understand how a particular phenomenon fits into the larger picture, this insight comes at a price; often, the actual process is understood to be the consequence of processes which cannot be traced in full detail, either because it concerns a history about which we have insufficient data (e.g., evolutionary histories of species, or even of particular DNA sequences) or because it concerns a system about which we know that we cannot know the actual state of affairs at a single moment (both for apparently ontological reasons, as in quantum physics, or for epistemological reasons, as in chaotic systems).

Despite these limitations, or, rather, even due to these limitations, science now is able to face more than the "garden" where reality is pruned so as to make it manageable to science; "wild" reality comes in sight again. To visualize the process: from the richness of our manifest images we have first gone down to the study of gross simplifications, and then reconstructed from insights about these simplifications an understanding of more complex phenomena. Perhaps one should rather envisage a reiterated process, with more than one consecutive cycle of simplification and building up again towards an understanding of complex phenomena. By the way, our current "manifest images" are influenced by the science of the last few centuries, as is clear from the pervasive use of scientific notions (including those borrowed from sociology [roles] and psychology and psychotherapy [conflict of interests], and technology).

As a consequence of the detour through the study of simpler systems, science now more fully understands "wild" reality in its variety and at the same time its own limitations in explanatory and predictive power. The scientific image understands reality in terms that seem to deviate in many ways from the way we experience "wild reality."

Reductionism and the Choice between Manifest and Scientific Images

At some places the distance between our manifest and scientific images may be minimal; at other places it may be more significant. If we find ourselves with two images, which one is more important? That depends on the purpose. It may well be that the "wild" richness of experiences is more important when we deal with one another as humans, when we long for consolation or for a sense of beauty. The scientific image, however, has gone through a critical process of articulation with precision and testing, and is therefore more adequate when we are after "intellectual adequacy," since that is what it has been selected for.

At the beginning of his contribution, Eberhard Herrmann uses as a criterion that the understanding of faith offered should be recognizable to some believers. This, however, is unnecessarily restrictive. In and through the sciences we have come up with all kinds of scientific images of the world which differ significantly from the way we experience the world, that is, our manifest images. "I experienced a tree" can be said in two ways, as a description and as a judgment. It can be a description about how something seems to me, without regard to the accuracy of that seeming. I may say "I experienced a tree, but then I realized I was mistaken." But experience is also used as an achievement word; "I experienced a tree" if it not only appeared to me that there was a tree, but there was a real tree which I saw or felt. "This second sense includes a judgment on the part of the observer about the accuracy of the subject's understanding of his or her experience" (Proudfoot 1985, 229). We cannot and should not seek to explain away experiences as they appear to the subjects. The self-description should not be reduced or denied, unless one has reason to believe that the description is intentionally dishonest. However, it is a fair game of science to explain the experiences as they appeared to the subject in a different way than the subject herself does. "*Explanatory reduction* consists in offering an explanation of an experience in terms that are not those of the subject and that might not meet with his approval. This is perfectly justifiable and is, in fact, normal procedure" (Proudfoot 1985, 197). Accepting a subject's experience in the descriptive sense as authentic need not imply the judgment that the self-description is correct.

One of the worries that is evoked by reductionistic explanations in terms different from those in which the subject describes his or her experiences is the fear that successful reduction would eliminate the phenomena considered. However, this worry is mistaken. Discerning the physiological basis for a trait affirms its reality. Genes are not less real for being understood as strands of DNA, and pain is not less real if physiologically understood. Rather the opposite: if the doctor can locate the physiological process underlying my pain, my friends will take my complaints with more seriousness. In most variants, "reduction is an alternative to, not a form of, elimination" (Schwartz 1991, 218). For instance, the common-sense notion of substance, say solidity, is underwritten by, explained by, and somewhat modified by the scientific account. We might have to give up some, or perhaps even all philosophical notions attached to substance, but we do not eliminate common-sense solids, including Eddington's "first" table. Any scientific description of the table will have to incorporate the fact that I cannot put my hand through the table (unless with considerable force and with major consequences for the table and for my hand).

The conviction that science is unable to account for "wild" nature is to some extent true: it is not able to predict events in full detail. However, science has over time become better and better at understanding complex phenomena (and not merely simple systems which are obviously inadequate models for understanding complex experiences). If we intend to be fair to science, we should not dismiss science on the basis of straw men, that is, simple models which can be dismissed too easily. Besides, we need to be realistic about phenomena in the world; if we have too perfect a view of human nature, for instance with respect to free will, rationality, perception, and the like, then we cannot see how humans would fit into the scientific image.[4]

4. For instance, even though quite different qua philosophers, both Mary Midgley (1994) and Daniel Dennett (1984) make clear that an analysis of human free will requires a realistic assessment of human nature; whether angels would possess rationality and free will is quite different from the question of whether humans do.

Part Two. Religions in the Context of the Scientific Image

a. Religion as a Phenomenon

As far as religions are concerned, two quite different challenges from the scientific image arise. One challenge is that science results in a view of the world which differs from the images generated by religious traditions. In this context, one may speak of a conflict between science and religiously motivated beliefs (e.g., creationism), and one could attempt to accommodate theological notions such as divine action to scientific insights and insights from historians, anthropologists, and so on (e.g., Peacocke), or reinterpret scientific insights to fit better the theological view (e.g., process thought). It is in this context too that debates about theological realism and the similarities and dissimilarities between theological and scientific claims flourish.

However, a naturalist view of reality not only has consequences for a theological view of reality, but also for the understanding of religions. Religions are phenomena within reality. Thus, they can be studied just like other human phenomena. The natural sciences in a restricted sense do not have much to contribute to the study of religions; this level of complexity and intractability requires approaches which may be less fine-grained and precise but are thereby able to take some of the richness of social interactions into account. However, even though the specific study of religions may be the business of others, such as anthropologists, sociologists, and psychologists, the perspective arising out of the natural sciences offers some outlines for views of religions.

One may consider the implications of the neurosciences, and thus the study of those aspects of our constitution which give rise to our "inner life," and one might emphasize the implications of the evolutionary understanding of humans, including their cultures and religions. Within an evolutionary perspective, one would primarily explain the emergence of religions along lines similar to the explanations one would advance for social phenomena such as political institutions and languages. The primary pattern of evolutionary explanation is functional: religions arose, and therefore probably contributed to the inclusive fitness of the individuals or communities in which they arose, and which in turn were shaped by them. An alternative could be that they arose as a side effect with the emergence of some other trait. Perhaps with the rise of consciousness questions about the origin and meaning of the world and of one's individual existence could arise, and as long as other explanations were not available, explanations in terms of spirits and personal powers in and beyond the world were attractive — in that sense, one would move on to the encounter between science and religion as views of the world.

As for the functional role of religion, various proposals may be considered, such as Ralph Burhoe's view that religions made the cooperation of larger groups of hominids, beyond close kin, possible. Another proposal places less emphasis on the role of religion in contributing to human cooperation and more on its role in our responses to intractable, apparently contingent features of our environment (e.g., Luhmann [1977] 1992, 26). Such proposals are in need of further specification. One might test their credibility by analyzing in greater detail how religions may have arisen and may have been sustained in the environments of various epochs, and what their adaptive value (via culture) may have been. The functions of religions may have changed over time as well. Here I will not defend one particular view of the function of religions but rather reflect on some general implications of such naturalist views of religions as functional cultural practices.

Religions with their rituals and myths have arisen in certain environments and have been shaped by the challenges that humans, or their hominid ancestors if we dare to go back that far, faced. Thus, these myths are rooted in natural reality; religious rituals may remain valuable means of dealing with the challenges we face in life, and religious traditions may well convey valuable insights. However, the question is whether we should take the vehicles — the rituals, myths, narratives, conceptualities, and so on — serious as cognitive claims. It is to this issue that we will now turn.

b. The Relevance of Origins for Religious Truth-Claims

To say that religions are, or were, functional is not necessarily to deny that their central terms refer to realities. However, if a religious claim purports to be about a supernatural reality, such as one or more gods, one might raise the question of whether the claim is right or wrong. For comparison I want to start with the example of observing trees.

On an evolutionary view, the adequacy of our language about trees, with notions such as bark, leaves, firewood, and so on, is intelligible since the language has been modified in a long history of interactions of humans with trees and with each other in conversations about trees. This web of causal interactions lies behind the adequacy of our language about trees. If one came across a culture with no past experiences with trees, it would be a very surprising coincidence if they had an adequate vocabulary for trees. We refer to trees, and we seem to do so in fairly adequate ways, because our language has arisen and been tested in a world with particular ostensible trees. Now back to religions and reference. On the naturalist view there is no locus for particular divine activities in a similar ostensible way. Thus, it is extremely unlikely that our ideas about gods would conform to their reality (Segal 1989, 79). Hence, an evolutionary view challenges religions not only by offering an account of their origin but thereby also by undermining the credibility of their references to a reality which would transcend the environments in which the religions arose.

One might propose a different analogy, not between religion and sense perception (seeing trees) but between religious claims and claims in mathematics and ethics. For instance, the philosopher Philip Kitcher wrote, in the midst of a discussion on sociobiology and ethics: "Even if [E. O.] Wilson's scenario were correct, the devout could reasonably reply that, like our arithmetical ideas and practices, our religious claims have become more accurate as we have learned more about the world" (Kitcher 1985, 419). An account of origins, how we have come to a certain conviction, does not in itself decide the truth of that conviction. To argue otherwise, conflating issues of origins of beliefs and of their justification, is to commit what is called the "genetic fallacy."

However, there are relevant differences between the status of mathematics and ethics, and the status of religious ideas. Mathematics may be seen as a second-order activity, growing out of the analysis of human practices such as counting and trading. Similarly, ethical considerations involve a second-order reflection upon procedures or standards which may be fruitful in resolving conflicts of interest with reference to an (unavailable) impartial perspective. As second-order activities, they aim at norms of universal validity, but these universal, "transcendent" claims may be construed without reference to a realm of abstract objects apart from the natural realm with all its particulars. Moral intuitions and judgments may be considered first-order phenomena, but they do not need a "supernatural" realm for their explanation nor for their justification.

In contrast, religions are first-order phenomena in which there is, in most cases, some form of reference to transcendent realities, denizens of another realm. Whereas such references in morality and mathematics may be reconstructed in terms of procedures for justification (and of some insights about human nature and the world in which we act), religions are much more tied to an ontological view of those realities: gods are either supernatural realities or they are unreal, nonexistent. In this sense, an account of the evolutionary origins and adaptive functions of religion is a much stronger challenge to the truth of religious doctrines than is a similar understanding of the origin and function of arithmetic or morality, since mathematical and moral claims are not so much seen here as truth-claims about reality, say about causally efficacious entities, whereas religious claims are often taken to be of such a kind.

Thus, whereas an account of ethics which avoids reference to a nonnatural realm would not affect morality, a similar account in theology would have more radical consequences, as it would undermine the referential character of statements which purport to be about a nonnatural God. In the next section, we will consider two strategies which have been employed to respond to this challenge for theology.

c. Attempts at Integration

Among those who are not willing to discard evolutionary theory or diminish its scope, and who also seek to maintain an understanding of religions as consisting not only of functional phenomena, but also of, in some sense, true claims about reality, at least two approaches can be found. Some have argued that the evolutionary process itself has certain qualities which make it revelatory of God, or perhaps even represent God. Others have argued that the religious metaphors should not be considered claims about a nonnatural reality or about the process of evolution as a whole, but rather as referring to phenomena within natural reality. We will return to this approach, but first we will consider representatives of the first option with its focus on particular qualitative features of the evolutionary process.

Qualities of the Evolutionary Process

Various thinkers have emphasized different qualities of the evolutionary process as theologically significant. Ralph Burhoe has not only offered some ideas about the role religions have played in our evolutionary past but has also made a theological proposal about the most adequate view of God. God is the Creator, the Lord of History — and that is the evolutionary process. Burhoe sees God as that reality to which one has to bow and adapt; in evolution that powerful reality shows itself as natural selection. Humans are not autonomous, nor can they pretend to be the Lords of History. Rather, our salvation lies in adaptation to the majestic reality that created us, and in which we live, move, and have our being (with reminiscences of Acts 17:28). Natural selection will crush any individual or group which does not adapt. Thus, science confirms what most traditional religions have always held: there is a power which creates and judges, punishes what is evil and rewards what is good.

There are other attempts at taking the evolutionary perspective seriously which articulate other views of God. The German Lutheran Gerd Theissen sees grace rather than power as the primary characteristic of God. He holds that evolution displays an increasing tolerance for variation, a tolerance which has become more pronounced with the emergence of culture; the ultimate limit corresponds to a monotheistic view of the deepest reality as God who is inexhaustible and therefore able to tolerate all variations. Rather than the stern God of judgment (by selection) which Burhoe envisages, Theissen offers a God who is primarily graceful, tolerant of variation.

Theissen moves from observations about beliefs which were functional in specific contexts, that is, those of the historical situations of the Israelites, to an ontological claim with universal scope about the tolerance for variation exhibited by the ultimate or central reality. However, evolutionary theory always considers adaptation with respect to actual environments, local realities. Some environments allow for a wide variety of organisms of various species to coexist; other environments are more restrictive. Claims about the central reality and unconditional tolerance have no place in such a perspective; evolutionary tolerance is always conditional on a specific environment. Thus, whereas I regard highly Theissen's analysis of the history of biblical monotheism as a developing protest against selection, I doubt the way he draws conclusions about "ultimate reality" from characteristics of the evolutionary process.

The Lutheran theologian Philip Hefner also seeks to relate religion and science with respect to "the way things really are," a term which Hefner uses in an attempt "to clarify what is meant by the terms *God* and *ultimacy*" (1993, 287). Hefner needs a positive view of "the way things really are," as gracious, offering beneficent support, since he identifies a normative proposal about a way of living with a hypothesis about reality. "The only persuasive ground for this commitment is the possibility that the hypothesis is a true, declarative picture of the nature of things" (1993, 187). This need not imply that we derive religious convictions from scientific insights; in the religious myths and their interpretations one may take it that reality is disclosed to us in such a way as to evoke spiritually and morally appropriate responses.

I doubt whether this link between commitment and truth is as close as Hefner seems to have it. Myths and ritual address deeper layers of human existence. To be effective at those deeper levels the explicit, consciously communicated words need not match the unconsciously received message. Even within science, an adequate picture need not be true; the Newtonian view of gravity as a force acting at a distance is not true, but it has been and still is very adequate for almost all practical purposes. It is obvious that effective moral behavior requires proper knowledge of our situation and of the possible ways to change it, but is the moral input in the choice itself dependent upon cognitive insights about the ontology of the world? I fail to see that the moral commands are dependent upon the "way things really are." Hefner writes: "Christian theology interprets this behaviour [altruism, love] as expression of basic cosmological and ontological principles" (1993, 197). An evolutionary view does not deliver such cosmological principles; love and altruism are phenomena which have arisen in certain contexts. The command to love would not be wrong if reality is indifferent rather than loving; love would still exist as a real phenomenon within reality even if one could not consider reality as a whole to be loving — unless one uses the phrase "the way the world really is" to refer not to the world as we experience it, but to a transcendental perspective on reality expressed, articulated, or disclosed through religious myths. In that sense, talking about aims and values in terms of "the ways things really are" has its advantages; it uses a figure of speech which expresses basic trust and refers beyond one's local environment.

Attempts to integrate a functional, evolutionary view of religious traditions with ontological claims by claiming certain characteristics of the evolutionary process as a whole turn out to be problematic. An alternative could be to focus on religious language as language used within particular, local environments, while avoiding an absolute ontological claim about "the way things really are," "ultimate reality," or the overall direction of the evolutionary process.

Nature and Nature's God

Lindon Eaves, geneticist and Episcopalian priest, agrees with the other authors just considered in treating religion as speaking in and about this reality, rather than about "another world." "Reality shapes itself" (Eaves 1991, 501). Nonetheless, it is useful to distinguish "nature" from "nature's God." Why can there be such a distinction?

> The process of natural selection also produces an "ought" within nature, in the form of the DNA-coded history of many past experiments with nature. The capacity to "dream," however fragmentary the dreams, and to conceive of an alternative world, may also be DNA's solution to potentially inhospitable environments. The "ought" and the "dream" are experienced as "nature's God," that is, as the existential pole of an evolutionary adaptive "is" embedded in nature. (Eaves 1991, 501)

In making a distinction between "nature" and "nature's God," Eaves avoids the problem of affirming qualities of the evolutionary process such as power, tolerance of variation, or creativity;[5] our God-language refers to a segment of our experiences with reality, especially some which are unconscious and intractable for us; "We bear in our genes [and, I would add, our cultural traditions] non-cognitive ways of functioning that have been adaptive in the past"; humans give a name and coherence to this heritage beyond immediate experience by locating it in reality beyond immediate experience (Eaves and Gross 1992, 272). Thus, Eaves and the theologian Lora Gross go on to consider the biological basis of religious notions such as grace and evil, community and diversity, sin and death, transformation and fulfilment.

Why would one use personal language in this context? Eaves considers the personal language to be metaphorical. However, in metaphors it does speak about important aspects of reality which would be less adequately addressed in nonpersonal language.

> Clearly, the "thou" is metaphoric. But the puzzle for biology is accounting for the power of the "thou" compared with the "it." That is, even if the "thou" is metaphoric, something is lost when we attempt to translate the religious reality to the language of "it," much as the

---

5. Burhoe emphasizes power, Theissen tolerance, and Gordon Kaufman (1993), not discussed here, creativity.

joy of sex is not always enhanced by understanding the neurobiology of orgasm. (Eaves 1991, 502)

I do not think that "the puzzle for biology" is to account for the power of personal over impersonal metaphors. In our evolutionary past (and in our present), people, and to a large extent also animals, have always evoked stronger responses of fear and affinity than inanimate objects. Whenever inanimate processes were experienced as unpredictable, a personal metaphor became quite prominent — spirits, demons, or gods of winds and water, for instance. Animism is a "natural" way of experiencing the whims of nature; many people even speak in such a way about and to their cars or computers.

The problem is not the power of personal metaphors but whether we can justify continuing to use such personal metaphors, even when we have become aware of their metaphorical character. Eaves makes an analogy with the joy of sex and the neurobiology of orgasm. There we use both kinds of language, whenever appropriate (depending on purpose and context). The personal and affective dimensions can be there, and be communicated to the other, and thus have genuine meaning and consequences, whatever further analysis the neurobiologist offers. The demise of dualism between matter and spirit, between the chemical basis of life and the affective and cognitive features in humans and their cultures, may undermine the last analogy for a dualism between God and the world. However, it need not deprive us of a rich language which, in different ways, makes sense of higher and lower levels of analysis — a language in which the metaphor of a "thou" to which we speak and sing may be appropriate for certain purposes, especially in our responses to phenomena which we do not control or understand, for which we feel grateful or which we are unwilling to accept.

Functional and Immanent Ontological Religion

We have considered two tendencies in theological proposals which seek to take an evolutionary view of everything very seriously. On the one hand, there is the tendency to focus on the evolutionary process as a whole, and to argue that it has certain features (power, tolerance, creativity), which justify a religious view of evolutionary reality. On the other hand, there is the proposal to consider different aspects within reality, such as the wisdom from the past which is encoded in our genes and articulated in religious metaphors, or the regulative ideals which humans construct.

In my opinion, the second approach has two major advantages. It is more in line with an evolutionary understanding of reality, which focuses on particular contexts, and it does not seem to justify an evaluation of the evolutionary process in positive religious terms, such as grace. It allows better for a contrasting role of religions, as systems which confront us with a sense of distance between what is and what should be, a prophetic role for religion, whereas emphasis on characteristics of the process as a whole aligns more easily with a mystical religious view which gives primacy to the sense of belonging to a harmonious whole. I do agree that there is a genuine role for reflections upon the whole, but they do not so much support answers (such as "ultimate reality is tolerant") as provide an awareness of limitations, limit questions which may be posed but will never be settled. As argued in section 1b, explanations in a scientific framework do not explain the framework itself.

I see particular religious traditions, which propose answers or responses to such limitations, as phenomena within reality, which have a certain role and reflect certain features of natural reality in a metaphorical way. As Eaves (1991, 499) formulated it, religions provide

> a symbolic and metaphorical framework for speaking (inadequately) of an overwhelmingly powerful and mysterious prevenient biological reality whose origins are lost in the mists of evolution and hidden from language and logic in the genetic code.

Religion is thus understood as related to "wild" parts of our experience and being; the parts hidden from language and logic, "hopelessly beyond science's powers to analyse" (Fowles 1979, 41). To some extent this is a return to the god of the gaps. We do not use religious language to account for lightning, since we understand lightning and are able to manipulate it by putting up lightning rods. However, we do use religious metaphors in dealing with aspects of reality which are "hidden from language and logic in the genetic code." However, the discredited strategy of postulating a god of the gaps has tried to fill apparent holes in natural processes as described by the sciences with the action of a supernatural being. Here, there is no similar transcendent ontological claim, as if we could show the impossibility of a natural process by which the aspects which are "hidden from language and logic" could have arisen.

The wisdom in our genes and our traditions stems from our tribal past; it need not be wisdom for today or tomorrow. Thus, whereas we should not and cannot deny our evolutionary heritage, critical analysis and normative reflection, as they arose in our heritage, remain called for.

d. Religious Naturalism

How does my naturalist view compare to other contributions with respect to the relationships between science and religion, such as the other essays in this volume? In this final section I want to explicate my view and method in comparison to more realistic and hermeneutical alternatives.

Renewal of Images: Experiential Adequacy

What would, in my opinion, be the best way to proceed with images and concepts offered by religious traditions as part of our heritage? I do think that the development of physics offers a helpful analogy. When we consider major transitions, such as those from Newtonian conceptions of space and time to Einsteinian views, or from classical to quantum conceptions of matter, we may be struck by the lack of continuity at the level of ontology, of conceptualization of reality. However, there is in these cases also continuity at less abstract levels of knowing, for instance with respect to predictions for the orbits of planets. The way from the older to the newer view is not via a translation at the level of theories, but rather one of developing new theories which do (better) justice to the experiences and experiments coded to a large extent also in the old theories.

Similarly in religion. We need not aim at continuity at an abstract level, which is one or more interpretative steps away from actual life. Continuity with the insights of earlier humans, including those found in the Bible and the writings of the early churches, should be sought at the level of life as lived. The more abstract levels, including notions such as the Trinity, the virgin birth, heaven, and even God, are to a greater extent constructions, and these constructions or interpretations may change drastically even though one seeks to be fair to the underlying experiences. Fundamentalists and those who reject Christianity because they think it has to be fundamentalist often make the error of conflating different levels. They take the original form of expression of human concerns and experiences to be as important as those experiences and concerns themselves. One may attempt to develop new worldviews in which everything of old has an equivalent, while ending up with a complete failure since the new images do not relate sufficiently to the experiences that led to their predecessors. A typical area is eschatology, where images of "another place," "a future perfection," and "personal life beyond death" may be updated in such a way that major underlying concerns, such as anger about injustice, are lost out of sight.

Thus, in my view, the best way to renew religious language and models is to think about the manifest images as they functioned for humans in earlier periods, and to find out as far as possible what the underlying concerns and experiences were. Insofar as we recognize those experiences and concerns and see them as our own, we can attempt to develop new images and models, new ways of dealing with them in images which are credible in our time, in the context of all else that we take seriously, including science.

This is unlike realism in the sense that it does not seek to protect (by reinterpretation or otherwise) the truth-claims of religious metaphors and models or an earlier age — because these metaphors and models are not so much understood as truth-claims but as language which was functional since it helped the individual while living his/her life and the community by creating and maintaining a culture.[6] Realists are, in general, less interested in the detour via the analysis of the human concerns and experiences that lay behind the images; they focus on the truth-claims which appear to be articulated in metaphors and models, whereas I think that we should first pay attention to the relevance these images had in the context they existed in.

Hermeneutical approaches give much more weight to the context of religious beliefs, the way they function for the believers. If a hermeneutical approach is used to keep scientific insights at a distance, the resulting view will not be credible or helpful in communicating ideas. However, a more open-minded hermeneutical approach fits well in the minimalist framework of religious naturalism given here.

6. There are many ways of describing different conceptions of religion (e.g., Sessions 1994); I have found the distinction between a propositional-cognitive view, an emotional-expressivist view, and a cultural-linguistic view to be helpful (e.g., Lindbeck 1984; Drees 1996, 31, 42). A functional, evolutionary understanding gives primacy to the role of religions in shaping cultures, the third view mentioned.

Limit Questions and Religious Traditions

The persistence of limit questions gives room for a theological approach which accepts the natural world as God's creation, while qualifying God's unique mode of creative action in such a way that no problems due to a naturalist view of the natural world can ensue. A disadvantage of such an approach is that it bypasses particular religious traditions with the orientation that they may offer for religious ways of life. An alternative is to consider theological views which take as primary data the richness of particular religious traditions. However, when these traditions are seen as evolved responses to reality, it is hard to see how one can move from traditions as adaptations to local environments to claims about some ultimate reality which is tolerant (Theissen), or in which "is" and "ought" coincide, since altruism and love express basic ontological principles (Hefner). Such claims seem to me to expect a deeper ontological foundation for tolerance or goodness in the natural world than is warranted. However, the emphasis on the value of particular religious traditions is important. Humans live in parts of the actual world, at particular times and places; their native tongue is not language, but a particular language; they are immersed in some culture. They also relate to particular religious traditions. Some people are totally immersed in a tradition; others are confronted with a variety of traditions and seek to respond to that variety.

Humans are not only beings enmeshed in their particular situations. They also speculate about the world beyond their local environment. In the sciences, such speculations have reached remarkable heights, resulting in the understanding of many phenomena and the discovery of new phenomena. In the speculations of science, we seem to reach beyond particularities, although the achievements of science are acquired through the study of details and not through reflections of a more general kind. In theological thinking there is a drive towards universality and abstraction which resembles the move in science from particular contexts to an understanding which covers different contexts. Wondering humans may receive answers from science, but beyond the answers arise further questions which science does not answer.

Wandering Humans: A Variety of Particular Traditions

Religious traditions are complex entities. Each one offers a particular language, with certain metaphors and concepts. A *way of life* may be suggested by parables, as for instance that of the Good Samaritan helping a stranger from another culture (Luke 10:29-37), by historical narratives (such as various accounts of prophets protesting against injustice, or of Jesus forgiving those who persecuted him), and it may be articulated in commandments, such as the Ten Commandments (Deuteronomy 5:6-21). Such a way of life need not always strengthen the conformity of the believer to the expectations of the larger community; it may also emphasize individual responsibility even where the individual goes counter to the interests of others. Such a way of life is not only a practical matter. It is oriented by an *ultimate ideal* which surpasses any actual achievable goal or situation. Thus, religious traditions include elements such as "the Kingdom," "Paradise," "Heaven," "Nirvana," immortality, emptiness, openness, perfection, or unconditional love. Such notions function as regulative ideals with which actual behavior is contrasted in order to evaluate it.

A tradition's way of life is affirmed and strengthened by the particular *forms of worship* and devotion of that religious tradition. Worship and other forms of ritual behavior express and nourish the individual and communal spirituality in relation to the joys, sorrows, and challenges of life and to the conceptions and ultimate ideals of the good life.

Religious traditions are not only ways of life; believers see their religious way of life as *rooted* in certain claims about historical events, ultimate destiny, or authoritative commandments. These claims are supposed to justify the way of life espoused by a tradition as corresponding to the way one should live one's life; justified because they derive from an authoritative source, because they deliver future happiness, or because they correspond to the way reality is intended to be or, deep down, really is.

Just as cognitive variety is not to be dismissed in the sciences, so too may religious variety be acceptable, natural, and valuable in a naturalist perspective. The variety of ways of life may well be a rich resource and a colorful element in our own time. Variety is to be expected, since we deal with human experiences (of various kinds in a wide variety of contexts), and different forms of ritual behavior and different guiding ideals of human flourishing may be entertained. However, no tradition is beyond dispute and beyond development. There is no reason to dismiss at once such complex cultural entities as religious traditions as being at odds with natural science, but neither do we have to accept our own tradition, or any other, without critical scrutiny or as a yes-or-no package deal. Change is characteristic of our history, and there is no need to exclude religious traditions from it.

A particular tradition (or stage of, or element in a tradition) may, of course, have to be rejected as outdated. One reason, which corresponds well with an evolutionary view, is that the actual circumstances have changed, and that therefore models of the good life or forms of worship may have to change. Such is certainly the case when we consider the human condition today: we are vastly more numerous, stand in a fundamentally different relation to nature (which is now threatened by us rather than we being significantly threatened by it); we are more powerful than before, and we are confronted with neighbors across the globe. In relation to such changes, traditional models and metaphors may be employed differently, or they may be understood as they always were but this may now be inappropriate to the circumstances (for example, since they fuel the exploitation of natural resources).

Not only have our circumstances changed, but so have our moral and spiritual sensitivities, for example with respect to conflicts between ethnic or religious groups, slavery, or cruelty to animals. Religious traditions, changing circumstances, a wider encounter with other cultures, and philosophical insights have all contributed to this process of change. We evaluate traditions also by the moral and spiritual life they support. These changes do not, in most instances, have much to do with science, though they reflect the general characteristic of a naturalist approach of relating the behavior of biological organisms to the contexts in which they live.

One more reason, but not the most important one, is the cognitive credibility of a tradition. If the images which support the way of life are not recognizable, or if the claims by which the way of life is justified have become incredible (and thus no longer justify it), then that too challenges the religious tradition, though more indirectly than challenges to the appropriateness of the circumstances of the way of life and to its moral and spiritual adequacy.

Granted that we may have to discard some traditions or may have to modify them, why would one keep alive any such tradition? The reason is, in my opinion, that they are useful and powerful. They are useful and powerful, not only for unreflective moments and persons, but also for reflective and well-informed persons. No human is only a rational being who could entertain all his motives and desires consciously and intentionally; the structure of our brains is such that much goes on which is not dealt with consciously. This is the risk involved in religious forms of behavior (since so much cannot be scrutinized consciously) and the reason for their importance: through religious metaphors and forms of behavior we address reality especially in a way which confronts us with ideals, with what ought to be, with a vision of a better world, or with images of a paradisiacal past or an ultimate comforting presence.

Wondering Humans: Limit Questions

There is another aspect of religious traditions, where we also reach beyond the local environment. Humans have, with the development of consciousness and communication, contemplated questions about the world in which they found themselves. Many of their speculative answers may have been functional; anthropologists and other scholars in comparative religious studies have found that creation myths and other cosmogonies are not merely speculative attempts at explanation, but ways of presenting and justifying moral imperatives and social structures. However, some speculations may well be useless, toy with the possibilities of thinking, or at least reach beyond what is sufficient for the circumstances of the moment. In earlier ages, answers to speculative questions may have been closely allied with the way the world was experienced, which is still to a large extent reflected in our manifest image of the world. In this manifest image, persons are the major agents from which action proceeds. Hence, it is not very amazing that animist ways of speaking about the world have become widespread; experiences with many phenomena are modeled after experiences with human agents. Sometimes such agents are understood as residing in the phenomena, say as spirits, and sometimes the agent is thought of as a god who transcends the phenomena but acts through them.

Such models are still with us; animist ways of speaking about cars or computers are common, and many persons discern intentions behind bad luck, such as being struck by a disease. I consider the belief in such intentions a remnant of earlier times when manifest ways of speaking were not yet corrected through the development of scientific images; such ways of speaking and thinking are interesting as phenomena, but they are not credible given our knowledge of cars and cancers. However, even though earlier answers have lost their credibility and questions may have changed their appearance, humans can still be wondering persons, contemplating questions that transcend our current answers. Religious traditions offer answers to such questions, but — more importantly, in my view — they are thereby also ways of posing such questions, and thus ways of nourishing sensitivity to such questions. Maintaining this speculative openness is one role of limit questions.

The openness expressed in the limit questions may induce a sense of wonder and gratitude about the reality to which we belong. Such a cosmological approach might primarily be at home with a mystical form of religion, a sense of unity and belonging, as well as dependence upon something which surpasses our world. The functional view of religion offers some opportunities for a prophetic form of religion, with a contrast between what is the case and what is believed ought to be the case. The contrast might be seen as a consequence of our evolutionary past, which has endowed us with wisdom that is encoded in our constitution and in our culture (including religious traditions).

Not everything that is "wisdom" of the past has the same characteristics. On an evolutionary view, the structures of our eyes and of our immune-system can be considered "wisdom of the body" which provides some useful capacities and defences. This "wisdom of the body" is experienced as a given; we could not choose to have a different eye color. Religious traditions are phenomena which differ from physical characteristics in that they embody an awareness of a reality which is different from the reality of our daily lives. Furthermore, this "other reality" is experienced in such a way that it reflects upon our individual and social behavior, for instance by promoting a quietistic acceptance or an activist rejection of social inequalities.

Such religious wisdom is to some extent independent of the actual situation which we face. Hence, it may serve as an external reference, an apparent Archimedean position outside the actual situation, in reference to which one might judge human decisions in the actual situation. However, such "prophetic" wisdom transcends the current situation but is tied to an earlier one. Hence, it may not be adequate in the new situation, where consequences may be different; blind application is never justified.

Another way to articulate a prophetic element is to argue that evolution has endowed us with the capacity for imagination, for reconsidering our situation from a different perspective. This capacity has as its limit the regulative ideal of an impartial view transcending all our perspectival views. The inaccessibility of such a point of view is beneficial since it protects us from fanaticism; if one were inclined to believe that one's view could be the final one, one would not be incited to self-questioning (Sutherland 1984, 110). When considered in relation to the radical concept of divine transcendence, all regulative ideals as they arise in particular religious traditions are relativized; they can never lay unrestricted claim to our allegiance.

We know, collectively, a great deal about our world. Our knowledge is also limited. Certain phenomena may be intractable, even though they fit into the naturalist framework. And limit questions regarding the whole naturalist framework can be posed but will not be answered. In a book of aphorisms, *The Aristos,* the novelist John Fowles has given a positive appreciation of such limitations to our knowledge.

> We are in the best possible situation because everywhere, below the surface, we do not know; we shall never know why; we shall never know tomorrow; we shall never know a god or if there is a god; we shall never even know ourselves. This mysterious wall round our world and our perception of it is not there to frustrate us but to train us back to the now, to life, to our time being. (Fowles 1980, 20)

I wonder how Fowles knows that we shall never know. He even knows *why* we do not know: to train us back to life!

"To train us back to life": the notion of such a purpose of our limitations is inadequate with respect to the evolutionary process which has saddled us with these limitations; it has simply happened that we are endowed with our capacities and our limitations. However, the emphasis on the wider context of knowledge, our lives, fits well. Our knowledge and our capacity for knowledge have arisen in the midst of life, and if we are to use them anywhere at all, it will have to be there. They allow us to wonder about that which transcends and sustains our reality, but all the time we wander in the reality in which we live, move, and have our being; to its future we contribute our lives.

References

Bonhoeffer, D. 1970. *Widerstand und Ergebung* (Neuausgabe). München: Kaiser.

Burhoe, R. W. 1981. *Towards a Scientific Theology.* Belfast: Christian Journals Ltd.

Dennett, D. C. 1984. *Elbow Room: Varieties of Free Will Worth Wanting.* Cambridge, Mass.: MIT Press.

_____. 1995. *Darwin's Dangerous Idea: Evolution and the Meanings of Life.* New York: Simon and Schuster.

Drees, W. B. 1990. *Beyond the Big Bang: Quantum Cosmologies and God.* La Salle: Open Court.

———. 1995. "Gaps for God?" In *Chaos and Complexity: Scientific Perspectives on Divine Action.* Vatican City State: Vatican Observatory & Berkeley: Center for Theology and the Natural Sciences (distr. University of Notre Dame Press).

———. 1996. *Religion, Science and Naturalism.* Cambridge: Cambridge University Press.

Eaves, L. B. 1991. "Adequacy or Orthodoxy? Choosing Sides at the Frontier. *Zygon* 26:495-503.

Eaves, L. B., and L. Gross. 1992. "Exploring the Concept of Spirit as a Model for the God-World Relationship in an Age of Genetics." *Zygon* 27:261-285.

Fowles, J. 1979. *The Tree.* St. Alban's: Sumach.

———. 1980. *The Aristos.* Revised edition. Falmouth: Triad/Granada.

Hefner, P. 1993. *The Human Factor: Evolution, Culture, and Religion.* Minneapolis: Fortress.

Isham, C. J. 1993. "Quantum Theories of the Creation of the Universe." In *Quantum Cosmology and the Laws of Nature,* ed. R. J. Russell, N. Murphy, and C. J. Isham. Vatican City State: Vatican Observatory and Berkeley: Center for Theology and the Natural Sciences (distr. Univ. of Notre Dame Press).

Kaufman, G. D. 1993. *In Face of Mystery: A Constructive Theology.* Cambridge, Mass.: Harvard University Press.

Kitcher, P. 1985. *Vaulting Ambition: Sociobiology and the Quest for Human Nature.* Cambridge, Mass.: MIT Press.

———. 1993. *The Advancement of Science: Science without Legend, Objectivity without Illusions.* New York: Oxford University Press.

Lindbeck, G. A. 1984. *The Nature of Doctrine: Religion and Theology in a Postliberal Age.* Philadelphia: Westminster.

Luhmann, N. [1977] 1992. *Funktion der Religion.* Frankfurt am Main: Suhrkamp.

Mackor, A. R. 1994. "The Alleged Autonomy of Psychology and the Social Sciences." In *Logic and Philosophy of Science in Uppsala,* ed. D. Prawitz and D. Westerståhl. Dordrecht: Kluwer Academic Publishers.

McMullin, E. 1994. "Enlarging the Known World." In *Physics and Our View of the World,* ed. J. Hilgevoord. Cambridge: Cambridge University Press.

Midgley, M. 1994. *The Human Primate: Humans, Freedom and Morality.* London: Routledge.

Millikan, R. G. 1984. *Language, Thought and Other Biological Categories*. Cambridge, Mass.: MIT Press.

_____. 1993. *White Queen Psychology and Other Essays for Alice*. Cambridge, Mass.: MIT Press.

Misner, C. W. 1977. "Cosmology and Theology." In *Cosmology, History, and Theology*, ed. W. Yourgrau and A. D. Breck. New York: Plenum Press.

Peacocke, A. R. 1993. *Theology for a Scientific Age: Being and Becoming — Natural, Divine and Human*. Enlarged edition. London: SCM, and Minneapolis: Fortress.

Polkinghorne, J. C. 1991. *Reason and Reality: The Relationship between Science and Theology*. London: SPCK.

Proudfoot, W. 1985. *Religious Experience*. Berkeley & Los Angeles: University of California Press.

Salmon, W. C. 1990. *Four Decades of Scientific Explanation*. Minneapolis: University of Minnesota Press.

Schwartz, J. 1991. "Reduction, Elimination, and the Mental." *Philosophy of Science* 58:203-220.

Segal, R. A. 1989. *Religion and the Social Sciences: Essays on the Confrontation*. Atlanta: Scholars.

Sellars, W. 1963. *Science, Perception and Reality*. London: Routledge and Kegan Paul.

Sessions, W. L. 1994. *The Concept of Faith: A Philosophical Investigation*. Ithaca: Cornell University Press.

Strawson, P. F. 1985. *Skepticism and Naturalism: Some Varieties*. New York: Colombia University Press.

Sutherland, S. R. 1984. *God, Jesus and Belief: The Legacy of Theism*. Oxford: Basil Blackwell.

Theissen, G. 1985. *Biblical Faith: An Evolutionary Approach*. Philadelphia: Fortress. (Transl. of *Biblischer Glaube in evolutionärer Sicht*, München: Kaiser, 1984.)

Weinberg, S. 1992. *Dreams of a Final Theory*. New York: Pantheon Books.

A Pragmatic Approach to Religion and Science

Eberhard Herrmann

I. Introduction

The Aim of My Contribution

The aim of my contribution is to present the implications of a pragmatic approach to religion and science for the science-theology debate. The philosophical model which I will use is applicable not only to religious views of life but also to nonreligious ones, which I find helpful in a growing pluralistic situation such as ours. I introduce the term "view of life" already here to indicate that I will not make any difference in principle between religions and such phenomena as existentialism, Marxism, or feminism as far as their function in our lives is concerned. By using the umbrella term "view of life" I will theoretically separate those phenomena that are not sciences but often are claimed to constitute alternatives to science or at least to be a complement to science. However, by the term "view of life" I mean neither grand-scale worldviews nor specific theoretical worldview assumptions. Instead, I want to refer to the ideas we humans make ourselves, in our relations to other humans and our environments, in order to cope with the concrete

I would like to thank Michael Scott for his comments and corrections to an earlier draft of this paper and Mark Sluys for his comments and corrections to a later draft. I would also like to thank Niels Henrik Gregersen and Wentzel van Huyssteen for their constructive criticisms before the publishing of this paper.

121

contingencies of life. The stress lies on the last part of this sentence. What I will label "views of life" are fragmentized as well as more systematized expressions of what it means to be a human being living with love and happiness, suffering and death. In this process of system-atization some expressions can stiffen and finally emerge as institution-alized worldviews. As far as I can see, it is only when views of life become institutionalized worldviews that there is a debate about the relationship between science and theology. But such institutionalization is not es-sential for views of life as far as the concrete contingencies of life are concerned. I will come back to this issue at the end of my paper when pointing out the implications of my philosophical model for religion.

There are people who claim that there is no meaning or truth in religion, while other people affirm that there is but disagree among themselves about how religion can be said to be meaningful or true. Plurality as such is no problem. It only becomes a problem if we raise truth-claims that we consider to be infallible. On the theoretical level there still is no problem. However, if our actions are rooted in what we accept as true, then living together may become impossible if one claim of infallibility collides with another. Thus, we need to find a way to discuss our different views of life critically, that is, on the level where we cope with the contingencies of life. Even if suffering and death, love and happiness are obvious realities in our lives which can be partly explained within limited perspectives, there is still something unex-plained. We just have to learn to live with this. Luckily, we are not wholly dependent upon our own individual resources in learning this. In our views of life considered as traditions we have access to expressions of the contingencies of life (see Westphal 1987).

A critical discussion should satisfy the following two conditions: First, an account should be given of religion such that at least some religious people can recognize their faith in it. I do not think it is possible to get support from all religious people. The opposition be-tween traditions, even differences within the same religion, is too great. Second, a philosophical model should be proposed whereby one can analyze religion as a human phenomenon without committing oneself to either a reductionist account of religion or the theory that there are religious statements referring to a transcendent reality.

As will be manifest to the reader, my approach in this paper is epistemological. This focus on epistemology explains why in this paper I prefer to use the word "statement" and not "proposition." I want to avoid the ontological question of whether or not we need to consider propositions to be some kind of abstract entity. However, to use the word "statement" is not without problems either. We have to distinguish between the expressed content of a statement and the making of it (Moser 1989, 14). Probably some philosophers would prefer to call this expressed content a "proposition." But because of the epistemological connection between the expressed content of a statement and the making of it, I still try to avoid using the word "proposition." When we make a statement and ascribe the truth-value true to its expressed content, it is presupposed that we have reasons for doing so. There is a logical distinction between the conditions for a statement being true — here again some philosophers would prefer to talk about propositions — and the conditions for our finding out whether the statement is true. Certainly, the latter do not make a statement true. However, I do not see how we could ever avoid considering the question of what the conditions for our finding out whether a statement is true are. I will come back to this issue when giving my reasons for not talking about knowledge-claims in religion.

On the one hand, since religion plays a crucial role in the lives of many people, the model must not be reductionistic, reducing religion to something else. On the other hand, the model does not presuppose divine revelation in the explanatory conditions of religion.

This latter restriction needs a comment. There are two groups of people who will probably not accept my emphasis on religion as a human phenomenon manifesting itself in versions that need to be critically compared with each other and with their secular equivalents. First, there are those religious people who raise knowledge-claims about the divine, and second, there are their critics who argue that these religious knowledge-claims are false. For instance, some Christians consider the Creeds as containing true statements about facts concerning God the Father, the Son, and the Holy Spirit. Some of their philosophical critics argue that these religious utterances look like statements but actually are not statements at all because we cannot falsify them. Both positions seem to presuppose that one has to justify knowledge-claims by referring to facts as parts of an independently existing reality. Those who accept religious knowledge-claims assert that this reference is shown by revelation. Their critics do not accept revelation as a criterion of reference and thus deny this way of trying to justify religious knowledge-claims.

As far as I can see, both sides neglect the point that by treating religious sentences as knowledge-claims, that is, as hypotheses, we do not do justice to religious belief. Religious expressions are not hypothetical in character but are in one sense necessary within the belief system. Therefore, I prefer not to talk about knowledge in religion. I know that words like "knowledge" and "knowing" are used, for instance, in the Bible and other holy scriptures and that many religious people would rather talk about what they call "profound" knowledge or knowledge that is quite different from ordinary knowledge. My point is not that a word like "knowledge" is used with different meanings. We use other words with more than one meaning also. What I am objecting to is that religious believers quite often claim that religious knowledge is different from nonreligious knowledge while riding on the fact that in the sciences there are procedures for deciding which knowledge-claims are justified, and thus they do not preserve the very distinction which they started with. Certainly, believers say there is a distinction, but, since they presuppose decision procedures just like scientists do, their knowledge-claims cannot be distinguished in this respect, so there is no distinction. All ordinary knowledge-claims must have decision procedures, and as far as I can see, religious ones do not, so they are not ordinary knowledge-claims. And if this is the case, then it should be emphasized in order to avoid confusion. In our Western societies we are conditioned to bring associations along with us from the scientific context to our talk about knowledge in other contexts. If we are aware that this is the case, then, certainly, there is no danger in using the word "knowledge" with different meanings. Unfortunately, we do not always notice the differences. Therefore, because it is important to make the difference between knowledge in science and knowledge in a different sense in religion explicit, it seems to be more fruitful to use another term for the latter, such as "insight" or "wisdom." Much confusion would then be avoided. Of course, we could reserve the word "knowledge" for religion and try instead to find other words for what we now mean by "knowledge" in the sciences and in everyday life. But this suggestion does not seem very practical.

The question of how to use certain words is linked to differences in context and conceptual framework. These two kinds of difference are interrelated with each other in the following sense. How to identify what is what in a certain context is determined by the conceptual framework that we consider to be relevant. The decision of which conceptual framework is relevant for a certain context depends upon how we are related to the context. The assertion that religion, faith, or revelation is a gift from God is by no means exempt from the rule that we are always confined by given conceptual frameworks. Even when we claim that we cannot analyze, criticize, or change revelation because it is a gift from God, we can only make such an assertion by means of ideas and concepts at our disposal. This, I think, at least partially explains the fact that we actually can be confronted by completely different views of religion, faith, revelation, and so on. Thus, in a kind of postmodernist spirit I do not claim that my view of religion is the true one. However, I will argue for this view being a plausible and fruitful one as far as the problem of plurality is concerned.

Let me continue on this track. We are dependent on our conceptual framework in the sense that we cannot think, talk, and act without ideas and concepts. This does not mean that we could not change them at all. It just means that, though undeniably possible, the categorical claim of what does or does not exist in an evidence-transcendent way, is not a plausible one. In relation to religion it means conflating different areas of utterances and not understanding the function of religious beliefs in our lives. Of course, we can assert that there are facts although we do not know them. However, when we want to state some fact about the world, that is, claim that the expressed content of the statement is true, we cannot decide whether this is true by transcending the evidence we have for it. In this respect, religion is no exception.

However, seen from another angle, to make a completely reductionist statement about religion would mean to transcend the evidence, too. We are not in our epistemic rights to maintain categorically that religion is nothing else but, for instance, the expression of infantile regression or of the conditions within class society. We can point out cases where it seems to be so. However, we cannot refer to evidence showing that religion is nothing else but that.

In general, although there is an ongoing change concerning what we can know and actually do know, we nevertheless are subjected to some epistemic constraints. They do not exclude ideas of what could be possible but they do exclude transforming at least some of these ideas into statements about what is the case. The implication of taking our epistemic constraints seriously in the sciences and views of life is the following. First, neither of them can provide us with infallible truth-claims. Second, the results of the sciences and what we express in our views of life do not lie on the same logical level. Scientific investigation provides us with knowledge that we can test directly or indirectly by observation, although observations always are theory-laden. I will come back to this issue later in my paper. Views of life provide us with expressions that we can experience as adequate expressions of what it means to be a human being. To propose a division of labor between the sciences and views of life means that the question whether integration between science and religion is possible, changes character. As a rule, the issue of integration is considered to be a matter of statements. This appoach, however, I want to question.

A Non-integrative Approach to Science and Religion in Regard to Statements

My reasons for trying to develop an approach to science and religion that is not integrative in regard to statements has mainly to do with the problems that result from the traditional treatment of the relation between science and religion. The focus is evidently on knowledge and truth-claims. There is a long discussion, especially within Christianity, about what to do when different truth-claims collide with each other. Which type of truth-claim has priority? The answer of the fundamentalists is, of course: the religious truth-claims. The fundamentalists are not against science in principle, only when its results are incompatible with faith. In that sense the fundamentalists advocate integration. Usually, however, the idea of integration goes in the other direction. Here we meet a strong version in the claim that we need to justify even religious truth-claims by scientific methods. A weak version is given by the claim that religious truth-claims do not contradict science but complete it.

Both kinds of integration presuppose, first, that the question of integration is a matter of statements and, second, that religious and scientific statements lie on the same logical level. One can question these two assumptions by questioning either the first or the second claim. Let us start with an example of a position according to which religious and scientific statements do not lie on the same logical level. We can choose the doctrine of double truth, according to which there are revealed truths and there are natural truths. Nowadays, we would say scientific truths. These two kinds of truth do not lie on the same logical level in the sense that they belong to different universes of discourse, because of their roots in different aspects of reality.

My reason for not accepting this kind of position is twofold. First, it presupposes that we can assert evidence-transcendent truths about what is the case. I have to confess that I do not understand how we could do that. Certainly, I am not opposed to the very ambition of avoiding a definition of truth in epistemic terms. To do this would be to advocate extreme relativism. There would then be no way of distinguishing between what we think is true and what is actually true. In practice, when we want to make statements, we choose those statements for which, in a given context, we have the most evidence. Sometimes we have equal evidence for statements that exclude each other; nevertheless, we have to make a decision if we do not want to be like Buridan's ass starving between two equally desirable stacks of hay. Now, when not only eating from the chosen stack but still thinking, a definition of truth in epistemic terms would not only allow us to consider these statements as separately true statements. It would even oblige us to go further and claim that both a statement and its denial are actually true. The difference between the two steps is that it is one thing to accept contradictions because in a certain situation we cannot settle definitely which side of the contradiction is the right one, and quite another thing to accept both sides of the contradiction as true. The latter position would imply that we could deduce whatever statement we want from the contradiction, including false statements. However, that would mean that we no longer could distinguish between true and false. In turn, this would mean that one of the main grounds upon which we make conscious and rational decisions would be undermined.

When discussing how to avoid relativism, we have to be aware of the fact that the noun "truth" is ambiguous. The claim that there are evidence-transcendent truths could mean that *something can be the case* without our knowing of it, or that *there are statements that are true* irrespective of whether or not we know that they are true. However, to assert the truth of statements about what lies beyond our epistemic abilities is not the right way to avoid the risk of relativism. It is one thing to accept that something can be the case without our knowing of it. It is another thing if we want to make certain truth-claims. Then we cannot assert things that lie beyond our epistemic constraints. To talk about statements being either true or false makes sense only if there is a relation to evidence, and that always means what we count as evidence. In some sense we need observational grounds not only when we have to decide which statements are true but also when we want to know which sentences can reasonably be used as statements. In this respect it is not meaningful to assert the existence of evidence-transcendent true statements.

My second reason for not accepting the doctrine of double truth is that it presupposes a statement view of religion. As far as I can see, religion mainly seems to consist of pictures, stories, and expressions that we use in molding our lives. Certainly, in religion statements are made, but since, according to my view, they are part of existential expressions of what it means to be a human being, they do not function like scientific statements.

At this point I will introduce the other way of questioning the common presupposition for both the fundamentalist and scientific versions of integration. Here one questions the first claim that the issue of integration is a matter of statements at all. Instead, the issue is taken as being related to the fact that science and religion have radically different functions in our lives. Regarding these differences I will argue that we need both sciences and views of life to cope with the different kinds of problem we meet in our lives.

I do not think that we can avoid considering ourselves as problem-solving beings. To survive both as individuals and as a species we have to cope with the problems that we encounter in our lives. For me there is nothing horrible in the thought of a universe without human beings. In this sense I do not think that we humans have intrinsic value. However, in a universe in which we exist, such conditions should surround us that make it possible that we can live a good life together. In this respect problem-solving plays a crucial role in our lives.

This does not mean that we necessarily need to define truth in terms of the successful solutions of problems. However, it would be foolish not to take account of the solutions to problems that experience has shown us to be successful, when arguing for the justification of truth-claims. This, of course, raises many difficult philosophical problems. One of them is the problem of realism.

II. The Problem Situation

Let me start with a short description of the problem situation. In our days, especially, two aspects are troublesome. They cause difficulties not only for the philosopher of religion. They are also a problem for society. Let us call the first problem the cognitive problem of religion and the second problem the problem of pluralism.

The Cognitive Problem of Religion

On the one hand, religious people want to say something substantial about what they experience as a transcending reality. They want to say more than that it is a way of satisfying our existential questions about what it means to be a human being. On the other hand, religious people know that they cannot say anything about the transcending reality other than by human language and within our conceptual frameworks. We can go beyond them in the sense that we can change them when they do not fit our knowledge and experience any longer. However, we cannot go beyond them in the sense that we could do without any of them. We have to use the ideas and the concepts given by the different contexts in which we live. In this sense the cognitive problem of religion is part of the general problem of realism.

There is something right in the realist intuition that we cannot define truth in terms of verification or acceptability. Let us consider the distinction between the definition and criterion of truth. According, for instance, to Hilary Putnam, a necessary condition for a statement to be true is that it could at least be justified. To justify either a statement or its negation we must consider circumstances as ideal for justification as we could hope to make them (Putnam 1983, 85). In this respect it is entirely reasonable to claim "that truth comes to no more than idealized rational acceptability" (Putnam 1990, 41). However, this is a question of criteria. If we assume that the idea of truth as idealized rational acceptability is taken as a definition of truth, then obviously this idea would open the door for relativism. Idealized rational acceptability means what we humans can conceive of as idealized conditions for justifying truth-claims. Following the limitations of my epistemological approach I restrict the scope of persons to humans, and do not include, for example, God. We cannot exclude that perhaps we may be wrong also with regard to the circumstances as ideal for justification as possible. The idea of truth as idealized rational acceptability, however, does not lead us into relativism, if taken as a criterion of truth.

When there is a clash between reality and how we conceive of it, reality, so to speak, offers resistance, and we have to change our views. It would be foolish to try to have it the other way around. The wall in front of me is a wall, which means that I cannot claim that there is nothing stopping me from going in any direction I want. Let me give another example of how reality offers resistance by pointing to the context of social life. I cannot treat people as I want without being confronted with the consequences. As experience has shown, sooner or later people will strike back. For instance, to advocate a segregating housing policy according to which some groups are forced to live together in areas with almost no opportunities for the individual will inevitably promote aggression.

Yet, on the other hand, in spite of all these realist intuitions, there is something right in the antirealist criticism that we cannot raise knowledge- and truth-claims without relating to conceptual frameworks and within them to our epistemic abilities. There is a lively debate about realism and antirealism. But it is not easy to follow it because it is not always clear where exactly the dividing lines are drawn.

Different Kinds of Debate about Realism and Antirealism

The fundamental realist intuition consists of the thesis that the world is objective or real in the sense of being independent of how we think of it. This implies that we cannot define truth in epistemic terms. The truth, that is, what is the case, is objective or real irrespective of whether or not we know it. From this perspective, realism is about truth and not about particular objects. I will come back to this issue when discussing epistemological realism and antirealism. Realism changes character when the meaning of "objective" and "real" relates to particular objects. These can be common-sense objects and, as with scientific realism, the entities postulated, for instance, by physicists. This kind of realism is not truth-theoretical realism but an ontological or metaphysical realism that is opposed to idealism. On the truth-theoretical level the antirealist points to the fact that, for instance, in theories made in physics we do not directly encounter the truth conditions of certain hypotheses. What we have to do with are idealized circumstances for persons similar to us for finding out whether or not these hypotheses are true. According to the antirealist this means that physical theories cannot be considered as descriptions of reality.

Two different conclusions have been drawn from this antirealist criticism. The first is the instrumentalist conclusion that theories do not describe or explain reality but are only used as instruments in scientific investigation. If the application of a certain theory contributes to making predictions, the theory will be accepted as a fruitful theory rather than one which in some way corresponds with reality. Against this one can argue, which leads us to the second conclusion that can be drawn, that if one were to adopt a consequent instrumentalist attitude, one would believe that scientific discoveries occur mostly by accident. Certainly, this happens. However, as the history of the sciences has shown, planned discoveries of planets, chemical substances, and so on, actually occur. This is an argument for some kind of realism, yet not in a strong sense, because strong metaphysical realism claims that there is one and only one true theory implying one all-encompassing world theory. By the way, some of the debates about science and theology presuppose this kind of strong metaphysical realism. Scientific and theological theories are considerd to be alternate all-encompassing world theories.

However, we do not know whether or not there is one and only one true theory. It is rather in the following weak sense that the argument establishes realism: It is the anti-idealistic assumption that there is a thought-independent world to know about. The assumption of a reality that exists independently of us is the logical and practical presupposition of everything we think, do, and say. Such a weak realism still lies on the metaphysical level since it is about what there is and how what is, is, although the questions are always given within a certain conceptual scheme. More precisely, in weak metaphysical realism what one is talking about is having certain ontological commitments rather than about claiming what there is. The focus, however, is on the epistemological questions about how we can identify the better explanations and fruitful theories, and distinguish between confirmed and falsified hypotheses.

I accept this weak metaphysical realism. So henceforth I will emphasize the epistemological aspects of the debates about realism and antirealism. To lay the emphasis on these aspects also gets support from our need to cope with what I have previously called the problem of pluralism.

The Problem of Pluralism

The fact that we have different conceptions of reality in the sciences, in everyday life, and in our views of life is no problem as such. It becomes a problem only when different conceptions of reality appear with the claim that they are infallibly true. In everyday life this happens when some people need a certain conception of reality to sustain or achieve a position of power. This happens also in religion when dogmatic absolutism occurs in the name of God. And in the world of science this happens in scientism. According to this latter view it will be possible in the future to develop a perfect science. Then we will know once and for all with regard to every aspect of life what exists independently of language and theory. Therefore, since we are on the way towards this perfect science, all of our knowledge-claims ought to be subordinated to scientific knowledge-claims.

Traditionally, one tries to cope with the issue of which conception of reality is the right one by playing the roles of adversaries. One defends one's own position and attacks the position of one's adversaries by means of ever more refined arguments. This strategy presupposes that the traditional truth-question is the only question, or at least a very important one, to deal with. According to the traditional conception of truth, everyone who claims to have knowledge has to establish some kind of correspondence between thought and reality. My proposal is, in a kind of postmodern approach, not to regard the traditional truth-question as the most important one. Truth is still crucial. However, I want to make the following two points. First, there are different questions of truth in different contexts — which takes us back to the debate about realism and antirealism again. Second, in one way or another there is a connection between the different questions about truth and the question of what constitutes a good life — which raises questions of value.

III. Some Steps toward a Solution of the Problem of Realism

For reasons that I will mention briefly, I will not base my argument on a discussion of metaphysical realism and antirealism. However, I need to say some things about them. Metaphysical antirealism denies what metaphysical realism asserts. It denies, first, that there is a world consisting of entities that exist independently of our ability of knowing of them. This is also a denial of weak metaphysical realism. It denies that there is a reality that exists independently of us and that is the logical and practical presupposition of everything we think, do, and say. To deny that something can be the case without our knowing it, I think, is absurd. As far as I know, antirealists do not raise such an outspoken claim. Nevertheless, some of them write as if they meant something like that. One of the most outspoken antirealists in the philosophy of religion is Don Cupitt. According to him, "Reality is a battle field, an endless struggle between many rival stories about what's going on.

Truth is the state of the argument, truth is the story on top at present, truth is a precarious and always shifting consensus" (Cupitt 1991, 20). The story on top at the present makes it tempting for us to think "that there are real stories out there apart from us. This, however, is not the case. Stories depend on language, and language is human. We make up all the stories, for our own purposes. We narrate the world, that is we produce the world, made intelligible within our stories about it" (Cupitt 1991, 79). This has the following ontological implications. "Fiction comes first. First the world has got to be fictioned into existence from nothing by some kind of story — religious, cosmological, evolutionary, historical or whatever — and only then can we find a place for talk of truth and falsity, relative to the world as thus produced within the story. . . . We have to get rid of the bogey of a realistic ontology, the notion that there is something out there prior to and independent of our language and our stories, and against which they can be checked" (Cupitt 1991, 81-82). If Cupitt had written that *for us* there is nothing out there prior to and independent of our language and our stories, I think there is an epistomological point in his criticism. Perhaps he just meant that. However, without the phrase "for us" it sounds like an ontological denial.

Second, antirealism denies there is one true theory that describes the world as it is, though this theory might lie beyond our epistemic abilities. Here I support the antirealist position. It can be that there is one true theory. Nevertheless, it may also be that there is not. We do not know. Therefore I think it is more fruitful to just focus — in an ongoing process of knowledge — on what we can know and try to do our best. This means that we can assert neither that something necessarily is the case nor that something impossibly can be the case. Thus, let us leave metaphysical realism and antirealism and turn to epistemological realism and antirealism.

Epistemological Realism and Antirealism

An epistemological realist denies that there is a definitely determining conceptual connection between how we think of reality and how it really is. According to the epistemological realist, reality does not consist only of the reality that we conceive by means of our ideas and through language. Truth is not considered a conceptual product. Instead, truth is considered to be a property of statements that correspond with reality or depict it (see Soskice 1985, 97). There has to be some link between the facts that exist independently of our epistemic abilities on the one hand and the sentences that refer to them and the content of one's thoughts on the other hand.

Against this claim the epistemological antirealists assert another kind of link, a close conceptual link between our talk about how we think of reality and our talk about how it actually is. Accordingly, it is necessary to understand — though not necessarily to define — truth epistemically. Let us see what this means by considering the semantic aspect of antirealism. In other words, let us look at semantic realism and antirealism.

As far as I can see, semantic realism embraces the following three claims. First, for a sentence to have meaning it has to be a statement about some possible state of affairs. Second, the meaning of a statement is given by its truth conditions and not by the conditions for our finding out whether or not the statement is true (see Moser 1989, 33). And finally, a statement is always either true or false irrespective of whether or not we know it. According to the semantic antirealist the controversial point is the claim that meaning is a feature of statements. Only some sentences are actually used as statements such that their meaning consists of their truth conditions, and only some statements are always either true or false.

The semantic antirealist develops a counterargument from an alternative idea about the meaning of sentences: We understand the meaning of a sentence when we know two things. First, we have to know how we use the sentence, and second, we have to know how we can test and argue for its truth, likelihood, reasonableness, and so on. With regard to our concerns this theory of meaning implies that the semantic antirealist divides all sentences into two classes: those which are used as statements and those which are not. Statements are in turn divided into those which are definitely decidable and those which are not definitely decidable (Dummett 1978).

Take the statement "The weight of my desk is ten kilograms." This is an example of a definitely decidable statement. We know, first, what the truth conditions of this statement are and, second, how to determine whether or not they are satisfied. A statement such as "The weight of my desk is ten kilograms," we can say, is always either true or false. The reason for this statement being definitely decidable is the wholly epistemic one that here we know exactly both what the truth conditions of the statement are and how to decide whether they have been fulfilled. In other words, the conditions for a statement being true and the conditions for our finding out whether it is true are identical.

Now, let us take examples of sentences that are not definitely decidable or not decidable at all. Although the statement "In a week it will be rainy" is not definitely decidable, it is not meaningless. We know when and how to use such a sentence and how to estimate its probability in spite of the fact that weather is notoriously unpredictable. In a trivial sense this statement is either true or false — next week. Nevertheless, this does not tell us anything about whether or not its truth conditions are fulfilled at present. We do not have the technical and theoretical means to decide this. However, there are procedures to which we can appeal if we want to choose the most reliable forecast.

Finally, let us take a sentence like "My neighbor's dog is gladly looking forward to midsummer." It would be odd to claim that this sentence is always either true or false. At present we do not know enough about dogs to know how we could settle the truth of such a sentence, that is, there is no evidence that could be used to reasonably assert it or deny it. That the dog is wagging its tail is something that we can observe. But whether or not this has to do with midsummer, we do not know. The sentence does not need to be meaningless because of that. Figuratively we could say that since we are longing for midsummer so intensely, it is a matter of course for us to suppose that every creature is doing so.

I also want to maintain that religious claims fall into the category of sentences that are not decidable at all, that is, that religious sentences are not statements. Furthermore, even here, we would need observational grounds to decide which religious sentences could reasonably be treated as statements that are true or false. However, we do not have procedures to test putative religious knowledge-claims at this level. As knowledge-claims they should be treated as hypotheses, but that is not the way we use religious sentences. Therefore I hesitate to use the word "statement" in relation to religion. Of course, it does not follow that religious sentences are meaningless. Whether they are true or reasonable and in what sense, can be determined by the way in which they are used. I will come back to this partly normative question later. Let us now close our discussion of epistemological realism and antirealism by summarizing its metaphysical implications.

If we accept the antirealist's criticism of semantic realism, the main metaphysical consequence is the following. We cannot assert anything about how reality is without taking account of our epistemic abilities and their constraints. We can have ideas of how reality could be or what it could be like. However, when examining whether these ideas are true, probable, reasonable, and so on, we have to do so within the frame of our epistemic abilities.

This does not prevent one from being a metaphysical realist, provided this is in a weak sense. However, metaphysical realism in a strong sense is excluded. Its central thesis is that by means of one and only one true theory we can tell what the independent reality is really like. Sometimes, researchers in certain areas come to the conclusion that they have developed a new theory that can explain reality. It may be that, given the evidence, it would not be rational to reject the theory. However, if we remember the history of the sciences we will realize that such an apparently persuasive theory probably will be replaced by a more fruitful theory. Metaphysical realism in the weak sense is more cautious. It is just the general view that there is a world even when there are no human beings. This is no theory or theoretical assumption but a logical and practical presupposition for everything we think, say, and do. The combination of this weak metaphysical realism with a certain epistemological antirealism is the background for the proposal of an alternative to either realism or antirealism in the above discussed sense, namely, internal pragmatic realism.

Internal Pragmatic Realism as a Third Way

The concept of "internal realism" is derived from the writings of the later Hilary Putnam. Against rationalism he claims that "internalism does not deny that there are experiential inputs to knowledge; knowledge is not a story with no constraints except internal coherence." Against empiricism he claims that internalism "does deny that there are any inputs *which are not themselves to some extent shaped by our concepts*, by the vocabulary we use to report and describe them, or any inputs *which admit of only one description, independent of all conceptual choices*" (Putnam 1981, 54). By using the concept of "internal realism" I try to take something from both the realist and antirealist positions. I also try to avoid what is not acceptable in the two positions. Antirealism is not acceptable when it denies that the world exists independently of us. The theoretical antirealists get hungry, too, interrupt their philosophical activities, and go for lunch. Our realist intuition gets support from such experiences of everyday life, although, undoubtedly, the antirealist doctrine is entirely consistent with all experience. Nevertheless, I prefer the realist consistency in any case. It strikes me as more adequate. However, when it comes to our truth-claims and knowledge-claims, some forms of antirealism are appropriate. The expressions of our experiences are dependent on language and mind. The realist should also allow this. Furthermore, reality always means reality as conceptualized by us, which implies that we cannot divide our knowledge and our experiences into, so to speak, unstructured matter and its interpretation. Our knowledge and our experiences are always already there in language form. However, in some sense we need a realist's opening. Otherwise our dependence on language would, by virtue of the differences of language in different contexts, lead us into a situation where communication would be impossible between different language groups. In such a situation, critical discussions of the different contexts would be excluded. We have to look for something that enables us in practice to distinguish between truth and falsity, better and worse in a nonarbitrary way. Overemphasizing the aspect of dependence on language makes it impossible to settle how the borderlines may be drawn between the different contexts so that we can still ask for truth and reasonableness. Thus, we have to find an answer to the question of how we can talk about reality as independent of mind and language. The problem is how to achieve this without undermining the thought that our knowledge and our experiences are always expressed in and given to us through language.

The objective of finding an answer to the question of how we can talk about reality as independent of mind and language is shared by the critical realist. However, the critical realist still clings to the idea that we can depict parts of reality by means of theories, and thus presupposes that there is an ontological division between us as subjects of knowledge and reality out there as an object of knowledge. In contrast, by pointing to the fact that reality means always reality conceptualized by us, the internal realist rejects this ontological idea of a gap between a subject and object of knowledge.

The internal realist still accepts the correspondence definition of truth, but only in its minimal form. According to the minimal correspondence definition, the claim that a statement is true means nothing more and nothing less than that things are as they are stated by the statement (Moser 1989, 4). If a correspondence definition of truth-claims more, as is done in both naive and critical realism, it amounts to the claim that we are able in some way to compare statements with unconceptualized reality. The internal realist denies that we have access to unconceptualized reality (see Putnam 1981, 130, 134).

This does not mean, to use Willard Van Orman Quine's formulation, "that we are stuck with the conceptual scheme that we grew up in. We can change it bit by bit, plank by plank, though meanwhile there is nothing to carry us along but the evolving conceptual scheme itself." However, "we cannot detach ourselves from it and compare it objectively with an unconceptualized reality. Hence it is meaningless, I suggest, to inquire into the absolute correctness of a conceptual scheme as a mirror of reality. Our standard for appraising basic changes of a conceptual scheme must be, not a realistic standard of correspondence to reality, but a pragmatic standard" (Quine 1961, 78f.).

Thus, one way of justifying statements about reality is closed to us. We cannot directly compare statements about the world with reality itself. The reality in which we live is reality only insofar as it is understood as reality by us. However, this does not exclude the possibility of justifying, testing, and falsifying statements. For instance, there are religious people who claim that certain diseases are caused by demonic possession. According to some of these people, this implies that the sick person can only be cured through exorcism. Now, this belief can obviously be questioned on scientific grounds and perhaps even falsified by medical evidence. Certainly, there are books on how to perform exorcism just as there are books on medical procedures. However, as far as I know, among the exorcists themselves there are no established methods for settling which explanations are better than those of another exorcist. This meta-level of criticism, that is, of critically comparing different explanations and the proposals for treatment connected with them, we have in the medical context. I do not mean that doctors are always right. Rather, as far as the medical context is concerned, we know the criteria by which we can critically distinguish between better and worse explanations. It seems to me that the possibility of such a critical discussion is an unavoidable presupposition of being able to put the logical distinction between true and false into practice in a nonarbitrary way. I want to emphasize that the critical comparison is not a comparison between two different conceptual schemes. It is a comparison which uses pragmatic standards to compare two different ways of putting the logical distinction between true and false into practice.

Thus, in spite of the internal character of my approach, it is realism in the following sense: there are presuppositions in putting the logical distinction between truth and falsity into practice and therefore of stating something about the reality of which we are a part and in which we live. Internal realism is not strong metaphysical realism, claiming among other things that by pointing to the independently existing reality we can decide which theory and description is the one and only true one. With regard to our example about the causes of disease, the strong metaphysical realism of the exorcists would mean that illness has its causes in a reality which is completely different and not dependent on us for its existence. Internal realism, too, affirms that there is a world independent of us but, having said this, does not claim either that a certain theory is the true and only true description of reality or that every theory is as good as any other.

This immanent perspective has, epistemically speaking, the following consequences as far as our conception of something's existence is concerned. Let me illustrate them by reference to historical scientific discussions about whether there may be another planet in addition to those already identified (see Stenlund 1987, 160ff.). On the one hand, we are always dependent on our conceptual system in, for instance, our descriptions of outer space when talking about the existence of another planet. On the other hand, the existence of such a planet is not causally dependent on a conceptual system required to describe outer space. Nevertheless, when talking about the planet as existent, there is dependence in an intentional sense, that is, in relation to what we observe. Now, our observations are not naked sense-data but theory-laden, in the sense that they are always framed by a given conceptual system. Therefore, the existence of the planet entails the existence of an object as a possible subject of direct or indirect observation according to the current theories about outer space. In summary, we can have the conception of something's existence without giving up the thought that we cannot go beyond our epistemic abilities in statements about reality.

Let us hear what the strong metaphysical realist would say about that. Such a realist claims not only that there is a reality existing independently of us, but also that by investigating this reality itself we can decide which of our statements are true. The existence or nonexistence of another planet can thus be talked about as existing independently of any relation it might bear to us. This means that there is no need to refer to the given planet as intentional object internal to our conceptual systems and theories. Certainly, I do not mean that I cannot conceive of the planet as a real object. However, as far as I can see, for us humans the link between the planet considered as intentional object and considered as real object is an internal one. This is because for us to talk about the planet as a real object presupposes talking about the planet as intentional object. The intentional planet is the logical presupposition of the real planet as far as we, as observers, are concerned.

Now, suppose that with regard to our example there is a certain accepted state of knowledge. In our historical example this situation has been preceded by many different kinds of conflict: scientific, religious, and political. The situation is such that by referring to the use of scientific theories to generate hypotheses that can be tested, one is persuaded by the evidence that there is another planet. In that situation it would be unreasonable to deny that the planet exists. It is not a proof of the existence of this further planet. It is just that the observational evidence persuades us to accept the claim that there is another planet.

We can apply similar reasoning to talk about the existence of God. God considered as an intentional object, however, is not thought of in relation to our positions of observations but in relation to our personal life situations and the existential experiences of the contingencies of life. Love and happiness, on the positive side, and suffering and death, on the negative side, are obviously realities in our lives. Nevertheless, we cannot understand them entirely, nor can we explain them away. This can be seen most clearly when we turn to the question of evil. While we can trace and explain why some sorts of evil occur, there is no purely intellectual solution to the problem of evil. There are kinds of evil that are incomprehensible.

Let us assume that there are experiences of God. According to the epistemological implications of internal realism it would go beyond our epistemic abilities to say that in these experiences we have physical contact with God. Rather, they are experiences of God in the sense that we can relate to stories in which God figures, to our own life-stories. When there is such a relation, we can experience the religious stories about God as adequate expressions of what it means to be a human being, so that, given a certain way of life connected with these stories, it would be unreasonable for one to give up belief in God. God as intentional object, internal to our religious stories and used in relation to our experiences of the contingencies of life, is the logical presupposition of God being experienced as real as far as our life situations are concerned.

The realism of our religious as well as nonreligious views of life, that is, clusters of expressions of what it means to be a human, does not have to do with the question of what is given in a spatio-temporal sense. Rather, the realism lies in the existential experience of our views of life as providing us with real life-options. Such a life-option can be a life in peace, in loving one's neighbor, struggling for equality of opportunity between men and women, or producing and distributing goods according to people's needs and abilities. We do not find such lives fully realized, and probably we never will. Nevertheless, life would be totally different if there were not people who tried to live according to their views of life. It makes a real difference whether or not there are such people. In this sense views of life contribute to and mold our way of life by giving it meaning and a point of orientation.

Views of life, considered as traditions, provide us with real life-options by means of stories. This needs to be done by stories for the following reason. On the subjective side the adequacy of expressions of our views of life requires us to experience those expressions as adequate expressions of what it means to be a human being. On the objective side the adequacy of the expressions of our views of life requires that those expressions are coherent. However, if we wish to preserve the experiential character of the discussion about adequacy, not every kind of coherence is appropriate. An adequate expression of what it is to be a human being is one in which we are able to identify ourselves. This presupposes, first, that we can see our own life as a story with a past, a present, and a future, and, second, that our views of life are stories or parts of stories in which we can recognize our own lives. These stories are of different kinds depending on whether they are about cosmic life, human life in general, or the individual life (see Holmberg 1994, 42ff.). In religion, "God" is a figure in such stories. They are fictitious if by this it is meant that the stories are not constituted by testable knowledge-claims. But they are not fictitious in the sense that they mediate insights into what it means to be a human being. In that sense they are conveying the reality of which we are part and in which we live.

Thus, the question of the existence or nonexistence of God, irrespective of whether or not we can know whether or not God exists, does not even emerge. The question is not whether there exists some divine entity, as if this could be resolved by scientific investigation. The question is rather whether our religious and our nonreligious views of life succeed in providing us with pictures, stories, and conceptions that adequately cope with the contingencies of life (see Brümmer 1993).

This is not just a matter of feeling comfortable about using these expressions. If it was only that, the criticism that religion is an illusion would be justified. It is mainly a matter of taking into account the fact that we experience limitations of many kinds. When we want to say something about these limitations we do this in forms of belief, but because of our epistemic constraints we cannot conceive of these beliefs as knowledge-claims, that is, as the expressed content of statements.

Rather we conceive of these beliefs as insights. Let me give an example. We know the difference between loving and unloving actions and between more or less loving actions. We know what unrequited love means. Sometimes it is difficult to make sense of our experiences and we start to reflect about love. This we do by means of the varieties of imagination, directly by means of our own ideas or indirectly by means of different kinds of story, novel, or drama. In this way we can also come to the idea of pure love. What it is, we do not know. We have come to an end. The idea of pure love is the expression of a limit. Religious believers also talk about God as pure love. This is not a knowledge-claim. Nevertheless, it is a belief about insights into limitations, beliefs that can be defended by pointing to the pictures, stories, and conceptions in which it is embedded, as well as to the way in which this context is related to the experienced contingencies of life.

Another example is the question about the end of life and the afterlife. We do not know what will happen after we die, but we reflect on it and form ideas. Some prefer the idea of resurrection, others the idea of reincarnation, and still others the concept of being dissolved and so entering the cycle of nature. These ideas are not knowledge-claims but beliefs that we can inquire into as to their place within a view of life providing us with pictures, stories, and conceptions that can be experienced as adequate expressions of what it means to be a human being. It is their connection with the pictures, stories, and conceptions of a view of life that makes these beliefs about our human predicament into beliefs that can be experienced as existentially meaningful. If furthermore they are taken as knowledge-claims, they have to be treated as hypotheses with all that this involves. But in this case we are looking for observational evidence and not for experienced adequacy of expressions of what it is to be a human being.

I suppose that many religious people would not agree. They would point out that religious life is about more than experiences and a good life. Furthermore, they would claim that we actually know many things about God, for instance, that God is omnipotent and omniscient. According to my internal realism we do not know this. However, as already argued, religious stories are not meaningless because of that. Furthermore, they can still be considered true, but in the sense of being adequate expressions of what it means to be a human being rather than in the sense of containing statements about states of affairs.

As we can see, there is a strong emphasis on the internal epistemic aspect of our conceptual presuppositions in internal pragmatic realism.

Although we can change them, we can never be without any at all. Nor can we make statements about states of affairs that lie beyond our epistemic abilities. We cannot know what these states of affairs would be like. Of course, the traditional realist is also conscious of our epistemic constraints. We need to balance the emphasis on language and our epistemic abilities by finding an opening to realism. Otherwise, this emphasis would lead us to a definition of truth in epistemic terms. Both the traditional and the internal realist are against such a definition but for different reasons. Most of the traditional realists, whether naive or critical, believe words refer to an independent reality. The internal realist believes we humans refer to reality as a reality conceptualized and understood by us.

According to the definition of truth in epistemic terms, truth is defined as justified assertability or warrantability, as verification or as experienced meaning. To see what is wrong with this definition of truth, let us repeat its relativist implications. I have already mentioned them at the beginning of my paper. In practice, when we want to make statements, we choose those statements for which we have most evidence. If there is equally strong evidence for contradictory statements, a definition of truth in epistemic terms not only would allow us to consider contradictory statements as separately true statements, but it would even oblige us to go further and claim that both a statement and its denial are actually true. The difference between the two steps is that it is one thing to tolerate a contradiction because in a certain situation we cannot settle definitely which side of the contradiction is the true one, and quite another thing to accept both sides of the contradiction as true. Since a contradiction entails any statement, the latter position would imply that we could deduce whatever statement we want from the contradiction and therefore also make false statements. However, that would mean that we could no longer distinguish between truth and falsity. In turn this would mean that one of the main grounds upon which we make conscious and rational decisions would be undermined.

To avoid this consequence, it is necessary to sustain the logical distinction between the epistemic and the ontological truth-aspect. Whereas in referring to the former we ask how to decide what is true, in referring to the latter we ask what actually is true. If we still want to stress the importance of our epistemic constraints, the way of strong metaphysical realism is closed so far as the ontological aspect is concerned. We do not have access to reality itself. Let us try the way of pragmatism.

A Pragmatic Version of Internal Realism

As far as pragmatism is concerned I want to avoid the following two things. First, I want to avoid defining truth in terms of the successful solution of problems. That we succeed in solving a certain problem is no guarantee of the truth of the statements involved in the proposals for a solution. The solution could have happened by accident or even be based on beliefs that are false. It would nevertheless be unwise if we did not take into consideration the solutions that experience has shown us to be successful.

Second, I want to avoid defining truth in terms of being experienced as meaningful or important. This would exclude the idea of objectivity because there are so many differences in our experiences of meaningfulness and importance. But obviously, a pragmatic approach can be combined with the idea of objectivity, though not in the form of the traditional claim of absolute objectivity. According to this traditional claim, objectivity has to be defined in terms of what is true, that is, what is the case irrespective of whether or not we know it. This would mean, however, that the difference between truth and rationality is disregarded, as well as the fact that problems are always problems at a certain place, at a certain time, and within a certain context of meaning. How to decide what is true is one issue. What is rational for us to believe and to do under the given conditions is another one.

Certainly, when defining "being true" as "being the case," our reasons for claiming that something is true can also be our reasons for considering it as rational for us to believe that it is true. This is the case for statements that are definitely decidable in relation to the observable evidence available. In all the other cases, however, the reasons for claiming that something is true are only a section of the reasons for considering it to be rational for us to believe that it is true. We need more and other kinds of reasons. For instance, it would not be rational to accept only statements that are definitely decidable and not statements that are probable. Furthermore, there are value questions where we have to decide how to apply our knowledge. More precisely, the question is when it is rational to apply which knowledge-claims in relation to which problems, bearing in mind that a problem is always a problem at a certain place, at a certain time, and within a certain context of meaning.

That we cannot identify the reasons for claiming that something is true with our reasons for considering it to be rational for us to believe that it is true, becomes particularly clear in situations in which there is a clash between different truth-claims and the clash is itself part of the problem. Just to point to the reasons for claiming that something is true as the only reasons for considering it rational to believe it being true, would only be to repeat the problem.

By distinguishing between truth and rationality we can avoid defining truth in terms of successful solutions of problems without disregarding solutions that experience has shown to be successful. In this way we need not claim to go beyond our epistemic abilities. Also, we need not accept the extreme antirealist's claim that everything is nothing but language, stories, texts. In the successful solutions of problems, comparing different contexts with each other, we can find the pragmatic realist opening needed to avoid relativism. It makes it possible for us to distinguish between true and false assertions according to the evidence we have. This does not exclude our defining truth in a non-epistemic way as that which is the case irrespective of whether or not we know it. However, it does exclude our talking of truth as true statements in a non-epistemic way.

IV. Implications for the Theory of Views of Life

In our lives we meet different kinds of problems. Some of them are practical, for instance, how to repair shoes or how to avoid destructive conflicts. Others are theoretical, for instance, mathematical problems. Others are caused by the fact that there are different theoretical presuppositions for explaining and understanding the reality in which we live and of which we are part. These theoretical presuppositions can be in the form of conceptual frameworks, theories, or limited hypotheses that are subject to direct testing. All these problems have to do with the question of knowledge, mostly implicit in everyday life and of a more systematized form in the sciences.

However, there are also other problems that we humans have to cope with in our lives. These problems have their causes in the contingencies of life. There are things in our lives that are obviously real but that we can never understand entirely or explain away. On the positive side there is love and happiness, on the negative side suffering and death. A solution to this type of problem does not mean the disappearance of the problems but rather one's finding a proper relation to them, that is, to learn to live with them.

The Division of Labor for the Sciences and the Views of Life

To be able to survive and to live a good life, both as individuals and as a species, we humans have to cope with the different problems we encounter. For that we need both to know the nature of the world and to accept values without which we would not know what to aim for and how to apply our knowledge. Our sciences provide us in systematized form with knowledge about the nature of the world in which we live. Our institutionalized views of life provide us with conceptions of what it means to be a human being and, as I will argue shortly, with values. The values function as guidance when we reflect upon how to apply our knowledge about reality.

Let me briefly comment on some of these points. I do not deny that this proposal of a division of labor between sciences and views of life is a normative one, that is, that it recommends a way of understanding religion. I know that many religious people are realists, especially in the metaphysical sense. But I nevertheless want to recommend this alternative view instead of the traditional realist one because of a combination of philosophical, moral, and religious arguments. Traditional realism raises a great many serious philosophical problems. I will not repeat them here. Morally speaking, not being realists who are religious, we become much more sensitive to the fact that it is we humans who are responsible for which religious notions and symbols we accept and how we use them. Religiously speaking, not being realists who are religious prevents us from trying to occupy a god-like perspective.

I have sketched the idea that there is a division of labor between sciences and views of life rather schematically. Certainly, I do not deny that we can learn many things outside the sciences. We can gain insights from crises and in everyday life we can rely on recurrent experience. However, when different knowledge-claims arise, I cannot see why we should not go to the sciences to decide which of our knowledge-claims are justifiable. There are many beliefs that work in practice and that are not grounded in theories and hypotheses. However, when we are searching for explanations, I cannot see how we could do without the sciences.

Criteria of an Acceptable View of Life

In principle, I do not make any distinction between religious and nonreligious views of life. They have the same function with regard to the problems raised by the contingencies of life. Let us see what the necessary criteria are, if we want to examine the role of a given view of life in contributing to a good life for us human beings. Of course, there are different ideas of what a good life is, and clearly a good life does not consist in only moral values. For the sake of brevity, let us stay on a concrete level. Primarily, a good life involves a certain amount of happiness and not too much suffering, that is, that life is at least subjectively experienced as being a good life. The balance between happiness and suffering will be achieved only, first, if we can consider our own lives as coherent stories, second, if we can consider ourselves as part of our surroundings and of the universe, and third, if we have good relations with other human beings.

Regarding the two first conditions we get the means to consider our own lives as coherent stories and ourselves as part of the universe from the expressions of our views of life. As to the second condition, it is here that we find most of the relations and overlappings between views of life, when considered as theoretical systems, and the natural, social, as well as human sciences. Scientific results can become included, for instance, in religion in different versions of the so-called teleological argument for the existence of God; or they can become related to religious beliefs by declaring the compatibility, for instance, of the theory of evolution with Christianity, or by pointing out the need of explaining the sciences from an all-encompassing perspective. I will come back to this issue at the end of my paper. The third condition is of a different kind and I will return to it shortly.

When criteria for an acceptable view of life are used in relation to other people's view of life, the criteria are, of course, external ones. But they can also be applied in reflections on one's own view of life when it starts to fail in coping with the realities of life. In this case one could say that the criteria are internal. They are external criteria again, when one compares different views of life with each other. It is this latter comparison that we cannot avoid making in our present increasingly pluralistic situation.

Our views of life may overlap with regard to some of their pictures, stories, and conceptions. Nevertheless, it is one or another of these expressions that is constitutive of one's own view of life, which means that we cannot adhere to two views of life simultaneously. However, it does not follow that from a general point of view only one view of life can be the right one, in the sense that an argument for one specific view of life is automatically an argument against every other, or that an argument against another view of life is thereby an argument for one's own. What we can do is to critically discuss our views of life with regard to their function in providing us with adequate expressions that are coherent and in which we can identify our own experiences of what it means to live with the contingencies of life. What actually is experienced as adequate by individuals differs depending on the differences in the conditions that govern our lives.

A view of life is acceptable only (1) if we can find in it such expressions of the contingencies of life in which we can (a) identify ourselves and (b) recognize the conditions governing our life; (2) if we can find in it ideas of what human life would be at its best; (3) if, by means of its pictures, stories, and conceptions, we can conceptualize the experienced tension between ideal human life and the shortcomings of actual life caused by our own faults or by events that are beyond our control; (4) if, by means of its pictures, stories, and conceptions, in the experienced tension between an ideal human life and our actual flawed lives we can develop a feeling for good and evil, right and wrong; (5) if, by means of its pictures, stories, and conceptions of real life-options, we can conceptualize our feeling for good and evil, right and wrong and thus create values; and (6) if, by means of these values, we can examine and criticize how we apply our knowledge and how we actually mold our views of life.

There is a risk that the application of these six criteria allows for too much. As they stand, they could also be applied by someone who is quite happy in oppressing other people or ascribing to them a lower value than other human beings. This is definitely not a good life for the oppressed. But neither is it a good life for the oppressor. Some of the personal potentials of the oppressor will never be realized because no close or profound human relation can be developed unless both parties are open and allow themselves to be vulnerable in a way the oppressor hardly can be. Thus, we need a restriction of the application of the six criteria for an acceptable view of life so that it does not extend to such cases of oppression. An acceptable view of life cannot imply that certain sections of humanity should not partake of the good life. In our days a most decisive aspect is the issue of equality of opportunity between women and men. Let us therefore add a seventh necessary criterion, (7) that the application of the other six criteria include taking all types of human beings into consideration.

The acceptance and application of these criteria make it possible to see religion as a human phenomenon and to scrutinize it as such.

These criteria presuppose the internal pragmatical realism sketched above. However, such a position does not exclude the possibility of talking meaningfully about God with the presupposition that one accepts what could be called "religious nonrealism." I am not fond of this kind of labeling since it is done from the perspective of strong metaphysical realism. The label is chosen in lack of a better one. Against strong metaphysical realism with its implication of considering the idea of reality itself as deciding the one and only one true description of it to be a meaningful idea, I want to focus on the epistemological aspect and its implications for choosing the proper attitude to religion. As a religious nonrealist one neither asserts nor denies that there is a divine reality independent of us. This does not exclude the use of religious pictures, stories, and conceptions. However, one does not transform them into knowledge-claims.

Different Definitions of Truth for the Sciences and the Views of Life

The proposed division of labor between our sciences and our views of life presupposes two things. First, it presupposes different definitions of truth, and, second, it presupposes that one can distinguish between definitions of truth and criteria for truth. I have the impression that we do not always uphold this distinction when we compare different so-called theories of truth with each other. It is one thing to say in an Aristotelian spirit that our claims are true when things are as we assert them to be. Some theories of truth, for instance, a certain kind of correspondence theory, the minimal correspondence theory of truth, take this position. This is a theory about the definition of truth (see Mackie 1973, 48ff.). As a definition it does not tell us how to decide which of our truth-claims actually are true. If it, as a definition of truth, claims more, we get the confusion of the definition of truth and the criteria for discerning truth. To settle the question which of our truth-claims actually are true, we need criteria. Other theories of truth, such as coherence theories, are about criteria.

It has been questioned whether it is reasonable to apply such a distinction as that between definition of truth and criterion of truth when we are overcome by certain experiences. These occur in situations where we get sudden illumination, an insight of truth, a deep impression or conviction of the truth of something. Surely, in such situations we do not apply criteria to settle the question of whether the claim of which we are convinced is actually true. Nevertheless, even here we can err. So long as there is no dispute as far as truth is concerned, there is no problem. However, when our different truth-claims collide with each other, we need criteria to decide which of them are justified. What we find self-evident or of which we have sudden insight might be denied by others referring to other experiences which have overcome them.

As I said previously, our sciences provide us with knowledge about reality. Here we look for truth by means of testing hypotheses. To be able to achieve knowledge, our hypotheses must satisfy at least the following two criteria. First, our hypotheses must be free from internal contradiction. Otherwise, we could deduce any statement from them. Second, there has to be correspondence, though not between sentences and reality. Instead it has to be between statements about such observations that we expect from the proposed hypotheses and statements about observations that actually occur.

Whereas our sciences provide us with knowledge about reality, our views of life have another function. They provide us with values that we need for having an idea of how to apply our knowledge of the reality in which we live. Here "being true" is defined as "being true to life," that is, as "being adequate to what it means to be a human being." We neither can understand entirely nor explain away the lived realities of love and happiness and of suffering and death. Nevertheless, we need expressions for them that we can experience, that is, feel as adequate. Otherwise we do not find the kind of relationship towards the contingencies of life that contributes to a good life for us.

As I have said, the criteria by which we settle the question of the adequacy of expressions of what it means to be a human being is, first, coherence. However, not every kind of coherence is appropriate for preserving the experiential focus of the discussion about adequacy. If we want to use the expressions of our views of life as adequate expressions of what it means to be a human being, they have to be stories or part of stories in which we can recognize our own life stories. In other words, when we experience expressions as adequate expressions of what it means to be a human being, we have the feeling of the expressions being true to the lives we actually live. This experience occurs only within given circumstances of time, place, gender, sex, occupation, age, social group, personal relations, and so on. We experience an expression of what it means to be a human being as adequate if we can say: "So it is!" In one sense this, of course, is wholly subjective. However, that does not mean that in our reflections on adequacy our conclusions are necessarily arbitrary. In our different traditions and contexts we have methods for determining which expressions are meaningful given the people who use them and the situations they find themselves in. From this perspective what is called theology in the sense of beliefs about God is no exception. The knowledge about what is considered to be meaningful in which context is also the basis for our understanding other people. Such an understanding, which is both intellectual and emotional, is important since it contributes to our good life in the following way. Because understanding allows us to explain and therefore appreciate differences in behavior and action, these differences are no longer threatening. People who are not frightened live a better life and do not feel the need to defend themselves by oppressing others.

The question of which expressions are meaningful to use for which persons in which situations again brings into focus the issue of conceptual dependence. Neither in the sciences nor views of life can we go beyond our epistemic abilities. With regard to the sciences, we have to formulate theories and hypotheses by means of the concepts available. Concerning our views of life, too, we have to formulate expressions of what it means to be a human being by means of the concepts available. In this respect there is no difference between sciences and views of life. As far as our views of life are concerned, however, there is a specific dependence as regards language insofar as the experience of meaning is crucial. We use theories and hypotheses to gain knowledge about reality. Whether we experience these conceptual tools or the results of our scientific activities as meaningful for our lives is another question. It is an important question too, but it is independent of the very process of building theories and testing hypotheses. We become interested in this question when we want to know how to apply the knowledge we have gained and in which direction our investigations should develop. As humans we cannot avoid considering this question. For this reflective activity we need values. We create them by experiencing the tension between life as it could be at its best and how flawed it presently is. Thus we can develop a feeling for right and wrong, good and evil. To make sense of this feeling, we need concepts. We find the ground for such a process of conceptualization in the pictures, stories, and conceptions of our views of life. The result of this process of conceptualization are values. They do exist but as the creation of us humans.

As I have said, our views of life consist in pictures, stories, and conceptions with which we can understand ourselves in relation to the contingencies of life. Thus, the question of the existential experience of meaning is crucial. However, this does not mean that we cannot distinguish truth, in the true-to-life sense, from experienced meaning any longer. In other words, there is still a difference between meaning and truth even as far as views of life are concerned. If we would not make this distinction, nothing more could be done but to realize that there are different meanings experienced by different individuals. Critical evaluations of the expressions of our experienced meanings would no longer be possible. For practical reasons, however, I think that it is necessary that the conceptualizations of what we experience as meaningful, and that means even our views of life, become subject to critical scrutiny. Not all views of life do form the basis for a good life.

The Question of Non-epistemic Truth in Views of Life

Certainly, in the sciences we settle the question of whether such and such is the case, given certain theories. However, it is not the meaning of the theories that determine whether something actually is the case. This fact has to be considered when the replacement of theories is discussed. From this perspective the question of the replacement of scientific theories by theological ones like creationism is no exception. That is, the meaning of such a theological theory does not determine what actually is the case.

In general, we cannot go beyond the constraints offered by our conceptual frameworks. We can change them when they do not fit our knowledge and experiences any longer, but we are never without any conceptual framework at all. Therefore it would not be rational to give up an established theory while there is no serious alternative. The logical possibility that things may not be as stated in the theory is not enough. As I argued previously, there has to be a relation to our position as observers. Let us assume that there exists a serious alternative to an established theory. Then it would not be rational to define away or reject either one of these alternatives. Because of our epistemic constraints, in some situations, we have to allow room for both of them, or to use the more common but ambiguous phrase, we have to allow "different truths."

The question is whether we can make the distinction between meaning and truth when it comes to our views of life. I think so. In our views of life we try to resolve the question of how to find adequate expressions of the contingencies of life. We can only do this by conceptual means. Of course, there is the possibility of nonverbal expressions too. Nevertheless, when we have to explain what they express, we have to do this by conceptual means again. In spite of this dependence on conceptual means, these means alone do not decide whether an expression is an adequate one or not. This is only the case when we actually experience the expressions as adequate. Although the experience of adequacy is subjective, we cannot choose whatever expression we like, if we want to say what it means to be a human being. We cannot go beyond the constraints given by our conceptual means, and they are always a social affair. Therefore it would not be rational to give up an established conception of a real life-option as long as there is no serious alternative to it. Let us assume that there is a serious alternative to an established conception of a real life-option. Then it would not be rational to define away or reject either one or the other as acceptable. In some situations we have to allow that both of them are acceptable.

V. A Final Remark

What about God? Does God exist? I want to point out again the internal relation between an intentional object and its real object. When dealing with knowledge about reality, existence is paradigmatically considered in spatio-temporal terms, that is, in relation to possible positions of direct or indirect observation. But God does not have a spatio-temporal location. When it comes to our views of life, the internal relation between an intentional object and its real object is of another kind. We know that what we call God, for instance, figures in religious stories. In one sense, these stories are fictitious if by that is meant not being a testable knowledge-claim. But stories are not fictitious in the sense of being illusionary because they mediate insights into what it means to be a human being. In this sense they are about the reality of which we are part and in which we live. When they adequately express what it means to be a human being, that is, to live with the contingencies of life, we cannot help believing these stories.

The question of whether religious faith is an illusion becomes irrelevant in its traditional metaphysical form. It is not the question of the existence of a divine entity as if it were a scientific issue of knowledge. The question is rather whether religious faith succeeds in providing us with pictures, stories, and conceptions that adequately express the contingencies of life. To what degree our religious or our nonreligious views of life do this must always be the focus for discussion and examination.

Obviously, my view of the different functions of the sciences and the views of life in our lives in a certain sense has negative implications for the traditional science-theology debate. Let us define theology as the intellectual activity of systematizing and clarifying religious beliefs. If theology is said to be on the same logical level as the sciences, then the same kind of criteria ought to be applied when critically discussing the knowledge-claims and truth-claims in science as well as in theology. Previously in this paper, I have argued for the view that we ought not to consider it to be meaningful to talk about knowledge in relation to religion. My impression is that in the debate between science and theology as a debate between scientific theories and hypotheses and theological theories and hypotheses, theologians are scarcely prepared to accept the scientific rules of the game, that is, to actually accept a confirmed scientific hypothesis as a falsification of one's theological hypothesis. Irrespective of the theoretical flaws of logical empiricism, I cannot help thinking that Antony Flew's critical question from the falsification debate in the fifties in relation to religion is still valid. "Just what would have to happen not merely (morally and wrongly) to tempt but also (logically and rightly) to entitle us to say . . . 'God does not exist'?" (Flew 1955, 99) What would have to happen for theologians who treat their beliefs as theories and hypotheses on the same logical level as scientific ones to actually give up their theological theories and hypotheses? Certainly, the theologian could claim that the scientist ought to accept the theologians' rules of the game in order to do scientific work. However, I do not think that this would be prosperous for the sciences.

Let us leave this track and consider theology to be the systematization and clarification of expressions of what it means to be a human being. As I argued previously in this paper, we need both knowledge and insights of what is valuable in life to know how to apply our knowledge and which aims to pursue. We have to conceptualize our knowledge-claims as well as our feeling for good and evil, right and wrong in order to solve the problems we meet in life. The conceptualization of the latter we carry out by means of the pictures, stories, and conceptions of our views of life. So, we need both testable knowledge-claims, that we achieve in the sciences, and expressions that we can experience as adequate expressions of the contingencies of life. The question is whether we in addition to such expressions also need theology. From my perspective the answer is that we have use for theology only if it contributes to giving us expressions that we can experience as adequate expressions of what it means to be a human being. This includes, as previously mentioned, expressions of life as cosmic life, of the life of humankind, and of the individual life. If theology as the systematization and clarification of expressions of these aspects wants to prepare for the experience of specific expressions as adequate ones, certainly, it would not be wise to neglect what has been achieved in science. From this perspective, theological criticism of science cannot be scientific criticism. However, it can be a criticism of whether certain achievements of science are good means to solve our different problems in life or relevant for coping with the contingencies of life.

From the perspective I have presented, science and views of life are both needed and of equal value. Let me bring to your attention once more that by views of life I do not mean grand scale worldviews. Rather, views of life have the function of providing us with expressions that we can experience as adequate expressions of what it means to be a human being. At this point someone may ask whether theology as one of the many alternative views of life is needed for an all-encompassing explanation, including the explanation of the sciences. My pragmatic answer is the following. If a theological all-encompassing explanation functions as a story about cosmic life that we can experience as an adequate expression of what it means to be a human being, that is, if it fulfills the earlier mentioned criteria for an acceptable view of life, then, if one believes in this story, it is rational to do so. However, it cannot be claimed that the story as such is necessary for coping with the contingencies of life. In summary, science is one thing; theology, if needed only to address the existential question of what it means to be a human being, is another thing. Nevertheless, as humans we need both to justify our knowledge-claims and to find adequate expressions of the contingencies of life.

References

Brümmer, Vincent. 1993. "Wittgenstein and the Irrationality of Rational Theology." In *The Christian Understanding of God Today*, ed. James M. Byrne. Dublin: The Columba Press.

Cupitt, Don. 1991. *What Is a Story?* London: SCM.

Dancy, Jonathan. 1985. *An Introduction to Contemporary Epistemology.* Oxford: Basil Blackwell.

Dummett, Michael. 1978. *Truth and Other Enigmas*. London: Duckworth.

Flew, Antony. 1955. "Theology and Falsification." In *New Essays in Philosophical Theology*, ed. Antony Flew and Alasdair MacIntyre. London: SCM.

Grube, Dirk-Martin. 1995. "Religious Experience after the Demise of Foundationalism." *Religious Studies* 31:37-52.

Holmberg, Martin. 1994. *Narrative, Transcendence and Meaning: An Essay on the Question about the Meaning of Life*. Stockholm: Almqvist & Wiksell.

Mackie, John Leslie. 1973. *Truth, Probability, and Paradox*. Oxford: Clarendon.

McFague, Sallie. 1983. *Metaphorical Theology: Models of God in Religious Language*. London: SCM.

Moser, Paul K. 1989. *Knowledge and Evidence*. Cambridge: Cambridge University Press.

Putnam, Hilary. 1981. *Reason, Truth, and History*. Cambridge: Cambridge University Press.

_____. 1983. *Realism and Reason: Philosophical Papers*, Volume 3. Cambridge: Cambridge University Press.

_____. 1990. *Realism with a Human Face*. Cambridge, Mass.: Harvard University Press.

Quine, Willard Van Orman. 1961. *From a Logical Point of View: Logico-Philosophical Papers*. New York: Harper and Row.

Runzo, Joseph, ed. 1993. *Is God Real?* London: Macmillan.

Soskice, Janet Martin. 1985. *Metaphor and Religious Language*. Oxford: Oxford University Press.

Stenlund, Sören. 1987. "Tankar om realism." In *Mystik och verklighet. En festskrift till Hans Hof*, ed. Olof Franck, Eberhard Herrmann, Martin Holmberg, Björn Sahlin, and Peder Thalén. Delsbo: Bokförlaget Åsak.

Stenmark, Mikael. 1995. *Rationality in Science, Religion, and Everyday Life: A Critical Evaluation of Four Models of Rationality*. Notre Dame: University of Notre Dame Press.

van Fraassen, Bas C. 1980. *The Scientific Image*. Oxford: Clarendon.

Westphal, Merold. 1987. *God, Guilt, and Death: An Existential Phenomenology of Religion*. Bloomington: Indiana University Press.

Wright, Georg Henrik von. 1986. *Vetenskapen och förnuftet. Ett försök till orientering*. Stockholm: Bonniers.

Science and Theology as Complementary Perspectives

Fraser Watts

IN THIS CHAPTER I will argue for seeing science and theology as complementary perspectives. Breaking the argument down into a number of more specific points, I argue that:

(1) science and theology are distinct discourses, different in their character, and should therefore not be run together indiscriminately;

(2) science and theology are linked in that both bear on aspects of reality, though they approach it from different perspectives;

(3) the philosophy of mind and brain provides a helpful analogue for how things can be described from different perspectives in a way that is complementary;

(4) in a similar way, science and theology can be seen as complementary, rather than offering approaches that are necessarily in competition;

(5) theological accounts should not be seen as deriving any support from the failure of scientific accounts;

(6) even though there is no need in principle to choose between a scientific and a theological approach to any particular question, a *particular* scientific account may nevertheless sit so uneasily with a *particular* theological account that the two can be judged incompatible.

(1) The Different Character of Theological and Scientific Discourses

In this first section, I will claim that science and theology are very different kinds of discourses, so different that there are serious objections to running them together indiscriminately.

There is a tendency for views about the similarity or distinctness of theological and scientific discourses to become polarized. At one extreme is the view that the functions of the two discourses are *so* different that they have *no* points of contact. This leads to the conclusion that science and theology are completely independent of one another, and that there cannot be a fruitful dialogue between them. At the other end of the spectrum is the tendency to minimize the difference in character between theology and science so as to establish the basis for fruitful dialogue on common ground.

In common with most other people concerned with the relationship between theology and science, I reject the view that theology and science are so radically different that there can be no proper contact between them at all. Nevertheless, I believe that the two discourses *are* radically different, and that this is frequently underestimated by those who want to see a fruitful dialogue established. Though I also want to see such a dialogue, I do not think it helps to exaggerate the similarity of theology and science. Of course, this is a difference only of degree or emphasis. Hardly anyone imagines that theology and science are exactly similar. My point is that the similarities tend to be exaggerated and the differences minimized.

The view that there is a radical difference between the discourses of science and theology is sometimes labeled a "two languages" view. Ian Barbour (1990, 13-16) presents a clear statement and critique of this position. On the "two languages" view, scientific language is about "prediction and control." It asks "carefully delineated questions about natural phenomena" but it cannot necessarily be expected to provide a general worldview. In contrast, according to linguistic philosophers who hold a two languages view, the function of religious language is to "recommend a way of life, to elicit a set of attitudes, and to encourage allegiance to particular moral principles."

Now, this analysis of science and theology presents an extreme and unconvincing view of both languages, as Barbour well knows. He goes on to present a much more nuanced view of the similarities and differences between theology and science. He recognizes that religious language serves a wide range of functions, some of which have no parallel in science. However, he acknowledges that religious language does make cognitive claims that are in some ways similar to those of science, even though "religion cannot claim to be scientific or to be able to conform to the standards of science" (Barbour 1990, 89).

This seems to me an admirably well-balanced view of things, and I have made similar points myself, albeit more briefly, in an earlier publication (Watts and Williams 1988, ch. 4). Religious language is both *more* and *less* than scientific language. It doesn't have the same role in dispassionate exploration and description of the natural world as does scientific language. On the other hand, it is broader in its scope and reference than scientific language, being personal and moral as well as making claims about the nature of reality.

My only source of unease with Barbour here is a semantic one. Like many others, he uses the term "two languages" to refer to the position that the languages of theology and science are completely different, with no points of contact. It seems to me that the term "two languages" really ought to be used in a broader sense for any position that acknowledges important differences between the two languages. In this broader sense, my own position might be seen as a "two languages" one, albeit not in the narrower sense in which Barbour and many others use the term.

The exaggeration of the similarities between science and theology is not new and has an interesting history. Since the dawn of the modern period, the "scientific revolution" in the seventeenth century, there has been a recurrent tendency to recast theology in the image of science. The "modern" (i.e., post–seventeenth century) enterprise of "natural theology" reflects this exaggeration of the similarity of theology and science.

The seventeenth century saw the development of what has been variously called a "spectorial" (Lash 1988) or "onlooker" (Davy 1978) consciousness. Observation, of as detached a kind as possible, became the paradigm of how understanding was reached. On this view, as Lash argues, there may be two domains of knowledge (i.e., two kinds of things to be known), but only one way of knowing is allowed, the observational way. Religious knowing is thus cast in the observational form that science dictates, giving rise to natural theology in its modern form. This is a radical shift from the earlier theological tradition which saw theology as approaching reality within its own frame of reference, more than being concerned with a separate "religious" domain of reality.

The trouble with this recasting of theology as a form of observational knowledge is that it does violence to the premodern tradition of reflection on the nature of God and distorts the distinctive kind of prayerful attentiveness which is a hallmark of religious reflection. Above all, it is wholly unsuited to discourse about the being that we call "God." Lash quotes here, to good effect, Hegel's evocative remark that "God does not offer himself for observation."

Those such as Murphy (1990) who argue that theology can be considered as a "research programme" comparable to those pursued within the natural sciences seem to be showing scant regard for the ground rules of a discourse that is embarked on the paradoxical business of what Burrell has called "knowing the unknowable God" (Burrell 1986). It is difficult to identify any data in theology that functions in the same way as data in science, and theology does not normally attempt to resolve disagreements by collecting new empirical data. Theological enquiry, though not completely nonempirical, has a more radically indirect relationship to data than does science. If theology is to preserve its distinctive character, it is right that this should be so.

In some ways it is puzzling that people should want to argue that theological and scientific discourses are essentially similar. If you are looking for an epistemological analogue of religious knowing, scientific investigation seems to be one of the least promising. The attempt to argue the similarity of theology and science is presumably a hangover from the time when science was the only criterion of rationality. In contrast, I would argue that there is a broad family of rationalities, many different ways of coming to knowledge and understanding, and that the rationality of religion is not especially close to that of science (see Watts and Williams 1988, ch. 5).

One of the best analogues of how people come to religious belief is perhaps how they come to conclusions about themselves or other people. The path to self-knowledge is an interesting one epistemologically. People have enormous opportunities to observe themselves, their thought processes, and their behavior. However, there are marked individual differences in the extent to which these opportunities are taken. Some people come to have a very shrewd understanding of themselves, while others are strikingly lacking in self-insight.

Self-knowledge involves a different use of evidence from that found in science, though the difference is not an absolute one. Patient attentiveness to the relevant facts has a place in both but is probably more central to science than to self-knowledge. However, self-knowledge, more than science, requires moments of insight in which people reach beyond the obvious conclusions. Self-knowledge is markedly affect-laden, and is entertained with less calm detachment than a scientific hypothesis. Also, self-knowledge usually entails a process of personal transformation. As we come to understand ourselves better, we feel compelled to make fresh commitments and to behave differently.

However, this contrast between the different modes of cognition found in science and religion doesn't mean that there can be no fruitful relationship between them. On the contrary, as O'Hear (1993) has argued, there can be a mutually sustaining harmony between religion and science. Establishing such a harmony, however, will involve overcoming the dualism between essentially personal and relatively impersonal modes of knowing that is one of the most deep-seated of all dualisms. It is perhaps one of the important tasks of those working on the dialogue between theology and science to overcome this dualism, but this cannot be done by pretending that theology is more like science than it really is.

As Barfield remarked about science and the humanities (though the point applies equally well to theology), "Perhaps each needs the clasp and support of the other in his half-blinded staggering towards the light. Perhaps there is not one prison cell but two: the non-objectifying subjectivity in which the humanities are immured, and the adjoining cell of subjectless objectivity, where science is locked and bolted; and maybe the first escape for the two prisoners . . . is to establish communication with one another" (1977, 140).

(2) Reference and Reality

Though issues about realism are considered elsewhere in this volume, it is essential for me to say something about them here, because the referential character of theological and scientific discourse is a crucial link in my argument. I will argue that both theology and science are referential, that they both refer in their different ways to aspects of the same real world, and that because of this they cannot be regarded as unconnected discourses.

Sometimes when philosophers talk about the "two discourses" or "two languages" of science and religion, they assume that *neither* of them are referential. This is often true in Wittgensteinian philosophy. For example, D. Z. Phillips (1976), seems to assume that theology is a "language game" to be evaluated wholly in terms of *internal* criteria. Reference to a "real" world is not assumed. (Whether this was a view that Wittgenstein held as firmly as some of his followers is a question of exegesis into which I will not enter here.)

It is thus possible (though it is not my own view) to see both theology and science as entirely non-referential discourses, each to be evaluated solely by internal criteria, and not evaluated at all by the extent to which what they say corresponds to the state of the real world. If this is so, the argument of the previous section (that they are distinct discourses of different character) will lead to the conclusion that they are *independent* discourses.

In contrast, I assume that they are both referential discourses. This assumption that both theology and science are referential discourses, and that the domains of reality to which they refer co-inhere, is crucial to avoiding the conclusion that theology and science are independent, unconnected discourses. I should clarify here that I am not assuming that the worlds to which theology and science refer are identical. I assume that theology is a high-level discourse, and that no aspect of reality is excluded from its purview. The sciences can be seen as being concerned in more detail with aspects of the wider reality that is the subject matter of theology.

In assuming that the discourses of theology and science are both referential, I am also not assuming an uncritical realism. I would agree with those such as Peacocke (1984) and Niekerk (this volume) who wish to maintain some kind of realist assumptions about the world, but who recognize that this cannot be done uncritically. What is sometimes left unclear, however, is exactly how "critical" realism differs from naive realism about the world.

In clarifying this, I suggest that it is helpful to follow people such as Hacking (1983) who make a distinction between being realist about *entities* and realist about *theories*. He wishes to maintain a realist view of a good many of the entities that science investigates (i.e., that they really exist and are studied within science) without necessarily being realist about the claims made in scientific theories (i.e., that the claims that scientific theories make about those entities are true or false on the basis of how the world is).

Harre (1986) makes a similar distinction between being realist about *reference* (i.e., about at least some of the things that scientific theories refer to), but nonrealist about the *truth-claims* of scientific theories. It is clear from how Harre constructs his detailed argument that he wishes to be as realist about science as possible. He takes seriously the intuitive notion of almost every working scientist that there *is* a real world that they are seeking to investigate, and he wishes to refute the totally nonrealist views of science by which some people are tempted, especially those who take a strong sociological view of science as nothing more than a social process. However, rather reluctantly, Harre feels obliged to concede that truth realism cannot be maintained, and that the only viable form of realism is referential realism.

Of course, this is not to say that every entity postulated by science necessarily exists or is yet known to exist. It often happens that entities are first postulated as explanatory constructs and only later does sufficient warrant accumulate to claim that they actually exist. To use one of the examples Harre gives elsewhere (Harre 1985), theories of disease in terms of disease-carrying particles were initially a speculative alternative to vapor theories, and were developed largely on the basis of general metaphysical considerations at a time when it was the scientific fashion to develop particle theories about almost everything. However, the gradual accumulation of knowledge about bacteria made it justifiable to claim that they really existed, and this was clinched when bacteria were observed under the microscope. At that point, it was no longer sensible to say that bacteria were merely hypothetical constructs.

On the other hand, there seem to be insurmountable philosophical problems in taking the detailed claims of theories about entities such as bacteria as corresponding exactly to the real state of affairs in an independent world. Nancy Cartwright (1983) has put this point punchily in the title of her book *How the Laws of Physics Lie*, meaning how they mislead us. Theories are, of course, *useful*, but that can be admitted without forcing the "bivalence" principle about their truth, that is, that they are either true or false, and can be shown to be one or the other. Scientific theories generally turn out to be useful approximations to the truth, and can in any case never be known to be more than that.

This raises the related question of whether theological discourse can be taken in a realist way. I have indicated that I believe that referential realism can be defended, at least as far as science is concerned. But what about theology? There are some theologians, such as Cupitt (1994), who have explicitly defended a nonrealist way of interpreting theology. If there are serious difficulties with interpreting science in a realist way, there are likely to be serious difficulties with theology too. If philosophers such as Harre, who are favorably disposed to realism, have felt obliged to abandon truth realism as far as scientific theories are concerned, it seems unlikely that it can be defended for theology either.

It has been increasingly recognized that scientific discourse uses "models" to depict what is being studied, and that these cannot be taken literally. Equally, it has been widely acknowledged that scientific statements cannot simply be divided into those that are true and those that are false. Scientific truth is always too much a matter of approximation for that. This all seems to be true of theology too, at least as much as of science. Theologians have long known that all talk about God is analogical, and that it is in the nature of God that he can never be fully known or exactly described in human discourse.

Indeed, it may be that the objections to truth realism concerning theology are even more radical and sweeping than those concerning science. God may be more radically unknowable than the natural world; it may be even more inappropriate to talk of theological "progress" than of scientific "progress." However, these are questions that I will not pause to pursue. My main concern here is to claim that, whatever the problems about truth realism in theology may be, it is still possible at least to retain referential realism. The word "God" can still be taken as referring to a being who really exists, whatever the problems in knowing his nature, or in saying anything exactly true about him.

Interestingly, Hacking (1983) uses theology as an example of how it is possible to be realist about entities but not about theories:

> It is possible to be a realist about entities but an anti-realist about theories. Many fathers of the Church exemplify this. They believed that God exists, but they believed that it was in principle impossible to form any true positive intelligible theory about God. One could at best run off a list of what God is not — not finite, not limited and so forth. (27)

The conclusion of my first section was that the different nature of scientific and theological discourse needs to be fully recognized rather than minimized. My further conclusion now is that, provided the referential realism of both theological and scientific discourse is acknowledged, they can still be seen as related to one another, rather than as being completely independent. Science and theology can be seen as describing aspects of the same total reality, albeit from different points of view and within different frames of reference.

There is a great deal more that could be said about this complex philosophical topic of realism. However, I am not attempting an exhaustive treatment. I merely need, as part of a broader argument, to be able to assume some version of realism and, given the difficulty of defending realism at all, I have tried to say enough to indicate a version of realism that I believe is defensible.

(3) Complementary Perspectives on a Single Reality: An Analogy from the Philosophy of Mind

Before suggesting how theology and science can be seen as complementary perspectives, it will be helpful to discuss briefly other related examples of complementarity. I will argue that mind-brain complementarity is one of the most relevant analogues.

Actually, the form of complementarity that is most often discussed in this connection is wave-particle complementarity in quantum dynamics. Following Niels Bohr's proposal that the notion of complementarity in quantum dynamics be extended to other domains, it has been suggested that science and theology can be seen as complementary (e.g., MacKay 1974; Reich 1990). However, others have been skeptical of this extension of the notion. Barbour (1974), for example, has wanted to establish strict criteria for the use of the concept of complementarity, and has argued that the relationship between science and theology does not exhibit the kind of complementarity that obtains between waves and particles.

It seems to me indisputable that the kind of complementarity that might obtain between science and theology could not be the *same* as that between waves and particles. Theology and science are different discourses, whereas "wave" and "particle" are terms within the same discourse. Moreover, we know *exactly* what the relationship is between waves and particles: it is fully specified theoretically. In contrast, there is clearly no such precision in the relationship between science and theology. If, following Barbour, we take wave-particle complementarity as the defining paradigm, then the complementarity of science and theology clearly fails to conform to it. However, an alternative response, which I favor, is to conclude that there are different kinds of complementarity, and that the notion can be used appropriately in different cases, provided we recognize that not all cases are identical.

It has also been suggested that complementarity arises *within* theology, and this idea is reviewed in a recent set of papers (Kaiser 1996; Loder and Neidhardt 1996; MacKinnon 1996). Specifically, it has been suggested that the theological claim that Christ is both God and man is an example of complementarity, akin to wave-particle complementarity. Again, this lacks the precision of wave-particle complementarity, though there are no doubt resemblances between the two cases. It is also no more helpful as a guide to the kind of complementarity that might obtain between science and theology because there we are again dealing with complementarity within a single discourse, whereas science and theology are different discourses.

I want to suggest that one of the best examples of how different discourses can bear on a single reality in a complementary way is to be found in how mind-language and brain-language relate to one another. By mind-language, I mean the "first person" language in which people describe their mental experiences. By brain-language I mean the "third person" descriptions that arise from the ways in which modern science is able to monitor the activity of the brain, by measuring its wave-like electrical activity by recording from single cells, by brain scans, or whatever.

These languages are, of course, very different, as many philosophers, including Thomas Nagel (1974), have argued. We have privileged access to our own experiences but can never know exactly what someone else's experiences are like. Equally, as Nagel famously argued, we can never know what it would be like to be a bat. On the other hand, we all have the same access to records of brain activity, whether they are records of the activity of our own brain or someone else's, or even the brain of a bat.

This is enough to show that experiential discourse is very different from brain discourse. The two discourses cannot simply be run together in a way that ignores the differences between them. However, I do not see any reason to draw the more radical conclusion that the two discourses cannot be related at all. It is reasonable to assume that experiential and brain discourses sometimes refer to different facets of a single underlying reality. The lawful relationships found between brain processes and mental experience supports this (Jeeves 1997). A science of experience has to proceed in different ways from a science of brain process, but it would be unwarrantedly doctrinaire to say that there cannot be a science of mental experience at all, or that experiential discourse cannot be related to the more objective brain discourse.

The relationship between brain and experience comes out most clearly when we are dealing with radical and correlated *changes* in brain and experience. Damage to the brain usually results in changes in experience, and there is a fruitful science of clinical neuropsychology relating one to the other. Also, the everyday changes in consciousness involved, for example, in going to sleep, involve both brain and experience.

The changes in the brain that take place as sleep approaches can be monitored in the changing pattern of the brain's electrical activity. The wave-like activity measured by electroencephalography moves through a series of predicable stages, with the waves becoming slower and larger. These changes continue as people move from light sleep through to deeper sleep, through four clearly delineated "stages" of sleep. It is also possible to collect experiential descriptions of going to sleep. These also follow an orderly sequence, with thought processes becoming more fragmented, then bizarre, ending with loss of orientation for time and place just before the onset of sleep. Incidentally, this illustrates how a science of experience *can* make reliable progress, even though it has to proceed in a different way from non-introspective sciences. Each person can, of course, only report on what going to sleep is like for them, but, when the reports of many different people are collated, a standard sequence of experiential changes emerges.

Moreover, the brain changes and experiential changes associated with sleep onset can be related to one another. People can be roused at different stages of the brain's movement toward deep sleep, and their mental experience ascertained. In general, there are very close correlations between the two. This leads us to talk about a single process of "going to sleep." We do not think of the experiential changes and the brain changes as being quite separate and independent. We see them as different perspectives on the single process of going to sleep; our different descriptions of it are regarded as complementary.

To take another rather different example, to say that someone is in an emotional state such as anxiety is to imply something both about their experience (that they feel frightened), and also about their physiological state (high levels of adrenalin) and their behavioral propensities (being tempted to escape). None of these by itself constitutes having an emotion. A classical case of emotion involves all three. The same is true of emotional disorders such as depression, which need to be described in more than one discourse to be described adequately. The different discourses about anxiety or depression are complementary.

The point of this discussion of the relation of mind and brain languages is to show that there is nothing strange or unusual about the idea that two discourses can be distinct (i.e., function in different ways and describe reality within different frames of reference), but yet be related to one another in a way that is complementary. Discourses about brain and about experience can both be taken as referring to different aspects of a "real" process such as going to sleep. This provides a helpful model for how theology and science might relate to one another.

I continue to assume that theology and science are distinct discourses which should not be confused — any more than descriptions of brain and experience should be confused. Nevertheless, I assume that they refer to related aspects of reality. As I have already indicated, the reality that is potentially the concern of theology is wider than that of science. However, it can reasonably be claimed that the reality with which science is concerned is also the concern of theology, but that theology approaches it from a different perspective, within its own discourse.

I thus wish to suggest that science and theology should be seen as offering complementary descriptions, rather as mind and brain discourse are complementary to one another. Though I believe the complementarity of mind and brain is one of the best analogues of the kind of complementarity that obtains between science and theology, the parallel is not exact. For one thing, theology and science are two discourses from among the multiple discourses that bear on reality, whereas mind and brain appear to be exhaustive within their own domain of reality. In this sense, emotion, which can be described using a wide range of discourses, social, experiential, physiological, and so on, may actually be a slightly closer analogue.

Another issue raised by the analogy is whether theology and science are both so obviously necessary as are mind and brain discourses. In fact, of course, not everyone does accept that mind discourse is necessary. It is sometimes said that, if mind and brain discourses are so closely related, we perhaps do not need both. Perhaps we should regard experiential discourses as being a shorthand, but potentially redundant, way of describing what could be described more exactly in brain language.

There are two objections to this. One is that it ignores the different character of first-person experiential discourse and objective brain discourse; only someone who ignored this difference in character could imagine that one discourse could be replaced by the other. The other objection is that the relationship between what different discourses have to say about, for example, going to sleep, or being in an emotional state, is not exact but only probabilistic. The exact correlations that would be required if one language were to be regarded as redundant, apparently do not obtain. The two discourses are thus complementary, but neither can be regarded as redundant.

The attempt that many have made to eliminate theological discourse and to describe reality exclusively in the naturalistic discourse of science seems rather similar to the attempt to eliminate mind discourse and to use only brain discourse. Similar arguments apply. Theology is different from science, so it is not rendered redundant by science. Also, the mapping of theological claims onto scientific ones is again not so close as to make theology redundant.

(4) Theology and Science as Complementary, Not as Competitors

It is a key consequence of the position that theological and scientific accounts are complementary that they are not necessarily to be seen as competitors. Of course, a particular theological account may be incompatible with a particular scientific one, a matter with which I will deal in the last section. My point here is that there is no reason *in principle* why a theological account should be seen as a competitor to a scientific one. It is a further consequence of this that theology has no vested interest in the failure of scientific accounts. It is simply a mistake to imagine that scientific failures leave more space for theological accounts.

This may all seem very obvious, but in fact there is only very patchy adherence to this position among those who write about the relation of science and theology. I will discuss the matter in relation to two main examples, the origin of species and the fine-tuning of the universe. Strangely, and for no good reason that I can see, many people seem to regard science and theology as complementary to one another concerning the origin of species but as alternatives to one another in relation to the fine-tuning of the universe. I want to urge a more consistent approach, regarding them as complementary in both cases.

As far as the origin of species is concerned, the nineteenth century saw a marked shift from seeing theology and science as alternatives to seeing them as complementary. The kind of natural theology associated with Paley based its argument on the lack of any credible alternative to a theological explanation. To take the famous watchmaker argument, Paley saw no plausible alternative explanation of the existence of a watch on the heath other than that it had been made by a watchmaker. In similar vein, he saw no plausible alternative explanation for the existence of something as remarkable as the human eye other than that there had been a designer (God) who had made it.

The argument hinged completely on the lack of an alternative account. Once an explanation of the origin of organs, indeed of species, in terms of natural selection became widely accepted, Paley's kind of argument collapsed. There are, of course, still some people who feel that they have to buttress their theological account of "creation" by arguing against natural selection, but they remain a minority.

Even before Darwin, some people had begun to argue for the compatibility of the theology of creation with a scientific view of the evolution of species. An early advocate of a complementarity view was Charles Kingsley, who argued that evolution was God's way of creating species (see Brooke 1991, ch. 8). Kingsley saw the theology of the creation of species as being complementary to the scientific account of the evolution of species argued by Darwin and Huxley, not as an alternative to it. By the end of the nineteenth century, the vast majority of Christian thinkers had followed his lead. There were various different ways of reconciling scientific accounts of evolution and theological accounts of creation, as Moore (1979) has documented. However, by the late nineteenth century most people saw theology and evolution as complementary.

The current situation is very different as far as the fine-tuning of the universe is concerned. It would be widely agreed that if anything in modern science points towards a divine creator, it is the fine-tuned universe, with its remarkable coincidences. The world is geared, in a highly improbable way, to produce stable matter and carbon-based life. The balance between forces of expansion stemming from the big bang and the gravitational forces of contraction are remarkably finely balanced. Carbon, which is crucial to supporting life as we know it, is an element that requires conditions that are highly improbable, but there are resonances which are exactly right for producing it. I could go on, but the facts here are universally agreed; the question is how they should be interpreted.

I suggest that such facts are readily consistent with theism, though they don't offer compelling grounds for concluding that there is a God because they can readily be interpreted in other ways. Following my general line about theology and science being complementary, I want to emphasize that I do not see this suggestiveness of a creator God as being dependent on the failure of the alternative explanations of the natural sciences.

Many of those who use the fine-tuned universe as the basis for a theistic argument seem to imagine that it will only serve this purpose if all alternative scientific explanations are shown to fail. This is reminiscent of Paley explaining remarkable phenomena in the biological world in terms of the agency of God because it was utterly mysterious how they might have arisen otherwise.

Swinburne, for example, sometimes appears to use this strategy. In his appendix on the fine-tuned universe in *The Existence of God* (1991), he takes the fine-tuning of the universe as presumptive evidence for the existence of God: "the peculiar values of the constants of laws and variables of initial conditions are substantial evidence for the existence of God, which alone can give a plausible explanation of why they are as they are" (312). He then surveys two of the main alternative non-theological accounts, the anthropic principle and the many universes theory. He regards both as being unpromising, and this provides support for taking fine-tuning as "strong confirming evidence for the existence of God" (322).

I am sympathetic, as it happens, to his criticisms of the two non-theological theories that he discusses. I am not suggesting that they are much better theories than Swinburne imagines, and that *therefore* a theological account of the fine-tuned universe must fail. My point is the more philosophical one that it is inappropriate to be pitting scientific and theological accounts against each other in this way at all.

However, the way Swinburne phrases things here may be an unfortunate lapse. He is, in my view, much sounder in his recent and more popular book, *Is There a God?* (1996). Here he makes no use of the claim that science cannot explain fine-tuning. He makes clear that, in invoking God to explain fine-tuning, he is not invoking God to explain what science cannot explain. "I am postulating a God to explain what science explains; I do not deny that science explains, but I postulate God to explain why science explains" (68).

Another example of the idea that scientific and theological ideas on fine-tuning are competitors, and one that is probably reaching a very wide audience, is the video on creation in the series, "The Question Is . . . ?," made by Russell Stannard. In many ways it is an excellent video, and sets out what might be regarded as a "state of the art" approach to these matters. The video, like Swinburne, sets out three different accounts of the fine-tuning of the universe, though not exactly the same three. The anthropic principle is not dealt with in its standard form. Instead, the video features Guth suggesting the possibility of an account in terms of "inflation" theory of the finely tuned balance between expansion and contraction. (Incidentally, this seems to be an advance. The anthropic principle is a sad mixture of muddle and special pleading, whereas I am sympathetic to Guth's idea that inflation theory, or some successor to it, will eventually produce a scientific account of at least some aspects of fine-tuning.) The voice-over on the video then summarizes things in these terms:

> So, here we have three possibilities. Either the universe was deliberately planned with life in mind. Or there are an infinite number of random universes. Or you believe that science will one day come up with an answer to the apparent coincidence. Which view is the right one?

Again, the implicit assumption seems to be that the explanation of fine-tuning in terms of a divine plan (the first alternative) depends on the failure of the other explanations.

I have seen no discussion of the paradox that many people adopt a complementarity approach to the origin of species but a non-complementarity approach to fine-tuning. There seems to have been no attempt to defend these divergent approaches in a principled way. I suppose someone might try to argue that one approach was appropriate to biology and the other to the physical sciences, but it is hard to see that a convincing defence could be made out.

(5) Scientific Ignorance and the Case for God

The real explanation of the divergent approaches adopted in these two contexts is surely that we have a viable scientific account of the origin of species, but we so far lack one for fine-tuning. The obvious inference is that theologians adopt a non-complementarity stance as long as they can get away with it (i.e., as long as there is no convincing scientific explanation) but that they switch to a complementarity approach when a good scientific theory is developed. This seems to be what is meant by "god of the gaps"; gaps in scientific understanding are used to insert strong theological claims. Most people claim to have abandoned "god of the gaps" arguments, but this does not stop them continuing to buttress a theological explanation of fine-tuning with the lack of an alternative scientific explanation.

This implicit approach, of taking a non-complementarity view as long as possible and then switching to a complementarity one when necessary, is rather reminiscent of Augustine's approach to the interpretation of the Bible. He advocated a literal interpretation unless it conflicted with something that was definitely established scientifically, but a symbolic interpretation if it so conflicted. The problem with this kind of approach is that, as knowledge advances, the number of points where literal interpretations are viable is always shrinking. Also, the ever-shifting boundary between literal and symbolic interpretations seems dangerously unprincipled.

Of course, one can readily see why people are attracted by a non-complementarity view of the relationship between theology and science, where science still leaves room for it. Where there is an absence of a scientific account of a puzzling phenomenon such as the fine-tuning of the universe, the lack enables people to argue, not just that fine-tuning *can* be seen theologically, but that it *must* be seen theologically. If it can be argued that fine-tuning requires theological argument, then this provides an argument for the existence of God.

While understanding the motivation for this, it seems to be wholly misguided. Pragmatically, it just doesn't work very well as an apologetic strategy. There must be very few people who have been led to conclude that there must be a God on the basis of the fine-tuning of the universe. Human ingenuity can always dream up other possible explanations, and an argument along the lines of "no other explanation is possible" always invites an ingenious riposte.

But also, arguments of this kind for the existence of God are unsatisfactory theologically. A clear distinction needs to be made between arguments that religious faith is *consistent* with rational considerations and arguments that it is *required* by rational considerations. The "five ways" of Aquinas are arguments of the former kind. Aquinas presupposed faith and showed that rational arguments could be used to buttress it; he was not trying to bring people to faith by rational arguments, and was too good a theologian to have attempted any such thing.

Views about the rationality of faith tend to become polarized. As I have argued elsewhere (Watts and Williams 1988), a middle path needs to steered in which faith is neither seen as splendidly irrational (as

Kierkegaard seems to have done), nor as the rational conclusion of an argument based on empirical data. Erecting such an argument overlooks the distinction between theological and scientific discourse, and perverts theology into something improperly close to empirical science. It fails to respect Hegel's dictum, which I have already quoted, that "God does not offer himself for observation."

It might be argued that, not only do we not have a convincing scientific account of fine-tuning at the moment, but that there never could be such an account. However, this seems an unpromising line to pursue. As far as I am aware, no one has advanced such an argument of principle, and it is not clear how they could do so. Also, in view of the fact that some scientists, such as Guth, expect a scientific account to develop, it seems foolhardy to try to argue that they are dreaming of something that is logically impossible.

A more promising line of argument would be that, even if we had a scientific account of fine-tuning, it would not explain everything about it. There would still be things that a theological account would be better suited to explaining. This line of argument can be firmed up by considering what is the proper scope of theological and scientific accounts, and suggesting that there is room for both.

It is often said that theology is about "why" questions, and science about "how" questions. This is only a first approximation to delineating the distinction between the two. "Why" questions are themselves quite heterogeneous, and there are certainly some "why" question that science can answer, especially biology — the function of a kind of animal behavior, for example. Also, not everything theology has to say is an answer to a "why" question. However, as far as fine-tuning is concerned, the how/why distinction is quite helpful. A future scientific theory may well give us an answer as to how the universe came to be fine-tuned, but there will probably be residual "boundary questions" (i.e., questions at the boundary of scientific enquiry) that call for a theological or metaphysical answer rather than a scientific one.

The analogy I drew in the last section concerning the relationship between experiential discourse and brain discourse also supports the position I am advocating here, that theological and scientific accounts are to be seen as complementary, not as alternatives. We do not generally try to decide whether something should be explained in brain terms or in psychological terms. Intellectual achievements, for example, are inevitably the result of processes which at one level are brain processes and at another level are conscious mental processes. Both mind and brain are involved in passing an examination. It makes no sense to ask whether a student used his mind or his brain to pass it.

Another relevant example from the philosophy of mind concerns human action. What at one level can be described in physical terms as mere movements of certain parts of the body can also be described as human actions. A hallmark of the latter is the way *intention* is built into how an action is described. However, clearly the two descriptions map onto one another. What can be described at one level as an intentional action can be described at another level as a mechanical movement. The two descriptions are again complementary, not competitors. Moreover, the two descriptions are linked to different kinds of explanations. When something is described as an intentional act, the appropriate explanation is in terms of the *reasons* for the action. When it is described as mechanical movement, the appropriate explanation is in terms of a different set of *causes*. The two kinds of descriptions are paralleled by two different but parallel kinds of explanation. Both are applicable, but under different descriptions of the action.

This is relevant to an objection that is often raised against offering a theological explanation (in terms of the purposes of God) for something that can be explained naturalistically. It is objected that this is "explanatory overkill," that one kind of explanation is sufficient. The point is that when a naturalistic explanation is available, a theological one should be eschewed as redundant. However, the fact that a naturalistic explanation is available doesn't necessarily make a theological explanation inappropriate. As the mechanical movement/intentional act analogy shows, complementary descriptions invite complementary explanations. Naturalistic and theological explanations can both be appropriate, explaining things in different ways.

(6) Assessing the Compatibility of Particular Theological Claims with Particular Scientific Claims

Though I have argued that theological and scientific accounts are to be seen as complementary to one another, rather than as competitors, it is important to emphasize that I am not suggesting that absolutely any theological account can sit alongside any scientific account. That would only be the case if one or both descriptions were non-referential, or carried no empirical claims.

Again, the philosophy of mind analogy that has been developed will help to make this clear. Though there may not be an exact one-to-one mapping of mental descriptions on to brain descriptions, there are certainly constraints on the range of mental events that are consistent with particular brain processes. Equally, while the same mechanical movement may subserve a variety of intentional actions, there are certainly constraints on the range of actions that can be implemented by a particular movement.

In a somewhat similar way, I would suggest, there are constraints on how theological and naturalistic accounts can map on to each other. However, the analogy cannot be pressed too far here. It is important to remember the distinctive nature of theological discourse. It is a mistake to take it as straightforwardly descriptive or empirical, even though it does contain truth claims.

The key question here is whether there are (or could be) any features of the natural world that would be *inconsistent* with the claim that God is the world's creator. Some have suggested, for example, that the multiplicity of galaxies in this enormous universe is difficult to square with the doctrine of God. I would suggest that this raises problems for some theological accounts, but not for all.

One assumption often made by theologians is the principle of "sufficient reason," that is, that God would not do anything unnecessary, anything for which there was not "sufficient reason." If you hold this doctrine, the vastness and complexity of the universe, much of which appears to be sterile, might be seen as unnecessary, and so inconsistent with the doctrine of sufficient reason of God.

However, this doctrine seems to me to be in no way a necessary part of belief in God. It would be equally possible to argue that the vastness of the universe, though much of it can be seen as in some sense "unnecessary," is fully consistent with the bountifulness of God. The nature of the universe might thus steer us towards a view of God that stressed his bountifulness rather than the constraining effects of the principle of sufficient reason on his actions.

Another example, from a rather different area of science, concerns the brain mechanism involved in special "religious" experiences. Religious experience takes many forms. In many cases, it is simply the experience of the world within a religious frame of reference, without having any distinct phenomenological quality, or needing to be seen as the experience of a different domain of reality from normal. However, there are also religious experiences which have a very special quality, making a powerful impact and having a special authority.

A theological account of such experiences can be given in terms of God's revelation of himself. However, it is also possible to give a naturalistic or scientific account. It must be presumed that, when people have special religious experiences, these are grounded in normal psychological and neurological processes. Religious experiences, however special they may appear to be, will inevitably make use of images and ideas from long-term memory; there is no way in which normal cognitive processes can simply be bypassed.

Equally, there will be neurological concomitants of such experiences. The scientific study of the brain processes involved in spontaneous religious experience is not straightforward methodologically, though there has been considerable work on the brain processes associated with meditation (see West 1987). There have been several proposals about what brain processes underlie special religious experiences. It will be helpful here to mention two current theories about the brain processes involved. I will suggest that one is less compatible with theological accounts than the other.

Persinger (1987) has developed a neurological theory of religious experience that emphasises the similarity between the brain processes involved in temporal-lobe epilepsy (TLE) and religious experience. The theory takes off from two key facts: (a) that religious experiences shows some similarity to the special phenomenal experiences associated with TLE, and (b) that there is a higher than normal frequency of religious experience in patients with TLE. This leads to the view that religious experience reflects the malfunctioning of the temporal lobes, albeit a malfunctioning not as radical as that found in TLE. Such an account might be seen to sit uneasily with a theological account in terms of God's revelation. In fact, Persinger's theory seems to be an unwarranted extrapolation from the limited similarities between religious experience and TLE phenomena; there are too many dissimilarities for the theory to be compelling.

An alternative theory, developed by d'Aquili (1993), is in terms of the normal "neural operators" of the brain. He suggests that there are two in particular which underpin religious experience, a "causal operator" that organizes disconnected strips of reality into a causal sequence, and (b) a "holistic operator" that creates a sense of wholeness that wins out over the fragmented nature of experience. This is a speculative theory, and I would not want to claim that it is necessarily correct. However, my point here is only the philosophical one that there is nothing in this account, unlike Persinger's, that need be seen as sitting uneasily with a theological account.

These are matters that require a great deal more explanation than they have received in the literature so far, and I will not attempt a more detailed exploration of them here. We are badly in need of clear ground rules for evaluating how well particular theological accounts and scientific accounts sit alongside one another. I sense that this will be a matter of judgment rather than of strict logic, not unlike the judgments scientists routinely make about how well a particular scientific theory sits with a body of data.

The important general point is that, if scientific claims can be regarded as consistent with theology (as is often claimed for the fine-tuned universe), then it must also be possible for scientific claims to be *inconsistent* with theology. (The only escape from this is to say that anything in science is consistent with anything in theology, but then the claim of consistency becomes rather vacuous.) The view of science and theology as complementary that I have developed in this chapter must carry the implication that particular pairs of scientific and theological accounts can be either consistent or inconsistent. If the possibility of inconsistency is denied, the inevitable conclusion is that theology and science are simply independent of one another.

References

Barbour, I. G. 1974. *Myths, Models and Paradigms*. London: SCM.

_____. 1990. *Religion in an Age of Science*. London: SCM.

Barfield, O. 1977. *The Rediscovery of Meaning and Other Essays*. Middletown: Wesleyan University Press.

Brooke, J. H. 1991. *Science and Religion: Some Historical Perspectives*. Cambridge: Cambridge University Press.

Burrell, D. B. 1986. *Knowing the Unknowable God*. Notre Dame: University of Notre Dame Press.

Cartwright, N. 1983. *How the Laws of Physics Lie*. Oxford: Clarendon.

Cupitt, D. 1994. *The Sea of Faith*. London: SCM.

d'Aquili, E. G. 1993. "Religious and Mystical States: Towards a Neurological Model." *Zygon* 28:177-200.

Davy, C. 1978. *Towards a Third Culture*. Edinburgh: Floris Books.

Hacking, I. 1983. *Representing and Intervening*. Cambridge: Cambridge University Press.

Harre, R. 1985. *The Philosophies of Science*. Oxford: Oxford University Press.

_____. 1986. *Varieties of Realism*. Oxford: Basil Blackwell.

Jeeves, M. A. 1997. *Psychology and Christianity: Partners in Understanding Human Nature*. Grand Rapids: Eerdmans.

Kaiser, C. B. 1996. "Quantum Complementarity and Christological Dialectic." In *Religion and Science: History, Method and Dialogue*, ed. W. M. Richardson and W. J. Wildman. New York: Routledge.

Lash, N. 1988. "Observation, Revelation and the Posterity of Noah." In *Physics, Philosophy and Theology: A Common Quest for Understanding*, ed. R. J. Russell, W. J. Stroeger, and G. V. Coyne. Vatican Observatory/University of Notre Dame Press.

Loder, J. E. and J. Neidhardt. 1996. "Barth, Bohr and Dialectic." In *Religion and Science*. See Kaiser 1996.

MacKay, D. M. 1974. "Complementarity in Scientific and Theological Thinking." *Zygon* 9:225-244.

MacKinnon, E. 1996. "Complementarity." In *Religion and Science*. See Kaiser 1996.

Moore, J. 1979. *The Post-Darwinian Controversies*. Cambridge: Cambridge University Press.

Murphy, N. 1990. *Theology in the Age of Scientific Reasoning*. Ithaca: Cornell University Press.

Nagel, T. 1974. "What Is It Like to Be a Bat?" *Philosophical Review* 83:435-450.

O'Hear, A. 1993. "Science and Religion." *British Journal of the Philosophy of Science* 44:505-516.

Peacocke, A. R. 1984. *Intimations of Reality*. Notre Dame: University of Notre Dame Press.

Persinger, M. A. 1987. *Neuropsychological Bases of God Beliefs*. New York: Praeger.

Phillips, D. Z. 1976. *Religion without Explanation*. Oxford: Blackwell.

Reich, K. H. 1990. "The Relation between Science and Theology: The Case for Complementarity Revisited." *Zygon* 25:369-390.

Swinburne, R. 1991. *The Existence of God*. Oxford: Clarendon.

_____. 1996. *Is There a God?* Oxford: Oxford University Press.

Watts, F. and M. Williams. 1988. *The Psychology of Religious Knowing*. Cambridge: Cambridge University Press.

West, M. 1987. *The Psychology of Meditation*. Oxford: Clarendon.

A Contextual Coherence Theory for the Science-Theology Dialogue

Niels Henrik Gregersen

> *There is no such thing as a unique scientific vision, any more than there is a unique poetic vision. Science is a mosaic of partial and conflicting visions.*
>
> Freeman Dyson, "The Scientist as Rebel,"
> *The New York Review,* May 25, 1995

IN THIS ESSAY I aim to outline a coherence model for the science-theology dialogue. Coherence means, generally, that different beliefs (or practices) are justified insofar as they are *interconnected* within a logically consistent and a substantially comprehensive pattern of thought (or practice).

Seeking coherence between science and theology, however, does not necessarily mean going for a grand unification of science and theology. A unification would only be possible if one of the disciplines could be shown to be derived from the other, or if one could develop a third metaphysical position in which the perspectival differences between science and theology are bridged. Historically, at least, it seems that none of these solutions has proven very successful. The derivative model for unification, the heir of rationalism, does not seem to do justice to the endemic richness of reality, and the received models of metaphysical bridging seem to presuppose a God's-eye view to which we could never have access. On the contrary, our knowledge is built up like a patchwork, in which the individual parts are derived from different contexts of life but still have to resonate with the overall orchestration of human experience.

A commitment to the *interconnectedness* of human knowledge thus has to be balanced by a sensibility to the *differences* in our approaches to reality. Think of water as a simple example of complexity: H_2O is not without further ado identical with "water." Water, rather, is a specific property based on the elementary level of H_2O but a property that only appears when there exists a sufficient concentration of H_2O under the right circumstances. Moreover, the "nature" of H_2O does not only consist of *intrinsic properties* given by its molecular structure but also of the *relational properties* which emerge when H_2O enters into a practically infinite number of chemical compounds; inside these systems as a whole, H_2O often gains new properties as a catalyst for further processes. In this case, the interconnection between the intrinsic properties of the physical components and the related chemical properties is rather strong. If we transcend the physico-chemical perspective, new relational properties begin to appear, and the ties between the different parts of our system of knowledge begin to loosen. On the level of living beings, H_2O may thus be approached in a variety of ways: as a resource for drinking, a tool for rinsing or refreshment, an element for swimming, and so on. Without the intrinsic physico-chemical properties, these new relational properties would not be possible. But only by the interaction with living beings are these relational properties of H_2O revealed. Finally, we may add to these biological functions the symbolic qualities attached to water in specific cultural contexts: water as a symbol for cleansing, as the element of baptism, and so on.

Now, if somebody asks "What is water, really?" or "What is the best description of water?" he or she falsely presupposes that one single and complete description of the nature of water is possible. In the view taken in this essay, this assumption is false due to the endemic richness of the relational properties of H_2O. The relational properties are as real as the intrinsic ones (though the first build on the latter). For the relational properties obviously exert a causal role that exceeds that of their constituent level (the molecules per se). I see no reason to doubt that the physico-chemical description is the best and only one we have on the constituent level of "water," but the physico-chemical perspective which approximates reality in one respect at the same time implies a withdrawal from other aspects of reality, in particular the relational ones.

From a theological point of view, this sensitivity to epistemic diversity (often associated with "postmodernity") should not be surprising. Some sort of perspectival pluralism is what one would expect if the world — itself constituted as a boundless variety — is created by the "multifarious wisdom" of God (Ephesians 3:10). For the present argument, however, it is not necessary to delve into theological motivations and metaphysical assumptions behind my adoption of a model for a multicontextual coherence theory. It is enough to show that the coherentist search for interconnections is essential in an interdisciplinary context, and that the fact of a multiplicity of perspectives both conditions and challenges the notion of rationality in both science and theology. The coherence model, therefore, does not rest content with highlighting the richness of our experience of reality. As noted above, the coherence model also imposes some rational demands on the debate: (a) a "logical consistency," that is, a noncontradiction between science and theology. Moreover, the coherence model that I am going to advocate is not conceived as a formal method, a mere grid. The aim is in particular, (b) to make possible an interconnection between science and theology that extend to the "substantial issues" between science and theology.

Part I offers a short account of my own view on the science-theology interface, with special attention to the asymmetries penetrating the dialogue between science and theology. Part II gives a more elaborated account of the contextual coherence model on the basis of Nicholas Rescher's theory of rationality. Part III compares the coherence theory as employed here with other influential options in the science-theology debate. I subsequently discuss theories of scientific realism and internal realism, and take a critical look of Nancey Murphy's program for theology, modeled after an empiricist philosophy of science. In Part IV, I present a test case illustrating the usefulness of the criteria of coherence through a theological appropriation of neo-Darwinian theory. Thereby, I hope to corroborate the claim that the coherence model is both descriptive and normative: it describes the kind of rationality which is already at work in the dialogue, and yet it is also able to protect against a priori divorces and premature marriages between theories in science and theology.

I. Asymmetries in the Dialogue between Science and Theology

a. The Disunity of the Sciences

Already inside the house of the sciences, we face quite different methods, purposes, and styles of reasoning. The logical positivists' catch-phrase of a "unification of science" has increasingly been shaken. Though the achievements of local unifications such as physics and chemistry are, in fact, impressive, they have been followed up by a likewise amazing diversification of other parts of the scientific enterprise. "Unification does work — and so does diversification," as recently pointed out by Ian Hacking (1996, 56). The extent of disunity inside the natural sciences comes to the fore in biology, where the disciplines of molecular biology are institutionally becoming still more divorced from the study of macroevolution (at Harvard, the first are classified as experimental, the second as historical disciplines). If we add to this picture the methodological diversity in disciplines like psychiatry, economy, and sociology, it is increasingly difficult to maintain the global thesis of "science" as a singleton, which will end up in a unified "world-view." This grandiose view does not capture accurately the scientific enterprise but is rather a construct hovering over the surface of the wild waters of scientific differentiations. The term "science" itself is thus shorthand for the many different sciences. However, rather than adopting a postcritical attitude of "anything goes," it should be noted that each of the scientific disciplines have developed self-stabilizing rational procedures through setting terminology, methods, confines of purpose, and so on. And for all, the precept "Connect!" is as valid as ever (Hacking 1996, 49). While the idea of one unified science may be wishful thinking, the ideal of interconnecting the multiplicity of the sciences — sometimes in strong ties, sometimes more loosely — seems to be essential to the very idea of science.

b. On Asymmetries in the Science-Theology Dialogue

According to the coherence model for science and theology, theology also faces the demand: "Connect!" But care is demanded when investigating possible interconnections between theology and the natural sciences. For in this case, we do not only meet *differences* of style, methods, and languages, but also some penetrating *asymmetries*. In contrast to the sciences, theology is not only an object-related discipline, entertaining the study of religions, or even merely the study of specific religious formation like Christianity. "Systematic theology" (in contrast to most forms of "religious studies" but in line with philosophy) also undertakes the attempt to interpret all the very different aspects of the world, "the world as a whole." Theology does so, however, with reference to and from the perspectives offered by the disclosive potentialities of a given religious tradition. In the case of a Christian theology, everything is related to the belief in God as the omnipresent creator, and as the liberator and redeemer of nature and humankind in Christ and Spirit. This means that a certain distinctiveness between the task of theology and the task of the natural sciences is unnegotiable. Nonetheless, the very reason why systematic theology is not a strictly empirical discipline in the first place displays why theology cannot divorce itself from the empirical sciences in the second place. Theology cannot measure up to its own standards if it is not able to relate the Christian belief in the omnipresent God meaningfully to the theories of the empirical sciences. In other words, theology falls short of its own agenda if it rules out a specified relationship with the sciences. *The interconnection with science is part* (but also only one part!) *of the justification of theology as a rational discipline*.

How different is the case in the natural sciences! The justification of scientific theories occurs in ramifications internal to science; thus science does not need to take into account a discipline like theology in the process of self-validation. In all practical affairs, science proceeds with or without religion, with or without philosophy. Only at the cutting edge of speculative disciplines like cosmology or theoretical physics do general worldview assumptions of religious or philosophical character potentially play a heuristic role (think of Bohr, Einstein, or Bohm). Likewise the ethical boundary questions may influence whether or not scientists may decide to undertake some projects. But as soon as a research field has been opened, the game of justification goes on according to internal standards.

Comparatively, theology is a far more *context-sensitive discipline* since theological content cannot be divorced from cultural context. Scripture needs a reader as tradition needs recipients, and the readers and recipients are steeped in a culture permeated by scientific ways of reasoning and "scientific" world pictures. In this way, the state of the art in the sciences cannot help but influence the self-understanding of theology; but not so the other way around.

The asymmetries of justification and contextuality between science and theology are partly rooted in the different languages of science and theology. While theology, like the human sciences, refines and delves into the language of everyday life, science de-contextualizes itself from common sense through the use of the formal *language of mathematics*. This de-contextualization also implies that the sciences are distancing themselves from religion — and other cultural endeavors. Methodologically, science is and has to be a-theistic (which does not mean anti-theistic).

Now, what then is the language of the science-theology dialogue? Obviously, it is not one of mathematics. Rather, the dialogue is a meta-discipline that forms theories about the place of science inside a broader framework of meanings and values, including religion. In other words, the science-theology dialogue is, in my view, about the *transdisciplinary interpretation* of the methods and results of science inside the broader perspective of different views of life, in our case that of the Christian tradition. It is only at this level (which always involves philosophical questions) that one can talk about a mutual support or a reciprocal modification between science and theology.

Thus, the coherence model proposed here acknowledges from the outset that theology cannot contribute to the construction of theory-building inside the natural sciences. The *context of justification* takes place intra-scientifically. It may well be the case that Christian faith has nurtured a favorable climate in which the empirical sciences could develop, though such an overall hypothesis is difficult to test (cf. Brooke 1991, 19-33). One can, in fact, point to several cases where Christian beliefs have influenced the *heuristic* of scientific theories; religious presuppositions have thus contributed to the *context of discovery* of many new scientific ideas (think of figures like Boyle, Newton, Priestley, Oersted, or Faraday). It would appear, however, that looking back on past heydays makes only limited sense in the present cultural situation. Today, the scientific enterprise is on a whole pursued independently of any religious support or inspiration. The same scientific methods and devices are used in New York as in Teheran and Beijing. Not even a heuristic function is very likely to appear, except perhaps for the speculative domains of science (like cosmology) and highly context-sensitive sciences (like ecology). From these observations, I infer the general rule that the real interface between science and theology is on the metadisciplinary level of (a) *interpreting the consequences of science for our perception of reality* and (b) *evaluating the different social functions* of science and religion.

Consequently, theology neither contests science nor interferes in its internal developments. The role of theology is first and foremost one of *reception*, one of listening (and since the theologian is only seldom competent in science, he or she should normally give priority to the established parts of science). The more *active and critical* role of theology, as I see it, is to make constructive proposals as to how to interpret (and how *not* to interpret!) the consequences of the sciences inside a larger cultural horizon (with special emphasis on Christian tradition). The theologian is here expected, by virtue of the context-sensibility of theology, to have a competence in evaluating different ways in which the sciences do or may resonate with religious viewpoints of reality. The theologian will, of course, perform this interpretative role sometimes in congruence, sometimes in competition, with other views of life, whether a-religious, anti-religious or those coming from other religious traditions. But the inner-theological function is both descriptive and constructive: how do the sounds of the singular pieces of human knowledge (the scientific theories) propagate into the whole orchestration of human knowledge? How can traditional ways of expressing faith be reconstructed in order to resonate better with science and express better the authenticity of the Christian perspective?

In this view, science cannot demand that theology hold a specific theological position. The reason is simply that science is an a-theological enterprise. However, again we face an *asymmetry* between the partners of the dialogue. Though the sciences cannot tell theology what to do, the soundings coming from the sciences indirectly — refracted, so to speak, through the frequency response of theology itself — affect the self-constitution of theology. In this roundabout way, science certainly does rule out some theologies (see below, Part IV).

This influence, of course, comes to the fore in those forms of theology that explicitly take the sciences into account. But even theologies that programmatically proclaim their distance from the sciences are nonetheless marked by their withdrawal. For negative feedback is still feedback. In fact, those positions saying bluntly "No" to the paradigmatic theories of modern science or those claiming an absolute independence vis-à-vis the sciences disconnect themselves from vital aspects of the classical Christian tradition; they are (albeit often involuntarily) changing the agenda of theology. Fundamentalists, for example, who insist on a literal reading of scripture, do away with the spiritual readings of the Bible which were the cornerstone of the exegesis of the Fathers; likewise, nonintegrationists like existentialists will tend to cut away the cosmological aspects of Christian tradition. From a theological point of view, the interface with the sciences seems indispensable.

To sum up: While the science-theology debate can hardly change the self-definition of the sciences, it does decisively change the worldview interpretations of science; the dialogue makes a difference in the way we perceive the character of the world that we inhabit. Moreover, since any theological interpretation of science inevitably has repercussions for the self-development of theology, the dialogue cannot but change the self-understanding of theology, though indirectly. In the search for coherence, any new piece of theological knowledge has to find its place inside the internal structure of a given theology. Theology re-describes itself as it goes along re-describing scientific findings and theories from a theological perspective. At the same time, theology corroborates its own theory as long as the theory can be successfully applied to scientific theories — or at least placed (more loosely) in a specific relationship to it.

The last qualification is important. For as we have seen, coherence theory does not imply a program for a unification or homogenization of all kinds of knowledge. The theory to be developed in the following is thus emphatically *contextual* in that it allows for a plurality of perspectives inside of the overall texture of human knowledge. Some concepts of human knowledge belong to local areas of human experience and are not generally applicable. Other concepts are meant to have a universal scope but lead into prima facie paradoxes, as is the case in quantum theory or in theologies of grace and human freedom. How much more is a conceptual plurality to be expected in the interface between disciplines such as science and theology! In fact, the need for an adequacy in relation to a specific problem area may suspend an easy ride towards coherence. But this suspension is only temporary, for the coherence theory insists that all pieces of human inquiry should be brought into "a characteristic relationship" to one another. Prima facie paradoxes may be tolerated, and a perspectival plurality is to be accepted as a fact of life, but the coherence theory does not accept an insulation of allegedly privileged forms of knowledge. Which criteria a contextual coherence theory may offer for a choice between theories is now to be investigated.

II. The Coherence Model in Outline

a. From the Chain of Knowledge to the Raft of Knowledge

Since coherentism, historically speaking, is the most significant alternative to foundationalism (DePaul 1995, 133), it may be convenient to begin by pointing out some differences between a foundationalist and a coherentist account of knowledge.

Coherentism does not follow the foundational view, according to which knowledge, metaphorically speaking, builds on *chains of arguments* where the force of "fundamental evidences" is transferred to less evidential cases. According to coherence theory, such logical chains of argument make up only a few limiting cases in the totality of human forms of knowledge. Normally, knowledge is corrobated internally if new sentences (about data) and new theories (about structural wholes) are able to relate meaningfully to received sentences and theories that we tend to hold as true (though their truth-claim cannot be warranted by absolute evidence, either). Coherentism thus argues within the *linguistically* formulated web of beliefs and knowledge.

What is knowledge, then, if it is not like the foundationalist chain of arguments? Metaphorically speaking, the coherence theory looks at human knowledge as an intersubjective enterprise, like a *raft with planks* of different size and color. The raft as a whole (the web of beliefs) is corroborated by the planks (the truth-candidates) that constitute that raft, and knowledge is enlarged when new planks are added which fit into the raft and strengthen its structure. No plank forms a raft in itself but is only a distinctive part of the raft, and belongs as such to the family of planks constituting the raft as a whole.[1] In the raft of human knowledge, some planks are no doubt more fundamental than others (think of physics and chemistry), and

---

1. Darwin's theory of macroevolution of 1859 may count as an example of a new scientific candidate that was able to coordinate quite different planks of empirical data into a coherent raft of knowledge: geological fossil records, geographical variations of populations, environmental fitness, cultural breeding experiences, etc. It was not until the 1930s, however, that Darwinism became a stable theory. At this time the neo-Darwinian synthesis was able to extend and refine Darwin's explanatory pattern to cover the new discoveries of microevolutionary processes in molecular biology (Kitcher 1993, 11-57). Thus, empirical data form the input to larger theories, but these inputs are themselves placed in a more general pattern of thought that relates the data to one another.

may — through the long history of raft-building — have attained a pillar-like function for substantial sections of the raft. No plank, however, lays the foundation for all other planks (physics and chemistry do not help in the improvement of economics, while mathematics does). Other planks may seem to have a flair of oddity around them, though they have shown themselves to be irreplacable by any other planks (think of art and religion). Every metaphor, of course, has its limits, and the raft-metaphor falsely suggests the idea of knowledge as additive or cumulative. In fact, the idea of coherence implies to the contrary that the addition of any new plank in the raft-building will have repercussions for all other planks. In extreme cases, revolutionary new planks may even compel us to undo parts of the previous raft-building and reconstruct earlier planks, as is the case in scientific revolutions.

b. The Redefinition of Data in Nicholas Rescher's Coherence Theory

In the following, I take my point of departure in Nicholas Rescher's version of the coherence theory as developed in his *Coherence Theory of Truth* ([1973] 1982) and expounded in synthetic form in *A System of Pragmatic Idealism* (3 vols., 1992-1995). The promise of Rescher's theory, as I see it, is the way it links the formal elaboration of a theory structure with an emphasis on the "data" which any theory has to account for in its structure. It is thus on the content-based ("pragmatic") level that his coherence theory puts the emphasis, while acknowledging that any thought pattern has to be self-consistent ("ideal"). The theoretical development and the practical use of a theory is thus seen as co-developing, and a succesful theory is one in which the two cycles reinforce one another. Therefore the stunning title, "Pragmatic Idealism."

Rescher fully acknowledges that science, especially the "schoolbook science" of relatively well-established knowledge, is "unquestionably the best bet that we have" when it comes to the "close-to-truth" character of our knowledge (Rescher 1992, 277). However, he departs from the idea of a foundationalist construction (an *Aufbau*) of theories on unquestionable data. While this move is no longer controversial in today's philosophy of science, Rescher's denial of a sharp distinction between *theory* and *data* is more provocative. This distinction is normally presupposed, for instance in the so-called Covering Law Model

(Hempel-Oppenheimer Model) for scientific explanation. According to this model, we have a constructive theory in the form of a general law that has the function of explaining *(explanans)* the relevant data *(explanandum)* in question, by way of subsuming them under the general law (e.g., Hempel [1966] 1991, 301-304). Rescher here proposes a new definition of a *datum*. Data are not givens, in the sense that we know them to be simply true. They only possess a prima facie truth (as for instance, an ethical intuition), but they are not conclusive truths before they show their attunement to the overall scheme of knowledge. Rescher distinguishes between the limit notion of "raw data" (the extralinguistic input) from the "experiential data" as these are transformed into linguistic units (data). "A datum is a proposition" (Rescher 1992, 166), since all our experiential data are mediated through our cognitive systems.

Data are to be considered as *truth-candidates*. In order for a given statement to count as a truth candidate, we assume that it is worth considering as presumptively true. This is the pragmatic point of departure for any theory.

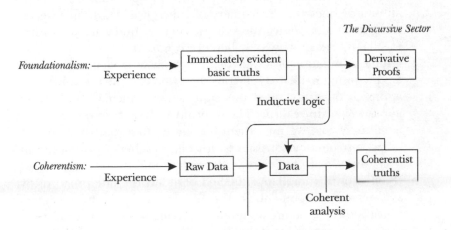

**The different role of data in foundationalism and coherentism
(Figure from Rescher 1992, 163)**

c. Differences between Foundationalism and Coherentism

Rescher points to a number of differences between the foundationalist and the coherentist approach, of which I only mention the following:

- On the foundational approach, *data* are wholly nondiscursive and fixed invariants, while on the coherentist account the data "represent a mixture of experiential and discursive elements" (Rescher 1992, 164).

- For the coherentist, "all knowledge is essentially of a piece" (163). Unlike the foundationalist view, the coherence view does not hold a sharp dichotomy between *general propositions* (for example, laws) and particular propositions. General propositions have the logical form of unifying interrelated data inside a network. In the same way, coherentism does not distinguish sharply between *immediate knowledge* (experience) and *derived knowledge* (propositions).

- For the foundationalist, knowledge is enhanced by an *ampliative method*, taking one's point of departure in a few, but putatively safe, data, and then moving outward by making inferences from a carefully circumscribed and tightly controlled set of initial propositions. For the coherentist the range of data is bigger; coherence theory does not need safe starting points but is content with a larger set of plausible and well-qualified prospects for truth. Only afterwards does the "machinery of coherence" start, and we restrict the number of truth-candidates that we find worth considering. Thus, the strategy of coherence is *reductive*.

- On the foundationalist approach, the body of evidence, the data, are presumed to form a self-consistent whole, while the coherence approach does not need this supposition, which in most cases appears to be unrealistic. The difficulty with data, in other words, is not only that we miss them but more often that they are too many and often inconsistent with one another. The important thing is not truth but significant truth!

- If one uses the ampliative method of induction, one proceeds by a *linear series* of argument. On the coherentist approach, one enters into a cyclical structure of judgment, trying to find a pattern that, so to speak, grows out of the data by systematizing those data that are able to form a consistent whole from some unifying point of view. Thus, there are *feedback loops* from the more general set of propositions to the initial data that were selected to go into the competition as truth-candidates. This procedure is also open for a reformulation of initial data if some of them prove to be incompatible with the new pattern in their original interpretation. Think, for instance, of a truth-candidate like "the sun arises over the earth," and its subsequent reformulation inside the coherent picture of the later heliocentric system.

• In the standard view, cognitively unified systems are only seen as organizers of what is accepted (from the safe home of safe data), while coherentism regards the systematization of knowledge as the "arbiter of what is acceptable" (157).

Now, of course, the standard objection to the coherence theory of truth is that it seems to be guided by purely logical or at least intra-linguistic connectives. Couldn't a fictive world or a fundamentalist world picture be counted as coherent, that is, as true? Rescher admits that this criticism would hit its target if we define coherence in a purely logical way (1992, 171). But it is here that the concept of data, as a mixture of experience and proposition, plays a central role in Rescher's argument. Coherence does not only mean *inner logical consistency* between propositions; coherence means a *systematic ordering of contentual propositions* that have grown out of experience (although we can never decide exactly how far our experiential data depicts the world as it is in itself). The coherentist best-fit analysis goes for a maximal attuning of the most data inside a systematization (Rescher 1992, 159). And the system is only strong if it continuously succeeds in incorporating data and thereby stabilizes itself.

d. The Theoretical and the Applicative Cycles of Control

Rescher points to two ways of evaluating competitive conceptual systematizations (Rescher 1992, 174-176). First, there is a *theoretical cycle* which controls the intellectual consistency of the conceptual schemes. Here we find a validation by the capacity of *theoretical self-substantiation*. Conceptual schemes are by their very nature *self referential*, that is, they are used on data, but also on the theory itself.[2]

Second, we have the *applicative circle* in which the evidences for pragmatic utility and fertility with respect to further research has to be shown. Here we face a validation by the *capacity of generalizing power,* of successful implementation on the relevant problems to be solved. The theoretical and the applicative circle are of a "symbiotic and mutually supportive nature," though the one goes for rational system-

---

2. Rescher's model of rationality is here congenial with modern systems theories such as Niklas Luhmann's (Luhmann 1990).

atization, the other for empirical progress. The structural closedness
of the theoretical proposal is a precondition for its empirical openness.
The double knife-edge of the knowledge system can be illustrated this
way:

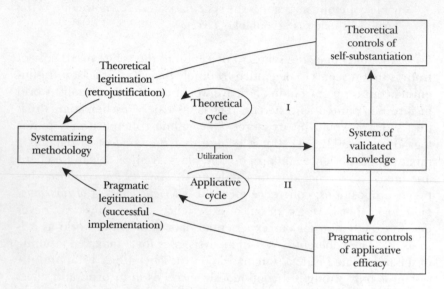

**The Twofold Cycle of Theoretical Self-Substantiation
and Empirical Generalization
(Figure from Rescher 1992, 175)**

In this sense, there is an inbuilt evolutionary dimension in Rescher's
version of rationality. The trials and errors of nature have their parallels
in the domain of epistemology. There might not be unilinear progress
in human knowledge, but there are procedures of revision that purge
the overflow of cognitive constructions and leave us with relatively
"better bets":

> After all, the articulation of cognitive systems is a matter of historical
> development, of repeated efforts at improvements in systematizing
> in the light of trial and error. We are faced with a fundamentally
> *repetitive* process of the successive revision and sophistication of our
> ventures at cognitive systematization, a process that produces by way
> of iterative elaboration an increasingly satisfactory system, one that
> is more and more adequate in its internal articulation or effective in
> its external applicability. (Rescher 1992, 177)

e. Coherence Theory and the Problem of Cognitive Pluralism

The empiricist criticism is one that has always followed the coherence theory as its dark shadow: "How can we know whether our cognitive systems are in contact with reality?" We have now seen an initial answer: Rescher's linguistic-experiential concept of data. The experiential inputs of the coherence machinery are only those data that we "believe" to be true; in this sense there is an inescapable pragmatic point of departure for any epistemology. But once the best-fit analysis begins and as it goes on, the applicative cycle gives us a form of pragmatic legitimation when it successfully implements the theory in ever new cases.

Another criticism raised against coherentism comes from the side of a pragmatic relativism. It may, therefore, be useful to outline how Rescher's version of pragmatism diverges from the pragmatism of Richard Rorty or Hilary Putnam. For if coherentism presupposes that all knowledge is "essentially of one piece," how then is it able to cope with cognitive pluralism?

Rescher finds cognitive or epistemic pluralism to be a fact of life that has to be taken seriously as a condition of human knowledge (Rescher 1995a, 64f.). But in contrast to the idea of a mere juxtaposition of unrelated conceptualities, Rescher argues for a *preferential pluralism* that demands that all players argue for the relative advantage of some conceptualities over relevant rivals. Rescher lists four fundamental positions vis-à-vis cognitive pluralism (1995a, 80; cf. 1995b, 195-223).

- The easiest way might seem to follow a *skepticism* which says that none of the alternatives are justified at all. Nothing goes. The inner problem of skepticism, however, is that it is a self-defeating position since it also applies to the skeptic; it is thus more an attitude than a philosophical position.
- A second position is the *indifferentist position* which says that we hold a truth, but there is no reason why we hold on to this particular position, except for the fact that we began this way or made the choice for it. Other ways might be equally enjoyable. Richard Rorty's pragmatism may exemplify this position.
- A third way would be a form of *syncretism,* saying that all (or certainly some) alternatives should be affirmed in their unrelated natures and simply juxtaposed, though they are internally incon-

sistent with one another. This seems to be a consequence of Putnam's version of pragmatism.[3]
- The fourth possibility, Rescher's own, is to argue for a *perspectival rationalism* (Rescher 1995a, 80). To be reasonable does not mean to possess the truth (that would be dogmatism) but to give *reasons* for preferring one solution over another to a given problem. To affirm is also to negate. Any search for truth has thus to be somehow "doctrinal," claiming something about something, albeit in a hypothetical mood which is open for revision.

In Rescher's model for coping with cognitive pluralism, there may thus be many different perspectives on any given subject-matter. But in the specification of a given perspective, one is to be preferred to another (except, of course, for cases of undecidability). A *perspectival pluralism* has to be accepted in cognitive affairs, since the context of inquiry differs, but this does not imply a *perspectival indifferentism*. There exists, for instance, no universally appropriate diet, but it is not a matter of indifference what a person eats and which kind of diet someone chooses. In the given situation, all things taken together, one diet will be more appropriate than others:

> On a perspectival approach, one and only one position is appropriate from a given perspective of consideration, but there are a variety of perspectives. No one doctrine is in itself "the right one"; none can make good an absolutistic claim to being uniquely right on general principles. We have no direct access to the philosophical truth except via the conditioning mechanisms of a cognitive perspective. (Rescher 1995b, 220)

Thus, context relativization does not drive us into a-rationalistic attitudes with respect to truth-claims (Rescher 1995b, 233). And even if rival theories are shown to be practically equivalent, they all have to argue for their position through the criteria of appropriateness, such as closeness to the problem, and the ability to appropriate the data in the applicative cycle. Rescher's preferential coherence theory can thus be seen as a pragmaticist alternative to Rorty's indifferentism and Putnam's syncretism.

3. Cf. Putnam 1987, 35: "That is, take the position that one will be equally 'right' in either case. Then you have arrived at the position I have called 'internal realism'!"

Rescher's theory disallows raising truth-claims that are not related to the relatively surer pathways of inquiry at our disposal. This would amount to the syncretism of private evidences. If syncretism proceeds by conjoining positions indiscriminately, the perspectival rationality proceeds by combining positions (Rescher 1995a, 92) so that the different perspectives retain a voice of their own and still fit with the overall pattern of knowledge. On this issue, the contextual coherence theory takes a middle course between different forms of incompatibilism which assert that different languages belong each to their own world (from Wittgenstein's language games to Putnam's internal realism), and the synthetic claims of a realism which asserts that we have access to a common perspective that allows us a panoptical view of reality.

The coherence theory thus offers a model for how to orient oneself rationally in a pluralistic world in which there exist no clear-cut logical connections between different visions nor any direct contentual identity between propositions. There is, for instance, no logical interconnection between the results of the human genome project and the theological doctrine of sin, nor is there a contentual identity between confessing "I am a sinner," and a genetic description of the peculiarities of that person's genome. Nonetheless, one should look for interrelations between the different perspectives on reality. A theological reinterpretation of the doctrine of original sin may in fact benefit from a theological redescription of the genetic boundaries and possibilities for being a human (see e.g., Hefner 1993, 123-144).

In place of the hard demand for interdependence in terms of mutual logical deduction, Rescher proposes the softer demand of a *contextual interlinkage.* Any position will have to stand in a "characteristic relation" with other positions which are also presumed to be true (in Rescher's sense of presumptive truth) with respect to a given set of data. Normally, there is an overflow of data of the most diverse kind (think of data from common sense, scientific research, and religious life). The demand, then, is to take into account that any change among the fellow positions (each referring to different data in the given context) has repercussions for one's own position. The demand of rationality is, so to speak, horizontal. Rationality is about finding pathways of interlinkage on the intra-linguistic level rather than on the extralinguistic level:

> The propositions classed as true in the context of the original set of inconsistent data *S* stand in a mutual dependency relative to *S:* every truth here stands in a characteristic relation of interdependence with

its fellows in the hypothetical sense that if the truth-status of some of
these were different (i.e., if they were to be classed as false instead of
true) then its own truth-status might well be affected. (Rescher [1973]
1982, 175)

But what could a "characteristic relation of interdependence" imply for
science and theology, and precisely *how* is the truth-status of theological
statements "affected" by science? This question relates to the *applicative
circle* of Rescher's theory, to which we return in Part IV. First, in Part
III, we shall seek a clarification of the *theoretical cycle* of the coherence
model when applied to science and theology by confronting the coherence theory with two problems: (a) the question of the "reality" of the
world beyond our cognitive schemes, and (b) the question of "empirical
data" inside theology.

III. The Coherence Model and Its Alternatives

a. The Coherence Model and the Many Faces of Realism: Rescher versus Putnam

"Metaphysical realism" we may define as the doctrine that the world
exists in a way that is substantially independent of our inquiry into that
reality. The paradox of metaphysical realism is then that it is a *taken*
position, not a given position, with regard to a reality that we take to
be *given*, not taken! But paradoxical or not, it seems to be a natural
attitude, a belief undergirding the conduct of most of our epistemic
practices. Metaphysical realism is thus endorsed by Rescher in consequence of his pragmatic stance (1992, 275).

Hilary Putnam nonetheless still finds a metaphysical realism too
"externalist." He wants to replace the idea of a metaphysical Realism
(capitalized) with an "internal realism" (lower case 'r'). Putnam does so
by defining metaphysical Realism as saying that the alleged thought-
independent objects, processes, or events "admit of only one description, independent of all choices" (Putnam 1981, 54; in italics). It would
appear, however, that even if one would share Putnam's point that the
presupposition of a "God's-eye view" is an abstraction from our day-to-
day realist intuitions, a general disregard of the notion of an external
realism would not follow. Or the other way around: saying that something like a "tree" exists whether or not I realize its existence, does not

imply that the nature of the tree can be described exhaustively in "only one description." The tree can be seen, for instance, (a) as an exemplar of a phylum or of a species, (b) as a specific morphological form, (c) as timber, (d) as an object of aesthetic valuing, (e) as a chemical compound, and so on. All of these descriptions might have a truth-relation to the existing tree. Likewise, to say that God exists independently of our God-talk does not imply that one linguistic representation of God would encompass the nature of God. In fact, theologians of all ages have denied a claim like this.[4]

In a later clarification of his own internal realism, Putnam finds three tenets in the doctrine of metaphysical Realism:

- *metaphysical Realism$_1$* thinks that "the world consists of a fixed totality of mind-independent objects";
- *metaphysical Realism$_2$* claims that "there is exactly one true and complete description of the way the world is";
- *metaphysical Realism$_3$* asserts that "truth involves some sort of correspondence" (1990, 30).

It would appear, however, that Putnam here makes a straw man out of his opponent. The three tenets in the definition by Putnam should at least not be mixed up into one idea of Metaphysical Realism. I, for one, would subscribe to metaphysical Realism$_3$ (truth involves correspondence) but oppose metaphysical Realism$_2$, according to which there is exactly one complete description of the world. I also think that some qualifications are needed with respect to metaphysical Realism$_1$ which claims that "the world consists of a fixed totality of mind-independent objects." My point would be that there can only exist a "fixed totality of objects" if the relations between objects are merely external. To use Putnam's own example: If we think of three objects as self subsistent and the relations between them as *external*, then we have a world of three entities:

x1, x2, x3

On the other hand, if we regard the relations between objects to be *internal* to the objects, any proposition on our part will end up having seven (possible) referents in the real world:

4. In his historical tour de force, John Macquarrie (1984) finds only Hegel and Whitehead as representing the idea of a thoroughly rational concept of God.

x1, x2, x3,
x1+x2, x1+x3, x2+x3,
x1+x2+x3

However, it seems to me that the fact that we have rival metaphysical descriptions of the world does not *eo ipso* imply the conceptual relativism that Putnam opts for. It would rather appear that we are confronted with two competitive "doctrinal" descriptions of the world. It might well be possible to show that the one description is more comprehensive — more coherent — than the other one. Both process thought (A. N. Whitehead) and systems theory (Heinz von Foerster et al.) take the seven-object description to be the more encompassing description of reality. From this broader description, the three-object description is understandable as a limiting case that abstracts from the internal relations (or relational properties) between objects. An important difference between these metaphysical positions, by the way, is that while the three-object logic only makes possible propositions about the status of the actual world of entities, the seven-object logic offers a way to form propositions about *possible constellations* between the objects in the future. In the formulation by A. N. Whitehead, propositions are not only statements but also "suggestions," invitations to reality (Whitehead [1933] 1967, 244).

Thus, there is a considerable difference between Putnam's incompatibility thesis, leading into a conceptual relativism, and a preferential pluralism developed alongside Nicholas Rescher's coherence theory. Our conceptions about what is to be counted as "real" and what has to be accounted for in a causal description, imply doctrines that can be discussed in a public realm, where we are obliged to offer reasons, as far as possible, for our choice of conceptualities.

b. The Coherence Model and the Claims of Scientific Realism

On the other end of the spectrum of positions concerning the problem of realism we have so-called *scientific realism*. Scientific realism goes beyond the bare-bones realism *that* there exists a mind-independent world with specific characteristics to which we aim to refer. It raises the additional claim that there exists some sort of correspondence between our scientific theories and the actual entities and structures of the real world. While metaphysical realism is directed against skeptical or idealistic ontologies, scientific realism is also directed against a positivism that wants to stay with the observables and their recurrent traits, and on the other hand, against a constructivism that interprets science as a mere instrument to cope with reality for our own purposes, regardless of the question of the nature of reality. Ian G. Barbour, in his *Issues in Science and Religion,* summarizes the contours of scientific realism in a helpful way:

> Against the positivist, the realist asserts that the real is not [just, NHG] the observable. Against the instrumentalist, he affirms that valid concepts are true as well as useful. Against the idealist, he maintains that concepts represent the structure of events in the world. The patterns in the data are not imposed by us, but originate at least in part in *objective relationships in nature.* (Barbour 1966, 168; Barbour's italics)

Thus, theories are not data. Nor are theories just theories about data since they intend to penetrate from observable data into the objective relations of the world behind the scene of data. Rather, we have a triangle of (a) *theories,* (b) *data,* and (c) *reality.*

Now, what is the stance of a coherence theory to the realist claims in scientific realism? I shall argue that coherence theory in fact supports scientific realism concerning the reference claims of science. In congruence with scientific realism, coherence theory denies the thesis of a complete incompatibility between scientific paradigms. According to a coherence theory, however, the testing of strict claims of scientific progress also demands a demonstration of conceptual progress as well as a translation of earlier successful theories in terms of the new theories.

According to scientific realism, the real is beyond the perceived data (though reality, of course, also expresses itself in the data). Furthermore, there exists a hundred years of theory continuity inside some of the sciences, and in this long period science has proven unreasonably effective. In Ernan McMullin's phrase, it could well have been that we lived "in a universe in which the observable regularities would not be explainable in terms of hidden structures" (McMullin 1984, 29). In fact, it was not until the eighteenth century that the scientific realist claim began to find some support on empirical grounds. This support consists of *fertility* in the prediction of novel facts, plus the *convergence* of explanatory models that are stabilized over a significant period of time in established sciences like physics, geology, and cell biology. In this sense, the criterion of internal coherence (beyond the boundaries of mere logical consistency) no doubt plays a pivotal role also in scientific realism.

Since Thomas Kuhn's book *The Structure of Scientific Revolutions* (1962), however, historians of science have disputed the idea of theory continuity even in the development of elementary physics. Larry Laudan, in particular, has pointed to some difficult cases for the scientific realist. The etheric theories of the late eighteenth and first part of the nineteenth century, for example, were by far the more successful explanation in the hard physics and chemistry of that time. This case is a counterexample of the scientific realist's empirical argument for the progress of science. In consequence, it is not only logically problematic but also empirically dubious to draw conclusions from the fertility of theories to the truth of their referents. Moreover, new theories do not always show an attempt to preserve the entities of earlier theories (Laudan [1981] 1991, 228f., 242f.). Kuhn and Laudan are thus representatives for an incompatibilist thesis over against scientific realism, parallel to Putnam's stance vis-à-vis metaphysical realism.

Laudan et al. have convincingly shown that the idea of a "convergent realism" through the general progress of the sciences is not unambiguously warranted by the history of the sciences. Ernan McMullin and other critical realists have therefore conceded that the realist claim cannot be held as a global thesis since it only extends to some of the more stable and successful scientific theories (McMullin 1994, 98). In other words, there is no rational reason to insist on a steady approximation to reality on behalf of "science" as such. Though most of us are inclined to *believe* in a progress in the natural sciences, grossly speaking, we only have *good reasons* to hold this view if we can pinpoint *where* and *when* progress occurs. Taking seriously the disunity of the sciences (see page 184) means therefore that one always has to argue piecemeal for the reality-claims of the different theories in the different branches of science.

On the other hand, Kuhn's and Laudan's historical test cases do not form any conclusive argument for a *global* antirealist thesis! It is, in fact, possible to show in some detail how concepts of later theories are able to incorporate the entities and structures to which the concepts of earlier theories referred. If the incompatibility thesis holds true, such a comparison would be a priori impossible. The coherence model, however, holds that this is nevertheless possible, though not universally.

The coherence model again opts for a *comparative* (indirect) procedure. Indeed, it may be the case that coherence is attainable only in a one-way direction. It could even be said to be a useful definition of a progressive theory, that it is able to translate, incorporate, and correct its predecessors, but not the other way around. Thus, there may be an *incompatibility*, seen from the point of view of the overflowed theory, while there may be a *coherence*, seen from the superior theory. Newtonian physics, for example, cannot translate Einstein's relativity theory, but relativity theory can, in fact, translate and critically incorporate classical physics. Relative progress may then be measured in terms of both the capacity for empirical specification and for semantic coherence. Philip Kitcher has recently pointed to the scientific progress involved in *conceptual clarification:*

> Conceptual progress is made when we adjust the boundaries of our categories to conform to kinds and when we are able to provide more specifications of our referents. (Kitcher 1993, 95f.)

The conceptual relativist of the Putnamian type would argue that each language creates a different world with different referents that cannot be compared since linguistic worlds are incommensurable. Let us nevertheless make a try and reconsider the ridiculed phlogiston theory of ether by Priestley, which is Larry Laudan's prime example.

Joseph Priestley (1733-1804) referred to ether as "the principle which is emitted in combustion and which is normally present in air"; Priestley therefore also referred to "dephlogisticated air" (cf. Kitcher 1993, 97-105). If we, with the hindsight of more than two hundred years, ask the question "Does the phlogiston theory have a referent?" the strict answer would apparently be "No," since no "principle" is "emitted" in combustion, and no hidden "ether" exists, either. Instead, Antoine Laurent Lavoisier (1743-1794) referred to "oxygen" as an "element" of the natural air. Despite all later refinements of chemistry, any chemist of today would think that Lavoisier found a real referent. The atomic structure of oxygen is well understood, and likewise the array of chemical constellations into which oxygen may enter. One could therefore interpret the development as a simple success story that demonstrates going from dark ignorance to true knowledge.

However, my point is that even here, in the case of the denounced ether theory, there is a continuity of both language and referent between Priestley and Lavoisier — when interpreted from the later theory. Lavoisier's own theory was in fact initiated by Priestley's account of his experiment. Lavoisier was in the audience when Priestley lectured in France, and a communication between the two chemists actually took place. But did they understand each other? Apparently yes. When reading Priestley's record of his experiment, his description is not wholly alien. He reports the following when he wanted to taste the dephlogisticated air that his test mice had been breathing:

> The feeling of it to my lungs was not sensibly different from that of common air; but I fancied that my breast felt particularly light and easy for some time afterwards. (Priestley 1775; quoted in Kitcher 1993, 100)

Anybody today easily recognizes the feeling of concentrated oxygen. At least on the phenomenological level of first-hand experience, communication between an ether- and an oxygen-theorist is not only possible but also fluent. It is on the theoretical level of explanation that difficulties begin. From the point of view of Lavoisier's later theory, however, one can translate Priestley's theory in a way that *preserves the intentional reference* of Priestley's theory. But why is the oxygen description better than the ether description? For two reasons, it seems. First, the description by Lavoisier is more specified with respect to its reference (an "element" is more identifiable than a "principle"); second, the elementary theory of oxygen is part and parcel of a research program that in two hundred years has shown a remarkable fitfulness inside chemistry. The conceptual progress is thus twofold, at once a higher level of specification empirically, and at the same time an increased coherence with other findings inside the web of chemical theories.

In much the same way, one can point to coherential backwards translations of earlier theories inside other branches of science: Mendel's "gene" can be reinterpreted as intentionally referring to the much more specified "gene" of the Crick-Watson model; the early Bohr-Rutherford model of the atoms can be reinterpreted as referring to the same entities as that of the orbital quantum theory of 1930s; Newton's corpuscle theory of light and the rival wave theory in continuation of Huygens are both interpretable in terms of relativistic field theories of light-quanta which have definite wavelengths, and so on. (Einstein and Infeld [1938] 1971, 257-265).

In these cases, I do not find reason to doubt the reality-claims of these sciences. Well-established chemical theories have shown an increasing empirical applicability inside a coherent explanatory scheme. The realist claims are grounded in the fact that the applicative and the theoretical cycles have historically reinforced one another. A corroboration by coherence has been achieved.

c. Coherence Theory and a Lakatosian Program for Theology

The coherence model is a general theory of rationality, not designed specifically for the natural sciences. This has the advantage that one does not need to change one's philosophy of rationality when proceeding from "nomothetic" sciences like physics to "ideographic" sciences like history and even to "systematic" disciplines like philosophy and theology. Coherence theory allows for the most different kind of data (seen as presumptive truth-candidates) like phenomenological first-hand experiences, religious experiences, traditions, scientific data — provided that none of these data are sacrosanct. All data are in need of conceptual framing, and likewise the other way around; that is, all theories need to show their applicability on data and to be clarified in their proper context.

What is an advantage in one respect, however, might be a failure in another respect. Nancey Murphy is among those who trace back the misconceptions of modern theology to its neglect of scientific empiricism: "I am suggesting that modern empiricist accounts of knowledge have created a crisis for theology, a crisis yet to be resolved" (Murphy 1994, 101). In her important book *Theology in the Age of Scientific Reasoning*, Murphy argues for a reconstruction of theology as an empirical research program. The thesis that "*(m)ethodology, not subject matter* has kept theology trailing behind in the age of science" (Murphy 1990, 127) might indicate the motivating drive behind her work. In particular, Murphy opts for Imre Lakatos's empiricist philosophy of science as a workable methodology also for theology. The question to be discussed here is whether her empiricist program is more workable than a coherence theory developed along the lines of Nicholas Rescher.

Like coherence theory, Murphy also endorses a *holistic* view of scientific knowledge. A postmodern empiricism acknowledges that our beliefs about reality are always formed in systems or webs of knowledge (Murphy 1990, 3-9; 1996). Science takes the form of grand scale research programs with no direct route to the particulars of data. With historians of science like Kuhn, Feyerabend, and Laudan, Murphy points to the difficulty in establishing a clear-cut line of demarcation between metaphysics and science. From the outset, therefore, it cannot be ruled out that theology can tranform itself into an empirical research program.

In the terminology of Lakotos, a research program consists of "methodological rules" telling us what pathways to avoid (negative heuristic) and which paths to pursue (positive heuristic). Any such research program (think of neo-Darwinism) entails a set of theories and a body of data. There will, however, always be a *hard-core level* of a program that cannot be directly tested (think of the idea that *all* life-forms have evolved in a uniform way). Thus, Karl Popper's idea of an instant falsifiability as the demarcation line between science and metaphysics does not hold. However, it is constitutive for a scientific theory that the hard core of the theory is connected with a network of *auxiliary hypotheses*. Internally, these auxiliary hypotheses serve as a "protective belt" around the hard core of the program. Externally, the auxiliary hypotheses link the general theory to empirical data which the whole theory claims to explain better than any other research program (think of mathematical models of selection; the biochemical DNA-RNA theory etc.). Thus, while the hard core delineates the negative heuristic (e.g., "do not look for separate species"), the auxiliary hypotheses are devices for the positive heuristic of the program (Lakatos [1978] 1992, 47-52; 92).

Now, according to Lakatos, research programs are not only succeeding each other, they are also simultaneously competing with each other. In continuation of Popper but in contrast to Kuhn and other incompatibilists, Lakatos aims at developing a rational reconstruction of the historical progress of science that at the same time provides a normative theory for deciding between competitive research programs. Nancey Murphy summarizes the following three main criteria for scientific progress from Lakatos:

(1) each new version of the theory (core theory plus its auxiliaries) preserves the unrefuted content of its predecessor;
(2) each has excess empirical content over its predecessor: that is, it predicts some novel, hitherto unexpected facts; and
(3) some of these predicted facts are corroborated (Murphy 1990, 59).

Above it was indicated how endogenous the preservation theory is to the coherence theory (ad 1). Furthermore, I would not doubt that a successful prediction of novel facts makes the strongest possible case for any empirical research program (ad 2-3). However, the immediate theological application by Murphy, saying that a rational theology can be evaluated according to its ability to *predict novel facts*, seems to me unworkable in the field of theology (as it would probably be in philosophy, also). Murphy's Lakatosian approach to theology builds upon three claims: (1) There do exist large-scale research programs in theology with empirically testable consequences. (2) Some of them have actually proven themselves to be, at least in part, empirically progressive. (3) Theology should be reconstructed as a forum for competitive research programs, aiming to predict "novel facts" (cf. 1990, 86, 183).

I would admit there are reasons that invite a Lakatosian approach along these lines. First, Christian theology seems in fact to be built upon a hard-core theory: that God the Creator exists, that God has revealed Godself in Jesus, that God is threefold, and so on. According to the Lakatosian scheme, it is not an anomaly if theology rests on such "dogmatic" or "metaphysical" tenets. No science is in fact unprejudiced: all data are theory-laden, and the justification of a research program is always circular (Murphy 1990, 184f.; 1994, 104-106). So far, Murphy can make a "you too" argument to the philosophers of science who want to rule out theology among the sciences (1990, 163; 1994, 119f).

Second, the Lakatosian approach directs the energy into the positive heuristic: the hard work of theology consists in the development of "auxiliary hypotheses" (like a theory of the need for revelation, of criteria for spiritual discernment of God) that are more proximate to the "data" of theology (like scripture, tradition, and religious experience). It is on the level of auxiliary hypotheses that we find a wrestling with the contents of theology in close contact with the different strands of data which a theology is expected to account for. The promise of a Lakatosian program for theology, as I see it, is its impetus for striving towards such specification of the *substantial* issues of Christian life and doctrine.

From the point of view of the coherence model, however, Murphy's insistence on theology's ability to predict "novel facts" appears to be somewhat awkward. The coherence model only demands that any (theological) point of view should be able to incorporate the most different kinds of "data" (specified as "candidates for something being presumably true") in such a way that the interrelations between theological and non-theological truth-candidates are specified (this demand, of course, also entails the possibility that theological hypotheses cannot stand a coherence test). But why should "accounting for" or "making intelligible" mean the same as "predicting novel facts" by invoking God as "explanation" of facts? At this point, two important differences between the coherence model and the Lakatosian model show up.

(1) To the coherence model, it makes no difference whether the data accounted for are novel or well-known, used or not used before. The process of interrelation and systematization goes on continuously and synchronously, and the criterion of success is comprehensiveness rather than the ability to predict specific outcomes in the future. *There is no reason to denounce a "post hoc theorizing" in general.* Prediction (which does play a decisive role in the empirical sciences) is itself a limited case of comprehensiveness, namely, with respect to new data.

(2) To the coherence model, "all knowledge is essentially of one piece" (Rescher 1992, 163). Of course, there might be different levels of abstraction. There is, however, no definite breach between theory and data, *explanans* and *explanandum,* since the demand of coherence is fundamentally one of interrelation and interaction between the different parts of knowledge. Causal explanation (A⇒B), for example, is a limited case of an interrelation (A⇔B), by which the exact specification of the relationship is made. There exist not only causal relations but also relations of logic and meaning. To Lakatos (and Murphy) however, the prediction of novelties is the hallmark of being a progressive rather than a degenerating science, if not a pseudoscience. Lakatos wishes explicitly to rule out the cases of a "post hoc theorizing":

> Thus in a progressive research program, theory leads to the discovery of hitherto unknown novel facts. In degenerating programs, however, theories are fabricated only in order to accomodate known facts. Has, for instance, Marxism ever predicted a stunning novel fact successfully? Never! (Lakatos [1978] 1992, 5)

Though Murphy proposes an improvement of Lakatos's concept of "novel facts," she still wants to conserve the independence between theory and data, so that the data remain "new" in relation to the theory:

> A fact is novel if it is not used in the construction of the theory T that it is taken to confirm. A fact not used in the construction of a theory is one whose existence, relevance to T, or interpretability in light of T is first documented after T is proposed. (1990, 68)

However, if scripture and theological tradition belong to the data of theology, "novel facts" would not be expected to be pivotal to any theory of theological data. To the contrary, a certain *replicability* — a continuous and successful application of a consistent view of reality — would seem to be a better criterion of rationality than predictive power. Murphy admits this problem, insofar as she is looking for "novel yet replicable fact(s)" (1990, 167). The favorite candidate of Murphy is the prediction of stable changes in attitudes and language usage among believers. By example, Murphy refers to the doctrine of the Holy Spirit in the book *The Divine Mother* by the Jesuit Donald Gelpi. Murphy thinks that Gelpi's historical and constructive work, if successful, "predicts that prayer addressed to the Holy Spirit as 'she' will become an accepted practice" (1990, 167). Provided that this new religious usage was not directly influenced by Donald Gelpi's work, it would, according to Murphy's definition, be "a novel fact" in the sense of "not previously used" as a confirmation by the theory itself.

It would appear, however, that Murphy here conflates two levels of theory: the *level of reasons* and the *level of empirical causes*. Gelpi in fact wants to show the applicability of feminine language to the Holy Spirit on theological grounds; Gelpi's case for such an appropriateness could well be made with reference to data from the imageries of scripture and tradition, new theories of the importance of metaphors, and so on — without any implicit reference to a future empirical change in the practice of prayer. Addressing the Holy Spirit as feminine could still be a reasonable option for a Catholic without being actualized in a larger social scale in the future. It seems to me that Rescher's perspectival pluralism does better justice to this multidimensional character of human knowledge, which is in some aspects metaphysical, in other aspects physical, in some aspects factual, in other aspects optional. Though these aspects are not unrelated, they are not reducible to one another.

Let us now turn to Murphy's prime example of a theological research program: Catholic Modernism around the turn of the twentieth century. If George Tyrell thinks that papal absolutism is a passing phase in Catholicism, it seems to me that he may be right for one of two sorts of reasons, normative or descriptive: (1) he might be right because there *should not* be any papal absolutism, since one *cannot* account in a sufficiently reasonable way for a papal absolutism on the theological and non-theological data of scripture, tradition, and religious experience; or (2) there will *not* be any papal absolutism in one hundred years time. It is logically fully consistent to endorse (1) without position (2), and position (2) without position (1). This shows — inevitably I think — that empirical facts of future history cannot decide the metaphysical question of normative statements and meaning. However, they are not unrelated, either: according to the coherence model, any anomaly — like the conflict between an acceptance of the absolutism of

papacy and the dismissal of claims of absoluteness in all other areas —
does place a specific burden of giving reasons for such an anomaly. In
an indirect sense, therefore, facts and values are interrelated.

Murphy, however, is not content with a coherential interrelation
between different sectors of knowledge. She demands from the side of
theology an explanation entailing God as *explanans* and empirical predictions as *explanandum*. However, since prediction of novelties is pivotal for
her theory, God must be seen as more than an explanation for the
existence and character of the world at large. (That would be "post hoc
theorizing.") Seeing theology as an empirical research program, Murphy
has to invoke God for explaining empirically why something particular
has happened or is going to happen. An example of this sort of theological
explanation, in continuation of some data themselves, is the following:

E_1 The Quakers freed their slaves, because God commanded them
to do so.

A more secular explanation would run as follows:

E_2 The Quakers freed their slaves because they judged that this was
the command of God (cf. Murphy 1990, 163).

Murphy seems to hold the position not only that E_1 is as appropriate
as the more guarded claim in E_2 but that there can even be better
reasons for holding the first rather than the second. At least, Murphy
underscores the possibility of competitions between theological and
scientific research programs when explaining religious experience
(1990, 199). A competition, however, means that the theological and
the scientific research programs want to explain "the same thing" only
with different predictions. Except for specific cases of doomsday proph-
ecy and so on, I cannot see how this program can work in practice.[5]

---

5. Murphy's empiricist emphasis also stands and falls with relatively strong
ties between the auxiliary hypotheses and the data. After all, Lakatos — following
Hempel's Covering Law Model — uses the method of hypothetical deductions. Also
in theological application, Murphy sometimes seems to presuppose logical deductions (Murphy 1990, 186): "The auxiliaries must be consequences of the hard core,
and the data consequences of the auxiliaries"), while she at other times admits that
the relations are only "quasi-deductive" (1990, 189). In the same vein, she also
admits "prediction" can be taken "in a sort of timeless sense" (1990, 190); in this
case, however, she can hardly rule out the possibility of "post hoc theorizing."

The coherentist alternative would be to place theology among the "systematic" disciplines (alongside philosophy) rather than among the "nomothetic sciences" like physics. The coherentist emphasis is about how to "make sense" of the different aspects of the world rather than how to give a "causal explanation" of specific processes of reality. The primary role of theology is therefore, in my view, to form proposals about *the interrelations of meanings,* seen from the specific resources of Christian tradition, rather than offering *causal explanations* in competition with non-theological alternatives. Important as it is to clarify the perspectival difference between theology and the natural sciences, it should nonetheless be underlined that theology cannot establish its "proprium" outside the world of the empirical sciences. The rational character of theology is exactly given with its *ability to redescribe* still broader ranges of experience, and with its readiness to revise its previous theories where they have become homeless in the texture of human knowledge (or ethics). This redescriptive ability of theological research could well include (in the line of Murphy's approach) new kinds of data "not previously used" by the preceding research traditions. New theoretical and empirical developments are primary examples of such "novel facts." In any case, the interpretative role of theology is about the "framing" of experience (data) rather than about the prediction of future religious habits.[6]

The difficult question for the coherence theory is, of course, *how* are we to determine whether our theological redescriptions are plausible or not, and *which* among them are the more plausible? I do not see any general answer to this question. The only possibility seems to delve into *particular areas* in science and theology. In other words, we first have to take our point of departure in the pragmatic problem-situation: in those areas that are most sensitive to contacts and conflicts between science and theology. Examples are "anthropic principle," "evolution and creation," "sociobiology and ethics." Second, in each case we should take our starting point, not in an assumed commonplace, as in foundationalism, but in those theological positions that have formed *elaborated clusters of theories* that propose how to *specify* the interrelation between (specific theories of) theology and (specific theories of) science. Only

6. Interestingly, Philip Hefner's looser application of Lakatosian concepts in his "Theology of the Created Co-Creator" does not raise any specifically empirical claims on behalf of theology but has rather a redescriptive, "framing" character: Theology has to do with an "interpretation" of scientific theories about empirical data (Hefner 1993, 23-25).

then do we come to the third level where the "coherence machinery" begins to work. The coherence works by sifting out the poorer solutions in order to rescue and further develop the potentials of the presumably better ones. Like evolution, the coherence model works by a *method of exclusion* rather than a method of amplification.

In this framework, Nancey Murphy's emphasis on the need for developing *middle-range auxiliary hypotheses,* so much closer to the empirical data than the general theological ideas, is of utmost importance. The difference is that while Murphy (more boldly) wishes to develop the incorporation of facts in accordance with the scheme of empirical explanations, I think that a more important role should be attached to the constructive elaboration of a theological semantics that is able to redescribe the phenomena already explained by the sciences.

What we can expect to find in the science-theology dialogue, then, is hardly progress in terms of a steady approximation to the realities of "God" and "world," but it may include elements of a *comparative progress* concerning the conceptual specification of the multiple interrelations between science and theology. After all, there is good reason to believe that those theologies of creation today which have learned (by "post hoc theorizing"!) to incorporate Darwinian theory are "better" — more encompassing, more specified — than the theology of creation by even a great theologian like Schleiermacher at the beginning of the nineteenth century.

IV. Darwinism: A Test Case for the Asymmetrical Coherence Model

Wentzel van Huyssteen has, in this volume, pointed to the "epistemic consonances" between theology and the sciences. In particular, he draws our attention to the broader concept of rationality in Rescher's epistemology that addresses not only the cognitive but likewise the evaluative and pragmatic dimensions of the pursuit of truth. The problem of consonance, however, should also be addressed on the *contentual* level. Nicholas Rescher's double-edged knife of coherence machinery (conceptual self-substantiation *and* pragmatic applicability) seems to me to be a promising tool to cope with the problem of cognitive pluralism also in the material interaction between science and theology.

This section shall thus be devoted to illustrating the applicative cycle of the coherence theory on a classical test case: creation theology and Darwinian theory. I shall investigate five levels of coherence: (a) data, (b) theories, (c) thought models, (d) metaphors, and (e) world-views. Before doing so, I wish to meet the claim raised by the non-integrative camp (in this volume represented by Eberhard Herrmann), that it is impossible to make theological statements so as to include scientific elements. Hybrid scientifico-theological sentences are fundamentally flawed, it is said. Not always so, I shall rejoin.

a. Coherence Theory and the Assessment of Hybrid Sentences

Let us think of two sentences like these:

(1) Human beings have evolved through a macromolecular structure of DNA and RNA by way of transmitting and recombining this genetic material from one generation to the other.

and

(2) God, thou creator of heavens and earth, help me to find my way through these days of sorrow!

Obviously, it would be a category mistake to fuse the contents of these two sentences belonging to different languages and situations. We would end up conflating a scientific statement and a religious prayer, an assertive speech act with a directive speech act, a global and a local statement, impersonal and personal language. The avoidance of such hybrids might be a central motivation behind conceptual relativism.

But would that mean that there are no possibilities of contextual interlinkage? I think not. For though utterances themselves are not always referential (they may have the form of expression, invocations, etc.), the speakers of such utterances in fact always presuppose some background assumptions (Searle [1979] 1996, 117-119). For example, one only invokes God on the presupposition that God exists, and within the perspective of an ultimate horizon of faith. In distinction from first-order religious utterances, theology can be understood as a way of transforming the pluriform and "wild" religious life (entailing first person commitments, second person prescription, doxological expressions, etc.) into a more disciplined and "tamed" second-order language. In this process, I would argue that theology may even construct *hybrid sentences* that combine scientific and theological elements. Consider a simple but typical example:

(3) Selection seems to be the way in which God continually creates and transforms the world.

The question is whether a sentence like this is meaningful at all. While nonintegrationists deny this, coherentists affirm the meaningfulness of such hybrid sentences.[7] A coherence theory, however, wants to qualify its affirmation of hybrid sentences. From a coherentist perspective, a hybrid sentence may not only make sense but is also rationally justifiable provided that it is possible to specify:

(a) *how* the theological content relates to the scientific content

and

(b) the proper *context* of a sentence like (3).

As to (a), one could say that the contextual interlinkage is attained through a differentiation of the actor-level (God "creates and transforms") and the level of the means (selection as God's "way"). For the meaning of the sentence it is important that there exist *no logical connection* between divine action and the presumed fact of selection. God possibly could create and transform in other ways than the game of selection (and does so, according to Judeo-Christian doctrines of creation, on both the physical and the psychological level). Therefore, one cannot make deductions in the other direction, from the nature of selection to the nature of God. The coherence model therefore pushes the further question: How is the idea of God's love compatible with the

---

7. By the way, if hybrid sentences were not allowed, many forms of religious language would be occluded also. Religious language is not very often formal and "clean," though liturgical praxis creates embryonic rules for conduct and religious intellectual traditions formulate grammars for speaking a religious language. However, religious language, as performed in meditations, prayers, hymns, sermons, etc., uses metaphors and symbols from the most different sectors of life, including science. When modern hymns refer to our planet not only as the "world" but also as the fragile and vulnerable "globe," we find a resonance of modern science inside religious language, looking at the globe from the outside space and knowing the fragility of highly developed life-forms. Obviously, religious language is inventive and therefore relatively anarchistic.

hard selection processes of biology? Thus, sentence (3) succeeds in establishing a "characteristic relation" (Rescher) between two different levels, and imposes on theology the burden of entertaining further inquiries.

As to (b), the question of the context of the sentence, it must be clarified that the same words can be used in different meanings. The word "way" in sentence (3) obviously refers to a global notion of divine action that should not be confused with local biographical perspective of "finding my way" in sentence (2).[8] In (3) we have thus a theological sentence that correlates a specific scientific theory with a likewise specific Christian belief. Obviously, we are in the context of secondary theological reflection, not on the primary level of religious perceptions.

This might all seem rather trivial. After all, the theological redescription so far was *generic* in nature, that is, we could as well have placed other scientific theories (big bang theory, quantum theory, etc.) as the means by which God is claimed to have created the world. The nontrivial character of the coherence model comes to the fore when the criteria of coherence are applied critically in the analysis of more *particular* theses inside science-theology debate. This is the aim of the following examples of contextual interlinkage, ranging from the issues of data and theories to the issues of thought models, metaphors, and worldviews.

b. Contextual Interlinkage

1: Redescription of Data

The simplest form of assimilation is an incorporation of scientific data. The history of the struggle of theologians to come to terms with Darwinism shows, however, that endemic problems arise already at this level. Theology always runs the double risk of either conflating theological and scientific language or of prematurely putting barriers to the coherence process. The evangelical spokesman for a religious Darwinism, Henry Drummond, may be said to have succumbed to the first danger, John Henry Cardinal Newman to the second.

In his *Ascent of Man* of 1894, Henry Drummond phrased his position in the following words: "Evolution is seen to be neither more nor less than

8. As to the difference between the global creator language and the local language of God as providence, see Gregersen 1997.

the story of creation told by those who know it best" (4). An assimilation of data, however, already imposes a demand for coherence on theology. Drummond wants to meet this demand by seeing evolution as the "method" by which God sustains and develops the world of creation, while the notion of creation is left to do with the origins of the world:

> There is only one theory of the method of Creation in the field, and that is evolution; but there is only one theory of origins in the field, and that is creation. Instead of abolishing a creative Hand, Evolution demands it. (1894, 421)

Drummond here proposes a kind of leveling between a theology of creation and Darwinism. He acknowledges that the concept of creation is homeless inside science but still he claims that scientists are either tacit about origins or they will have to take recourse to the idea of God. Drummond does not ask, however, whether his own synthesis measures up to the criterion of adequacy with respect to the *peculiarities* of theological and scientific data, respectively. His appraisal of Darwinism is a generic adoption, not a specified account on the interrelation between science and theology. This lack of specificity has consequences. Drummond is utterly optimistic concerning the evolutionary trend in general, and he therefore applies evolutionary principles to all areas of human culture. Thus, on the theological side Drummond opts for a wholly immanent God who is expressing the divine will in the very course of evolution:

> Those who yield to the temptation to reserve a point here and there for special divine interposition are apt to forget that this virtually excludes God from the rest of the process. If God appears periodically, He disappears periodically. . . . Positively, the idea of an immanent God, which is the God of Evolution, is definitely grander than the occasional Wonder-worker, who is the God of an old theology. (1894, 428)

While the denial of any doctrine of divine intervention is a real theological option (Drummond's position here echoes the position of earlier Christian Darwinists like Charles Kingsley or Aubrey Lackington Moore), it becomes increasingly clear that Drummond does not only see *God as acting in and through* the processes of evolution — evolution being the "method of God" — but evolution is nothing less than an increasing *revelation* of God:

> Evolution is Advolution; better, it is Revelation — the phenomeno-
> logical expression of the Divine, the progressive realization of the
> Ideal, the Ascent of Love. (1894, 435)

But if nature in this straightforward way is "God's writing" that "can
only tell the truth" (1894, 427), then Drummond runs into quite a few
incoherencies. On the biological side, Drummond clearly overstates
Darwinism. Darwin's evolutionary theory is not a global world-
explanation about physics, biology, and the welfare of human culture.
Without noticing the inconsistencies of data, Drummond in fact endorses a Spencerian metaphysics of evolution rather than a Darwinian
theory.[9] Drummond neglects all the elements of Darwinian theory that
are not consonant with his overall theological theory, like the wasteful-
ness of nature, the neglect of the individual, the disappearance of love
in the selection processes, and, most importantly, the absence of
guarantees of an overall evolutionary progress. Also from a theological
point of view, his position may be judged as inconsistent with theological
data. Drummond's position implies that God is not only omnipresent
but also manifest everywhere. The Christian conviction of the ultimate
good of salvation is conflated with inner-historical progress, eschato-
logical hope with expectations for the immanent future to come.

　　Drummond's synthesis is thus in a deep (though concealed) conflict with biological as well as with theological data. His proposal neither
matches the criterion of comprehensiveness with respect to data nor
the criterion of adequacy with respect to the particular data. As we have
seen, inner consistency does not suffice as a criterion for rational coherence; it is no coincidence that the title of his book was not "Descent
of Man" but "Ascent of Man."

　　I have gone into some detail with Drummond's position in order
to show that a coherence theory does not support conflatory syntheses
that do not account for the distinctiveness of different data and theories.
Coherence does not mean creating a homogeneous world picture but
demands a circumspection with respect to data. The ideal of coherence
is the constructing of a complex raft-building of human knowledge.

　　The other risk consists in an unwillingness to take the evolutionary

---

9. In his magistral study, James R. Moore (1981, 217-251) has shown that the
majority of liberal theologians in fact were metaphysical Spencerians or "Darwini-
cists." According to Moore's analysis, the more orthodox theologians were more
likely to be Christian Darwinists who took account of Darwinism as a specific biological theory.

theory into account as a fact. I can be rather brief on this point, since the examples of an ad hoc barrier with respect to science is easily seen as entailing an incoherence. John Henry Newman himself introduced evolutionary ideas in his work *On the Development of Christian Dogma* of 1845, and he thus might be expected to have been theologically prepared for Darwin's later theory of 1859. A closer look, however, shows that Newman's concept of development was organic rather than Darwinian. Evolution is seen as a harmonious branching of a tree which also needs some continuous pruning. Moreover, when it comes to the descent of human beings from apes, Newman altogether refuses this possibility since it is in conflict with the "sufficient ground I determined to come from heaven" (Newman [1870] 1979, 207). Not only is this an ad hoc argument, but it is an argument which wants to give theological data a priority in areas that are closer to scientific than to theological domains. We have to do here with the fallacy of misplaced concreteness.

2: Critical Incorporation of Theories

It is only on the level of theories that we find more serious efforts at reinterpreting Darwinism theologically. Above, we saw that one cannot incorporate data theologically without redescribing the scientific theories accounting causally for those data. We find an outstanding example of an attempt like this in Frederick Temple (who eventually became archbishop of Canterbury). In his Bampton Lectures, *The Relation between Religion and Science* of 1884, Frederick Temple not only took the evolutionary narrative for granted, he also adopted the principles of variation and selection in Darwin's biological theory. He was even able to engage in the conflict between Darwin's and Lamarck's different interpretations of evolutionary mechanisms, a conflict that was not settled at that time.

Nevertheless, Temple did contest Darwin's gradualism on two points: (1) the emergence of life from matter, and (2) the emergence of morality from life. In the case of the emergence of life, he could point out that the current scientific theories failed to explain the phenomenon of life. Temple took this failure to be a fundamental one (1884, 171); at this point, he argued *ex ignorantia*, from the actual ignorance of the sciences of his time, and rather than expecting progress in the sciences, he took recourse to a causal theological explanation in terms of a "miracle." Any such argument *ex ignorantia* is risky, of course, but from a coherential point of view, Temple's step was possible, given the actual ignorance of microevolutionary processes of his day. However, given today's scientific truth-candidates concerning autocatalytic chemical processes, Temple's position would certainly fail in a test of coherence.

Less risky and more convincing even today was Frederick Temple's argument with respect to values. Here it was the built-in universality in the claims of morality that Temple could not see as evolved from animal life-forms:

> Evolution may lead the creature to say what is hateful and what is lovable, what is painful and what is delightful, what is to be feared and what is to be sought; it may develop the sentiment which comes nearest of all to the sentiment of reverence, namely, the sentiment of shame; but it cannot reveal the eternal character of the distinction between right and wrong . . . the principle of the Moral Law, its universality, its supremacy, cannot come out of any development of human nature any more than the necessity of mathematical truth can so come. It stands not on experience, and is its own evidence. (1884, 179f.)

Temple here states a difference of *meaning* between the particular and always conditioned route of emergence and the universal and unconditional character of moral demands. As such, he can be interpreted as arguing for a perspectival difference between the *causal question* of origins (the realm of the Darwinian theory) and the *meaning question* of the consequents of these origins (the realm of philosophical and theological analysis). Evolution and morality are in this sense put into a "characteristic relation" to one another.

What is then the formal difference between Newman's argument and Temple's, in terms of coherence? The difference is that Temple, in contrast to Newman, was able to work out his dual perspectival theory in detail while pointing to the fact that not only the status of morality but also the status of mathematics presuppose a departure from the realm of the historical vicissitudes. Like ethics, science itself is about laws that exist prior to the evolutionary development, and prior to their discovery by the human mind (Temple 1884, 127-132). Thus, in Temple's case there is no ad hoc barrier. On the contrary, he makes his case by appealing to the criteria of coherence both where there are similarities and where there are differences between science and theology.

The Danish theologian Eduard Geismar, publishing his book on *Kristendom og udvikling* (tr. *Christianity and Development*) in 1903, may be seen as a theologian who combined elements from both Drummond and Temple, and formed them into a coherent structure. With Drummond, Geismar points to the fact that natural mothering instinct is the source of moral altruism; yet following Darwin rather than Drummond, Geismar also traces the root of brutality back to parental care and group-formation, since these phenomena are always combined with an aggression towards nonkin and outgroups. Geismar points out that the feeling of solidarity inside the group at the same time creates feelings of a conspiracy, very much like those of criminals (Geismar 1903, 27-34). With Temple, Geismar therefore takes the view that morality cannot be understood fully as a physico-biological phenomenon. In contrast to Temple, however, he wisely avoids interfering theologically in the biological explanation of history: "The *origin* of a specific attitude says nothing of the *legitimacy* of this attitude" (Geismar 1903, 39).

This overall solution of Geismar might count as an example of a position that balances cognitive coordination and perspectival plurality with respect to the data and theories of his time. We are here in the midst of a discussion which has continuously taken place from Thomas Huxley up to the recent discussions between sociobiology and theology.

3: Stimulation by Thought Models

More neglected in the science-theology discussion but not less important is the interaction of *thought models* between science and theology. Already in the very first post-Darwinian controversies, the hardest debates were in fact not about the descent of man and apes from common ancestors (the "data" level); the far grander issue was the complex of ideas clustered around the notion of *teleology*. The effect of Darwin's theory of selection (the "theory" level) was in fact an abolition of a widespread idea of design in the natural theology of that time (the "thought model" level).

Notions of design, however, are not uniform. In the doctrinal tradition of Thomas Aquinas, the idea of teleology can be found in the notion of God's eternal plan *(ratio)* for creation. The teleology thus both begins in God and ends in God, in the return of history to the confrontation with divine judgment. Inside natural theology, however, ideas of teleology were seen as having their proper ends within the world of creation. A transition took place from transcendent to immanent teleologies. But also inside natural theology, the notions of design were pluriform. In particular, in William Paley's *Natural Theology* of 1802, the thought model of teleology was found in the many cases of an apparent "prospective contrivance" (Brooke 1994, 56-58). The eye seems created for the light, and vice versa, and anyone perceiving such an aptitude would conclude that it was intended to be so, just as we infer from finding a watch that there has been a watchmaker. It was this appearance of a preestablished contrivance that Darwin was able to explain naturalistically, in terms of a preceding selection process devoid of any notion of final causality.

Often this story is pictured as the ultimate downfall of teleology. And in fact, the idea that contrivance and fittingness prove the existence of God broke down. The ideas of a transcendent teleology in the doctrinal tradition, however, widely survived. In a Lakatosian terminology, one could say that an important auxiliary hypothesis fell down but not the hard-core notion of divine design. New auxiliary hypotheses therefore had to be developed. As John Hedley Brooke has recently shown, one of these ideas was that the laws of nature, in particular the principle of selection, were themselves designed by God (Brooke 1994, 58-61). Frederick Temple was a proponent of this view. Temple refers to Paley's argument that the evidence of design would not be lessened if the watch was so constructed that in the course of time, it would produce another watch like itself. According to Temple, the teleological argument is even stronger on the basis of evolution:

> It would become more marvellous than ever if we found provision thus made not merely for the continuance of the species but for the perpetual improvement of the species. (Temple 1884, 112)

It is in this context of rescuing Paley's argument for design that Temple made his famous saying: "He did not make themselves, we may say: no, but he made them make themselves" (1884, 115). Again, for an evaluation of Temple's attempt to rescue the design argument it is important whether Temple argues in an ad hoc manner or not. I think in fact that Temple may be said to provide a new form of teleology that takes Darwinian gradualism into account. Temple's notion of divinely designed laws encompasses the laws of the constituent parts of matter, the laws of gravitation, the laws of chemistry, but "above all the law of life, the mysterious law which plainly contains such wonderful possibilities within itself" (1884, 116). In this redescription of reality, the many ad hoc contrivances of Paley are still valuable on the phenomenological level of everyday life, but they no longer have the status of being a proof for the existence of a providential God. Stimulated by the emerging

Darwinian thought pattern, however, Temple adds a transformed picture of a continuous though manifold display of one coherent divine intent:

> To the many partial designs which Paley's Natural Theology points out, and which still remain what they are, the doctrine of evolution adds the design of a perpetual progress. Things are so arranged that animals are perpetually better adapted to the life they have to live. The very phrase which we commonly use to sum up Darwin's teaching, the survival of the fittest, implies a perpetual diminuation of pain and increase of enjoyment for all creatures that can feel. (1885, 117f.)

From this quotation, however, it also becomes clear that Temple did not face the real challenge of Darwinism, namely that the selection process is continuously "red in tooth and claw." First, a general evolutionary "progress" is not guaranteed by Darwinian theory. Second, "progress" does not diminish waste and pain, it rather increases the sensibility to pain as well as to pleasure. Nevertheless, even if Temple's theological incorporation of Darwinian throught models was far from complete, his theory was a substantial advance in relation to Paley's.

When a later Bampton lecturer like A. R. Peacocke refers to the "propensity" for increased complexity as "built-in and intended by God" (Peacocke 1993, 156, cf. 65-69, 152-157), he can be seen as a twentieth-century follower of Temple's general approach. The generic approval of the laws for development, however, is qualified by Peacocke in at least two important respects. First, Peacocke guards himself from the general optimism of a Frederick Temple. From an evolutionary point of view, pleasure is not overthrowing pain; pleasure and pain have a common root in the capacity for sensibility. Second, Peacocke's theological Darwinism also includes an element of chance. Chance is no longer seen as the antipode of order. Rather, to have a flexible order, a proportion of chance is expedient. God does in fact throw the dice, but "the dice are loaded" (in the expression by Karl R. Popper). According to the coherence criteria of specificity and comprehensiveness, we find a new relative progress.

The restructuring of the design model is one example that shows how scientific thought models have been catalysts of an internal theological reconstruction of thought models. Another example is the reevaluation of the *principle of locality* implied in neo-Darwinian theory. There might be a general upward trend in evolution, but the alterations that have led to improvements are always taking place in local settings.

It is the mutations of *individual organisms* (mutations happening spontaneously or due to accidental environmental circumstances) that introduce novelty into the gene pool of a *population* that in the end might lead to a substantial change in the *species*. Evolution is shortsighted but with far-reaching effects. Redescribed theologically, it is always in the *local processes* that God's creation and renewal takes place, though with consequences for the entire further course of evolution. From this purview, it would seem apt to supplement the picture of evolution as a continuous law-like process with a picture of the local histories of evolution, putting a new emphasis on the importance of the individual processes (Gregersen 1994, 138-141). Thus, the Darwinian thought pattern implies that our ideas of "types" and "species" are abstractions relative to the actual processes. Type-specifications do not designate self-identical substances; they are rather abbreviations for similarities between organisms that have adjusted themselves to a narrower or broader aspect of life-niches, and are able to reproduce themselves.

The principle of locality may also offer a new way of understanding the nature of *laws of nature*. Natural laws may themselves be seen as the conjoined product of general mathematical laws *and* of the parameters stemming from local processes (think of the laws of genetics). It is therefore reasonable to think (though it is still controversial) that our mathemical modeling of the probability distributions of biological processes are not designating self-identical laws: they rather summarize typical constellations of the interaction between organism and environment. "Laws," then, are neither eternal necessities nor are they depicting everlasting properties in objects. Rather they point to *typical interactions embedded in local situations*. On the physical and chemical level, these situations are so uniform that we are able to measure the propensities. But as pointed out by Karl R. Popper, in many cases "the propensities cannot be weighted because the relevant situation changes and cannot be repeated. . . . It is unique" (Popper 1990, 17).

This sense of uniqueness of the world and of the principle of locality seems to me all-important also for a theology of creation. Rephrased theologically, it is in the midst of the peculiarities of biological life that the future course of evolution is to be decided. A creative transformation of patterns and probabilities takes place in the course of evolution.[10]

---

10. I have proposed an extensive interpretation of such autopoietic processes in terms of a theology of creation in Gregersen 1998.

4 and 5: Metaphors and Worldviews

The incorporation of data, theories, and thought models is in my view the level where the coherence model works best by bringing the interlocutors in science and theology into a rational procedure. There are two other examples of contextual interlinkage, however, of equal importance, though less susceptible to rationalization.

One such linkage is the *exchange of metaphors* between science and theology. A more recent example of an inventive cross-fertilization between biology and theology has been made by Holmes Rolston in his article "Does Nature Need to Be Redeemed?" Rolston here redescribes the theological concept of creation through the biological metaphor of "birthing." Just as in the process of birthing, pain and superabundance are simultaneously present in the world of creation. Rephrased theologically, God continuously creates through the suffering of the individuals *(creatio per passionem)*. The symbol of the cross points at the co-presence of death and new life, and a similar co-presence takes place in the midst of creation. Thus the metaphor of "birthing," adopted from biology, has internal repercussions in theology for structuring the relationship between the first and the second article of faith. On the other hand, Rolston also applies a theological metaphor on biological phenomena: The pain of the prey is "re-deemed" by the pleasure of the predator, Rolston says (1994, 212f., 217-219).

This is not the place to discuss Rolston's model extensively. My point is only that an exchange of metaphors may take place between theology and biology, whereby new interpretations of nature are opened up. Just as metaphors in theology are important heuristic tools for constructing new theories, so also at the cutting edge of science, metaphors serve to open up a new field of study. An exchange of metaphors between science and theology, however, would always await a clarification on the levels of data and theories in order to be justified.

Another important level is the interlinkage between science and theology on *the level of worldviews*. I think, however, that there is a bold step from reinterpreting scientific theories theologically (or philosophically) to developing a world picture. The vestiges of such attempts are, to me at least, not very appealing though sometimes admirable. One may think of the work of Paley, Haeckel, and Teilhard de Chardin as examples of theological, scientific, or hybrid scientifico-theological worldviews, respectively. "About evolution, theory itself has again and again been distorted by biases flowing from over-simple, unbalanced world-pictures," Mary Midgley rightly remarks (Midgley 1985, 5-6), and she points especially at social Darwinism and the "Escalator Fallacy": the idea of a general progressivism. It may be prudent to remind ourselves that neo-Darwinism is a biological theory of genes and local environments, not a theory about everything from gas to genius.

History thus gives us reason to think that the maps of our world-views involve a massive elimination of facts that we have no reason to disbelieve. They should therefore be taken as practical guides rather than as well-established pictures of reality. On the other hand, as Midgley also reminds us, world pictures are unavoidable, since they comply with our deep-seated striving for unity of knowledge and need for a practical orientation.

In this context, a coherence theory of the Rescher-type would impose on any worldview both a criterion of *comprehensiveness* with respect to the totality of data included and a criterion of *circumspectiveness* in the way by which a problem-area is seen from different angles. Worldviews should be able to *specify* their relation to different data, coming both from within and from without the sciences, and make clear how they relate the different areas of experience, knowledge, and values to one another. By definition, a worldview can therefore not be "scientific" in the strict sense of claiming that the scientific approach is sufficient. But neither can a rational worldview be antiscientific. The neglect of well-established scientific models for understanding the world would in itself be a sign of a failing circumspectiveness, since the sciences represent some of the "best bets" we have. Worldviews are thus maps of reality, although a map is not the world itself, but only a practical guide for orientation.

Even though the coherence theory takes all knowledge as being essentially "of one piece," a pragmatic coherence theory certainly opts for a practical reasoning that proceeds piecemeal in the construction of overall orientations, drawing from the data and theories of various contexts of human knowledge. The coherence theory starts neither from putatively safe data, nor does it begin with a massive elimination of more questionable data. Rather, we begin in the multitude of data, scientific and nonscientific, and then proceed slowly by ruling out the incredible elements of human knowledge. Thus, the coherence theory does not claim to purport universal solutions to worldview questions. But it does offer some guidelines and some criteria for the pursuit of truth also in worldview matters. Respecting perspectival pluralism means being committed to an intellectual versatility that gives justice to each context of human inquiry (from physics to religious life), and yet at the same time opting for the comparatively surer pathways inside each domain. From here — from the most specified theories inside science and inside theology, respectively — the search for a consonance on the contentual level takes its point of departure.

The practical implications for the science-theology dialogue are obvious: the dialogue partner of theology should primarily be the most established scientific theories representing the best available truth-candidates. The attempt to pick up scientific dialogue partners friendly to theology but on the fringe of the sciences in order to "find space" for theology is in itself a symptom of an irrational procedure. The same goes for the theological dialogue partner of science. The theology expressed in the science-theology dialogue should not be confined to the bleak remnants of an eighteenth-century theism which does not do justice to the religious developments of the twentieth century nor address the concerns of theology as discipline. The debate should be led with the currently highest developed (i.e., most specified) theories inside theology. The demands of a twofold cycle of theoretical self-substantiation and of empirical applicability thus forces any option inside the science-theology dialogue into learning processes in terms of interrelating methods and contents.

V. Conclusion: The Via Media of Coherence Theory

We have seen that the coherence model, by opting for the precept "Connect!" aims at something more than a mere "compatibility" between different truth-candidates. The model looks for more elaborated exchanges on both the methodological and the substantial level. The demand is that different perspectives of reality must be coordinated into a larger web of beliefs and practices. This web of cognitive and evaluative elements, however, does not consist of relations of a hypothetico-deductive nature. Given the actual disunity of the natural sciences, and given the even more differentiated situation in the human sciences, the ideal of mutual logical interrelations between science and theology is misplaced. I have therefore opted for a *contextual coherence theory*. The demand of coherence implies for theology that it should be able to clarify how, and in what sense, developments in science have reverberations for the understanding of faith, and how theology should cope with these reverberations in terms of eventually revised internal self-descriptions, in terms of external redescriptions of scientific data and theories, in terms of an appropriation of thought models and scientific elements of worldviews, and in terms of a potential exchange of metaphors. Likewise, the coherence theory imposes the demand on science to engage in a broader trans-disciplinary interpretation of natural science in a cultural context, which includes the fact of the existence of religions, some of which are able to give a reflective account of the relation of God and the world.

Where a foundational view of human knowledge sees knowledge as a chain of arguments, leading to secure conclusions from a few allegedly safe evidences, the coherence model sees the structure of human knowledge as consisting of different planks with different colors and functions. Though the coherence model always prefers stronger ties of interconnection, it also allows for looser connections between different epistemic approaches to reality. In this respect, the coherence model can be seen as steering a middle course between critical realist and nonintegrative approaches to the interface of science and theology, though coherence is closer to the former than to the latter.

The coherence model is not content with *non-integrative models* of science and theology, since these do not allow for any cross-fertilization of perspectives between scientific and religious views of life. The different semantic worlds are left as they are without any exchanges on the level of cognitive contents. Non-integrative models argue for compatibility by placing views of life and science on quite different domains of human existence.

While the coherence model is more demanding than non-integrative models, it is in some respects more modest than *critical realist models* of the science-theology dialogue. Coherence theory, in the version developed here, follows critical realism in the insistence that the truth we are pursuing in science and theology is about "reality." The *definition of truth* is simply "to be in accordance with reality"; this is what we mean by truth, and reality is what we want to know more about. But coherence theory, as presented here, does not have to insist on the claim that human knowledge, in general, entails a steady "approximation" to reality. What is an intimation to reality in one respect (cf. examples of scientific progress), may well lead to a withdrawal from other aspects of reality. Coherence theory also rejects the possibility that isolated "propositions" can be shown to be true by "corresponding to facts," mundane or divine, since propositions are always imbued by background assumptions of a more general kind. When it comes to evaluating competitive truth-claims, the internal coherence between linguistically formulated sentences and theories therefore seems to be the only workable *criterion of truth* that we have at our disposal (Rescher [1973] 1982, 1-5).

The coherence theory is thus *holistic* in the sense that scientific theories or theological proposals are seen as cognitive nets where the meaning of singular sentences is only given within larger frameworks: the theory as a whole (in science) or the language system of Christianity as a whole (in theology). The credibility test of more encompassing views of life cannot, in fact, consist in a direct comparison with reality. Rather, the justification of truth-claims is only possible in the indirect way of being in accordance with a wider pattern of other statements that we consider to be true. Only in this roundabout manner can the realist assumption inside science as well as inside theology be redeemed.

The coherence model, as employed here, is distinguished from attempts that fasten a theory of rationality too tightly to a specific empiricist philosophy of science, as we saw in the case of Nancey Murphy's employment of the Lakatosian model for science. I have argued that the advantage of the coherence theory is that it allows for a rational competition between different meta-scientific — philosophical or theological — views of reality. Nicholas Rescher's version of the coherence theory, applied to the science-theology dialogue, avoids cutting up theology according to specific empiricist models of knowledge, while it demands that theology should take into account the strongest possible nontheological truth-candidates, including those of the sciences.

In this perspective, the strength of the contextual coherence theory is that it allows for a *cognitive plurality* of theories and visions within a *common framework of rationality*. Acknowledging the fact of cognitive plurality in human knowledge, the expectation that science and theology should be put together in one overarching language appears to be exaggerated. A more modest procedure in which hybrid scientifico-theological sentences are clarified and appropriately leveled seems prudent. We have seen how the coherence model offers a set of criteria — related to the levels of data, theories, thought models, and so on — that have been functioning in the practical judgments of theory-choice for more than one hundred years of interface between science and theology. The fact that the model has worked shows its utility and effectiveness.

References

Barbour, Ian G. [1966] 1971. *Issues in Science and Religion*. New York: Harper.

Brooke, John Hedley. 1991. *Science and Religion: Some Historical Perspectives*. Cambridge: Cambridge University Press.

_____. 1994. "Between Science and Theology: The Defense of Teleology in the Interpretation of Nature, 1820-1876." *Zeitschrift für Neuere Theologiegeschichte* 1:47-65.

DePaul, Michael R. 1995. "Coherentism." In *The Cambridge Dictionary of Philosophy*, ed. Robert Audi. Cambridge: Cambridge University Press.

Drummond, Henry. 1894. *The Lowell Lectures on the Ascent of Man*. London: Hodder & Stoughton.

Einstein, Albert and Leopold Infeld. [1938] 1971. *The Evolution of Physics: The Growth of Ideas from Early Concepts to Relativity and Quanta*. Cambridge: Cambridge University Press.

Geismar, Eduard. 1903. *Kristendom og Udvikling*. Copenhagen: Gad.

Gregersen, Niels Henrik. 1994. "Theology in a Neo-Darwinian World." *Studia Theologica* 48:125-49.

_____. 1997. "Three Types of Indeterminacy: On the Difference between God's Action as Creator and as Providence." In *Studies in Science and Theology* vol. 3, ed. N. H. Gregersen, Michael S. Parsons, and Christof Wassermann. Geneva: Labor et Fides.

_____. 1998. "The Idea of Creation and the Theory of Autopoietic Processes." *Zygon* 33/3 (forthcoming).

Hacking, Ian. 1996. "The Disunities of the Sciences." In *The Disunity of Science: Boundaries, Contexts, and Power*, ed. Peter Galison and David J. Stump. Stanford: Stanford University Press.

Hefner, Philip. 1993. *The Human Factor: Evolution, Culture, and Religion*. Minneapolis: Fortress.

Hempel, Carl. 1991. "Laws and Their Role in Scientific Explanation." In *The Philosophy of Science*, ed. Richard Boyd et al. Cambridge, Mass: MIT Press.

Kitcher, Philip. 1993. *The Advancement of Science: Science without Legend, Objectivity without Illusions*. New York/Oxford: Oxford University Press.

Lakatos, Imre. [1978] 1992. *The Methodology of Scientific Research Programmes: Philosophical Papers Volume I*. Cambridge: Cambridge University Press.

Laudan, Larry. [1981] 1991. "A Confutation of Convergent Realism." In *The Philosophy of Science. See* Hempel 1991.

Luhmann, Niklas. 1990. *Die Wissenschaft der Gesellschaft.* Frankfurt: Suhrkamp.

MacQuarrie, John. 1984. *In Search of Deity: An Essay of Dialectical Theism.* London: SCM.

McMullin, Ernan. 1984. "A Case for Scientific Realism." In *Scientific Realism,* ed. Jarrett Leplin. Berkeley and Los Angeles: California University Press.

_____. 1994. "Enlarging the Known World." In *Physics and Our View of the World,* ed. Jan Hilgevoord. Cambridge: Cambridge University Press.

Midgley, Mary. 1985. *Evolution as a Religion: Strange Hopes and Stranger Fears.* London: Methuen.

Moore, James R. 1981. *The Post-Darwinian Controversies: A Study of the Protestant Struggle to Come to Terms with Darwin in Great Britain and America 1870-1900.* Cambridge: Cambridge University Press.

Murphy, Nancey. 1990. *Theology in the Age of Scientific Reasoning.* Ithaca: Cornell University Press.

_____. 1993. "The Limits of Pragmatism and the Limits of Realism." *Zygon* 28:351-360.

_____. 1994. "What Has Theology to Learn from Scientific Methodology?" In *Science and Theology: Questions at the Interface,* ed. Murray Rae et al. Grand Rapids: Eerdmans.

_____. 1996. "Postmodern Apologetics, or Why Theologians Must Pay Attention to Science." In *Religion and Science: History, Method, Dialogue,* ed. Mark Richardson and Wesley J. Wildman. New York/London: Routledge.

Newman, John Henry. 1979. *An Essay in Aid of a Grammar of Assent.* Notre Dame: University of Notre Dame Press.

Peacocke, Arthur. 1993. *Theology for a Scientific Age: Being and Becoming — Natural, Divine and Human.* London: SCM.

Popper, Karl. 1990. *A World of Propensities.* Bristol: Thoemmes.

Putnam, Hilary. 1981. *Reason, Truth and History.* Cambridge: Cambridge University Press.

_____. 1984. "What Is Realism?" In *Scientific Realism. See* McMullin 1984.

_____. 1987. *The Many Faces of Realism: The Paul Carus Lectures.* Lasalle, Ill.: Open Court.

_____. 1990. *Realism with a Human Face.* Cambridge, Mass.: Harvard University Press.

Rescher, Nicholas. [1973] 1982. *The Coherence Theory of Truth.* Washington: University Press of America.

_____. 1992. *A System of Pragmatic Idealism,* vol. 1, *Human Knowledge in Idealistic Perspective.* Princeton: Princeton University Press.

_____. 1995a. *Pluralism: Against the Demand for Consensus.* Oxford: Clarendon.

_____. 1995b. *A System of Pragmatic Idealism,* vol. 3, *Metaphilosophical Inquiries.* Princeton: Princeton University Press.

Robbins, J. Wesley. 1993. "A Neopragmatist Perspective on Religion and Science." *Zygon* 28:337-350.

Rolston III, Holmes. 1994. "Does Nature Need to Be Redeemed?" *Zygon* 29:205-229.

Searle, John. [1979] 1996. "Literal Meaning." In *Expression and Meaning: Studies in the Theory of Speech Acts.* Cambridge: Cambridge University Press.

Temple, Frederick. 1884. *The Relations between Religion and Science.* London: MacMillan & Co.

Whitehead, Alfred North. [1933] 1967. *Adventures of Ideas.* New York: Free Press.

Contributors

WILLEM B. DREES is the Nicolette Bruining Professor of Nature and of Technology from a Liberal Protestant Perspective at the University of Twente, The Netherlands. He is also a staff member of the Bezinningscentrum at the Free University, Amsterdam, The Netherlands.

NIELS HENRIK GREGERSEN is Associate Professor of Systematic Theology in the Faculty of Theology, University of Aarhus, Denmark.

EBERHARD HERRMANN is Professor of Philosophy of Religion at the University of Uppsala, Sweden.

KEES VAN KOOTEN NIEKERK is Associate Research Professor in the Faculty of Theology, University of Aarhus, Denmark.

J. WENTZEL VAN HUYSSTEEN is the James I. McCord Professor of Theology and Science at Princeton Theological Seminary, Princeton, New Jersey, United States of America.

FRASER WATTS is the Starbridge Lecturer in Theology and Natural Science in the Faculty of Divinity, University of Cambridge, Cambridge, United Kingdom.

Index

Abductive inference, 66-67
Absolutism, 36, 38, 41, 80, 107,
 131, 138, 189, 196, 209
Accountability, 38, 40, 45
Adequacy: empirical, 45, 57, 60,
 100, 216, 217; epistemological,
 21, 81, 105, 107, 108, 110, 167,
 188, 194; experiential, 41, 45,
 88, 96, 98-101, 103-4, 111-12,
 126, 136, 140-42, 148, 150-55
Analogy, 61, 164, 168, 175-76
Anthropology, 102, 116; anthropic
 principle, 10, 81n.29, 172, 211
Anti-foundationalism. *See* Nonfoun-
 dationalism
Antirealism, 37-38, 65-66, 130-37,
 145, 164, 202
Apologetics, 44, 77, 173
Aquinas, Saint Thomas, 80n.28,
 173, 220
Aristotle, 98, 149
Atheism, 77, 186
Atkins, Peter, 95
Augustine, Saint, 82, 80n.28, 173

Barbour, Ian, 2-3, 16, 52, 62,

72n.17, 74n.19, 81n.29, 158-59,
 165, 201
Barfield, O., 161
Berkeley, George, 53
Bible, 71, 74, 111, 124; interpreta-
 tion of, 16, 111, 173, 187. *See
 also* Scripture
Big Bang theory, 82, 170, 215
Biology, 3, 23, 58, 80, 90, 97-99,
 109, 172, 174, 184, 189n.1, 201,
 206, 217; and divine agency,
 171, 215; informing religious no-
 tions, 108, 110, 224; and moral-
 ity, 220; sociobiology, 84, 104,
 211, 220
Bohr, Niels, 61-62, 165, 185, 204
Bonhoeffer, Dietrich, 88
Braithwaite, R. B., 70-71, 78
Brooke, John H., 23, 221
Brown, Harold, 7, 20-21, 24-29, 33-
 35
Burhoe, Ralph, 103, 105-6, 108n.5
Burrell, David, 160

Cartwright, Nancy, 163
Chance, 94, 222
Chaos-theory, 97, 97n.2, 99

233